Answering God

Answering God

Towards a Theology of Intercession

Robert Ellis

PATERNOSTER

First published in 2005 by
Paternoster Press

11 10 09 08 07 06 05   7 6 5 4 3 2 1

Paternoster Press is an imprint of Authentic Media,
9 Holdom Avenue, Bletchley, Milton Keynes MK1 1QR, UK
and
P.O. Box 1047, Waynesboro, GA, 30830-2047, USA

British Library Cataloguing in Publication Data
A catalogue record for this book is available from the British Library

ISBN 1-84227-340-X

Cover design by 4-9-0 Ltd
Typeset by Textype, Cambridge
Print management by Adare Carwin
Printed and Bound by J. H. Haynes & Co. Ltd., Sparkford

Contents

Introduction

Further let me ask of my reader, wherever, alike with myself, he is certain, there to go on with me; wherever, alike with myself, he hesitates, there to join with me in inquiring; wherever he recognizes himself to be in error, there to return to me; wherever he recognizes me to be so, there to call me back: so that we may enter together upon the path of charity, and advance towards Him of whom it is said, 'Seek His face evermore.'

Augustine[1]

* * *

As a local pastor and worship leader for twenty years, week by week I was asked to lead the prayers of my congregations. How can such an activity be made sense of given what else my fellow church members and I believed about God?

As I led those intercessions in church week by week two encounters stand out. In the first, someone complained to me that 'The trouble with you is that you lead prayers as if you expect God to do something!' For *that* regular worshipper, intercessions should be more helpfully understood as a form of meditation. He was suggesting that the language of prayer be altered to reflect this understanding in order to preserve its integrity.

On another occasion, a GP in my congregation passed on some reflections he had on a 'randomised controlled trial'

---

[1] Augustine, *On the Trinity* 1/3, p.19; http://www.ccel.org/fathers2/NPNF1-03/npnf1-03-07.htm#P192_60603.

on over a thousand cardiac patients in Kansas City, which he had read about in a reputable international medical journal.[2] The trial set out to answer the question: does intercession work? Seventy-five people were recruited to pray, and divided into teams. All had to agree with the following statement: 'I believe in God. I believe that he is personal and concerned with individual lives. I further believe that he is responsive to prayers for healing made on behalf of the sick.' They were not previously known to one another, and all reported at least weekly church attendance. The patients were randomly allocated into two groups – those prayed for by the teams, and those not. Neither patients, nor relatives, nor staff of the hospital knew about the study. Whenever a patient was admitted he or she was allocated to a prayer group, his or her first name only being passed to the prayer group leader, with no other information. The group prayed for the patients over the next twenty-eight days, and all medical records were reviewed by doctors, scoring points on an agreed system according to a wide range of clinical outcomes. Patients prayed for during the trial scored on average 11 per cent better than those not prayed for. The researchers were aware of the difficulty of variables in such situations, but went on to discuss both natural and supernatural explanations. The authors knew they needed to be modest in their claims. They had not proven that God answers prayer, or even that God actually exists. 'What they have observed is that when individuals outside hospitals speak or think the first names of hospitalised patients with an attitude of prayer, the latter appear to have better outcomes.'[3]

Many others have tried to 'measure' the 'success' of

---

[2] I am grateful to Michael Whitfield for drawing this article to my attention: W. S. Harris, M. Gowda and J. W. Kolb et al, 'A Randomized, Controlled Trial of the Effects of Remote, Intercessory Prayer on Outcomes in Patients Admitted to the Coronary Care Unit', Archive of Internal Medicine 159 (1999), pp. 2273–8, on line at http://archinte.ama-assn.org/cgi/content/abstract/159/19/2273.

[3] Ibid., p. 2278.

intercessions. But even some sort of statistically respectable result leaves almost as many questions as ever. Some of them are practical: can one be sure that other people were not praying for people in both control sets? Others are more theological: it seems a bit tough on the 50 per cent not prayed for that God did not help them as much because they were put in the wrong group!

This book will not address the question of how we may or may not know whether that research project yielded helpful results. While I will suggest that we might understand how it is possible to believe that God may indeed respond to our prayers, the whole question of when God does so must remain shrouded in mystery. We cannot be sure beyond doubt whether prayers are answered or not. We live by faith. But we also hear the command and invitation of scripture to 'ask, seek, knock', and this study will, I hope, shed some light on our thinking on praying for the sick, and others.

Barth comes close to defining Christians as 'people who pray'.[4] Scripture commands our prayer and shapes it. The Psalter, and many other passages of scripture, provides the vocabulary and grammar of much of our prayer. (Indeed, it comes as something of a shock to those such as me from a Baptist tradition when they first discover that the set offices of other traditions are almost entirely scripture texts ordered into a pattern of prayer.) The Bible contains a number of prayers, and many more references to prayer and teaching on it. Because of the central place of the Bible in prayer, and the practice of prayer that is our concern, the Bible itself will prove a useful place to begin this study. This is not done in any simplistic spirit of hoping to find easy answers to the questions that we will consider. On the contrary, we will find the Bible already prefigures some of those questions even if it does not formulate them precisely. We will certainly also hope to find clues and pointers that we can usefully carry on into the later stages

---

[4] C.D., III/3, pp. 264f.

of our study. The biblical witness is a witness, in part, to the way in which believers have wrestled before God over these things, just as we do today. Their striving must resource ours. That said, it will also be clear that I am not attempting to offer a detailed or definitive account of the scriptural evidence. Apart from the many commentaries, there are excellent books – notably those by Balentine and Cullmann – that do just this. My purpose is rather different: in having a specific interest in intercession, and in wanting to move from scripture (a trajectory of enquiry established) to wider discussion. This means that a self-denying ordinance must be observed frequently: I have not usually got involved in some of the more complex textual matters, interesting and important though they sometimes are, but instead have had to remain with the theological readings of the texts as we have them.

But a further reason for starting in this way and at this length with scripture is another key theological point. Too often, I contend, discussions of intercessory prayer and the problems associated with it are hamstrung by being too abstract. These matters are discussed as if some generic concept of God was in mind, and the problems were entirely philosophical or logical. While I treat these questions seriously and as real questions, I am also keen to make sure that the problems of intercessory prayer are discussed in relation to the God in whom Christians believe, the God and Father of our Lord Jesus Christ, the God – if you like – of the scriptures.

Christian prayer is offered to the God and Father of our Lord Jesus Christ, the God of the scriptures. The chapter discussing the biblical material will be trying to understand for what sorts of things the people who worship this God might pray, and whether such prayers might really have any effect – for we recognise also that God knows what we need or want before we ask, and always cares for God's creatures with gracious loving kindness, even when judgement rather than grace is what is deserved. We shall conclude, and argue thereafter, that we are encouraged and commanded to pray not only for spiritual goods, or the coming Kingdom, but also for 'daily bread' in its widest sense. Our prayers make a real difference because – and this is the significance of the previous paragraph – the God to whom we pray is the God and Father of our Lord Jesus Christ: *because of who God is.*

These themes are further discussed by reviewing a number of historically influential theologians. In their writing we see either an interpretation of intercession that is distinctly passive, with our prayers making little difference except to our own demeanour or attitude (rather like my first worshipper above); or, alternatively, a way of speaking about God that seeks to show how God 'makes room' for our prayers. The third chapter returns to the question 'Who is God?' In it we consider first the God and Father of our Lord Jesus Christ as the Triune God, the God who is Father, Son and Holy Spirit. This doctrine of the Trinity, rather obscure and rarefied as it sometimes seems, is an important part of the argument I will seek to make in associating the identity of God with the 'problem of prayer'. Then we consider God's relationship to time, and divine knowledge and divine power, before trying to imagine divine action. In the final chapter we consider briefly some of the explanations often offered to account for intercessory prayer, and I will suggest a particular way of configuring the issues in the light of all the questions considered – outlining an understanding of intercession as a significant, viable, though far from simple way in which we are invited and required to work with the Triune God.

The God and Father of our Lord Jesus Christ is the personal reality who calls and claims us, each one, and enables our response through the Holy Spirit. As personal reality this God is, at root, deeply mysterious, and prayer to and in God will and must remain ultimately a deep mystery. This book, while probing and teasing at the edge of that mystery, cannot resolve it. To attempt or pretend to do so would suggest a form of reductionist approach to God that is even more doomed to failure than any attempt to 'explain' fully any human person. If I cannot explain my friends, my loved ones or myself I certainly cannot fully explain God. But probe and tease around the edge of the mystery we must, because God requires of us our 'rational worship' (Rom.12:1), and because our faith ever drives us on in search of meaning. As long as that meaning which we seek does not become an idol, a substitute for the God who calls and claims us, our faith will go on seeking understanding because it must. That our theology thus becomes not only the restless yearning of our selves for meaning, but also the rational worship which we offer to God, makes this whole enterprise a thoroughly doxological one: theology as praise.

Meanwhile, just as we must not mistake our clumsy concepts of God for the reality who calls and claims us in Jesus Christ, so we must not confuse our reflection upon and wrestling with the issues of prayer with prayer itself. It is my hope that this book will enliven and encourage all who pray to do so with vigour and with hope – hope in God, Father, Son and Holy Spirit, to whom be the glory, now and for ever, Amen!

* * *

The nature of our English language makes it difficult sometimes to indicate in print a difference between a prayer (something prayed) and a prayer (one who prays)! I have adopted therefore throughout this book the rather clumsy device of writing the latter (one who prays) like this: 'pray-er'. I have endeavoured to begin to use more inclusive language but have not altered quoted material; nor have I entered into discussion or adjustment of traditional Trinitarian language. That would be a task for another day.

* * *

I would like to thank not only the various groups who have discussed these issues with me over the years, but also some individuals: my former Superintendent minister in Bristol, Dr Roger Hayden; my college Principal, Professor Paul Fiddes; and Robin Parry of Paternoster – all offered just the right encouragement at the right times to give my momentum the required assistance. I am grateful to Regent's Park College for the sabbatical leave in which I finally wrote the book. Thanks are due also to my wife and family, Sue, Gareth, Tim, Ceri and Nick, for being supportive while keeping me earthed in more everyday matters. Finally I would like to thank the congregations of the two churches where I have served as minister, and from whom I received so much – not least the privilege of being invited to lead them in worship and prayer week by week. It is to the congregations of Spurgeon Baptist Church, Bletchley and Tyndale Baptist Church, Bristol that I dedicate this book with thanks, and with my prayers for them.

1

Starting with Scripture

The God who Commands us to Pray

'Do not worry about anything, but in everything by prayer and supplication with thanksgiving let your requests be made known to God' (Phil. 4:6). What is the point of intercessory prayer? Why should we 'make our requests known'? Is it an exercise in bringing our will into line with God's, or is it a genuine dialogue in which our desires in some way determine what God wills to do? Is prayer really an opportunity for us to answer God by becoming the vehicles of God's will, or is it a gracious moment through which God answers our hopes and longings? Is there any proper limit on what may be desired in prayer, on the sort of prayer that may be heard? And are there certain conditions upon which such requests might depend? Should we pray for ordinary and everyday things for ourselves and loved ones? Or should we confine our prayers to praying for God's Kingdom, or for more obviously spiritual qualities, like love or wisdom? How do such requests fit in with God's purposes, which some say have been established from all eternity? Such questions indicate something of the scope of this study, and in starting with scripture we will find that, rather than their being the preserve of philosophers, they are also questions wrestled with in the Bible.

The Old Testament

The instincts of many Christian readers may lead them to the New Testament as the place where they will most naturally find help in understanding and articulating a Christian concept of prayer. Certainly, in terms of *teaching about prayer*, notably from Jesus himself, that is true. However, the Old Testament gives us more examples of 'prayer in the raw', prayers 'just prayed' rather than reflected upon or taught about. In offering this material to reflect upon, the Old Testament will give us valuable insights into prayer and indeed into the nature of the God to whom we pray.

Looking to the Old Testament to give indications on the practice and theology of prayer (the latter being at least partly implied in the former) we will find a mixed and complex picture emerging. Often scholars seem to have assumed that the Psalter is the main reliable guide to an Old Testament perspective on prayer,[1] but – depending perhaps on how tightly it is defined – prayer may be said to be present throughout the Old Testament. Sometimes it appears to be natural and conversational in tone, while at other times more formal and literary. As Balentine notes, sometimes writers have displayed a predilection to consider one of these types of prayer more 'authentic' than the other – rather as judgements are made in church life, in fact – and thus a more worthy subject of study or a more reliable guide to 'true religion'.[2] But all elements and examples of prayer need to be considered if the Old Testament is to yield its full riches for us.

The view of God that emerges from eavesdropping on the prayers of the Old Testament is, suggests Balentine, of one who is personal, accessible, loving, powerful, and compassionate.[3] These terms are predominantly relational,

---

[1] See Samuel E. Balentine, *Prayer in the Hebrew Bible: The Drama of Divine–Human Dialogue* (Minneapolis: Fortress, 1993), pp. 16, 236f.
[2] Ibid., p.19ff.
[3] Ibid., p. 265.

and they are the 'controlling metaphors'[4] used in the Old Testament as it seeks to describe God for us and invite us into relationship with God. It will be important for us to understand prayer in these relational terms – prayer is neither some impersonal and quasi-magical transaction, nor is it some austere and arid spiritual exercise by which we train our souls. Prayer is an expression of, and a deepening of, the pray-er's relationship with God, who is personal, accessible, loving, powerful and compassionate. When Clark Pinnock looks at the Old Testament he tells us that he sees 'Yahweh's creative desire for loving relationships and covenant partnerships. It seems God did not create the world to exercise total control over it.'[5] This God enters into dialogue with humanity through prayer, and is a partner with his people through covenant. This partnership may not be a partnership of equals, but it is nevertheless a partnership.[6] Prayer is an expression of, and opportunity for, this covenant partnership. More than this, when we hear the pray-ers of the Old Testament in petition for others or in repentance over sin, we hear those who stand four-square on what we might call the 'God-ness of God', saying in effect 'You alone are God' (2 Kgs 19:5).[7] Who is this God?

God Involved in all Events and Processes

The division of the world into sacred and secular, so common today, would have been a quite foreign conception to the ancient Israelite. In all things God's hand was evident. Blessings religious and temporal came from Yahweh, as did all manner of misfortune. Crucially, this was never worked through into a thorough deterministic

---

[4] Terence E. Fretheim, *The Suffering of God: An Old Testament Perspective* (Philadelphia: Fortress, 1984), p. 11.
[5] Clark Pinnock, *Most Moved Mover: A Theology of God's Openness* (Carlisle: Paternoster, 2001), p. 25.
[6] Balentine, *Prayer*, pp. 261-3.
[7] See ibid., ch. 5.

scheme. With what may appear as anthropomorphism, God is pictured as becoming angry when men and women act against the divine will, and human freedom always seems assured despite enigmatic passages which hint at a more complex understanding. God's providence extends, in a direct way, over all of nature, over the corporate life of humanity, and over the destinies of men and women. Everything and every event is related to God's will and care.[8]

This 'holistic' understanding of the world and God needs to be understood at the beginning of our study for two reasons. (1) It betrays a world view very different from the one that prevails in the twenty-first-century Western world. Our contemporaries often have what amounts to a 'deistic' view of the world: as if (if there is a God) God is now not involved in its normal running. Indeed, even the language of 'divine intervention' implies such a view where God is seen as normally passive and only extraordinarily active. The question of 'world view' will keep recurring. If one believes and hopes that God will impinge upon the world in any way, then a model for the way in which God and the world are related must be in one's mind – either explicitly or implicitly. (2) It explains the nature and scope of the prayers observed in the Old Testament in particular.

According to Johannes Herrmann, then, the Israelite can ask anything of Yahweh, the creator and sustainer of the whole world, and can ask for material as well as spiritual blessings. In fact, even in the Psalms the material often seems more prominent, but 'it may also be said on the other side that in the Old Testament generally man's existence is seen as a unity, so that physical and spiritual needs are closely related for the praying Israelite'.[9]

---

[8] cf. Walther Eichrodt, *Theology of the Old Testament*, vol. II (London: SCM, 1967), pp. 162–75.

[9] J. Herrmann, 'Prayer in the OT' in G. Kittel (ed.), *Theological Dictionary of the New Testament*, vol. II, G. W. Bromiley (tr.) (Grand Rapids: Eerdmans, 1964), p. 792.

This ability to pray for material as well as spiritual blessings is significant. Heiler demonstrated in his classic study of prayer that the most primitive petitions were, amongst other things, very 'down to earth'. More 'advanced' religions tended to eschew such requests, but Christianity (especially in its world-affirming, highly incarnational emphasis) has once more made such things proper, says Heiler.[10] Jesus will teach his disciples to pray for 'daily bread', a very 'down to earth' request indeed.

'Primitive Traditions' and Difficult Texts

Despite Heiler's positive observations, primitive prayer also has other, less commendable traits, some of which *may* be detectable in the Old Testament. Some scholars believe, for instance, that there may be signs of magical practices, though they are now buried in layers of tradition pre-dating the text as we have it. Joshua arrests the sun in Joshua 10:12ff., not something that the most ardent modern prayer triplet would usually attempt! The sun and moon are addressed rather than Yahweh, *perhaps* indicating that his words were originally an incantation rather than a prayer, but if so the editor has inserted the saving grace – 'Then spoke Joshua to the Lord' – to put this right. The texts at 2 Kings 4:33 and 17:21 may have editorial glosses to similar effect. However, whatever is going on here it would be wrong to represent it as typical: 'Obviously in Yahweh religion there is a force at work to crowd out the magic which had penetrated from primitive religion, and to replace it by prayer.'[11]

> It is in reality almost impossible to separate the questions of 'What is God like?' and 'How should I pray?' Prayer is in large measure theology moving into action and testing out its own understanding

---

[10] F. Heiler, Prayer: *A Study in the History and Psychology of Religion* (Oxford: OUP, 1932), chs I, III, IV and IX, esp. pp. 251ff.
[11] Herrmann, 'Prayer', p. 795.

of the divine nature of reality . . . a close correlation is perceived to exist between the way in which the deity or deities are thought of, and the kind of prayer that they will deign to hear . . .[12]

This relates very much to the issue of 'world view' that we touched on above. How we understand God and God's nature is reflected in the way we pray; and the way we pray will reflect who we think God is. This is evident from all the biblical material we shall review, and it will be an important element in our later considerations. We will see that who we think God is affects decisively the way we pray. The Old Testament does not speak with one voice on this question with regard to every detail, but we might take Balentine's lead in recognising the first indications: God is personal, accessible, loving, powerful and compassionate.

Some Old Testament traditions appear to exhibit a somewhat ambivalent attitude to intercessory prayer. Consider the Deuteronomist's account. 2 Samuel 12:16–18 shows David interceding for Bathsheba's child: the request of prayer here is turned away. But in a curious passage in 2 Samuel 24:10–25 we see David interceding for his people after Yahweh inflicts plague on the land as a punishment for David's census. The text is difficult.[13] At one point (24:16) Yahweh seems to have repealed the punishment, but the story continues as if this were not the case, with Yahweh relenting again in verse 25 after David's worship and intercession. The image of God seems decidedly anthropomorphic. Can we really speak of this passage in terms of the 'Warmth of Mercy' as Davis does, when 70,000 are wiped out by pestilence before the 'warm mercy' kicks

---

[12] R. E. Clements, *The Prayers of the Bible* (London: SCM, 1986), pp. 3, 7; cf. Oscar Cullman, *Prayer in the New Testament* (London: SCM, 1995), p. 5.

[13] Ralph W. Klein discusses the possibility that this passage was originally three separate stories: *1 Samuel* (Waco: Word, 1983), p. 282ff. W. McKane also considers the difficulties by contrasting 2 Samuel 24:1 with its parallel at 1 Chronicles 21:1: *1 & 2 Samuel* (London: SCM, 1963).

in?[14] Whatever theological rationale the Deuteronomic author might offer, this passage seems problematic, and not just textually.

In 1 Samuel 2:25 the very possibility of intercession in certain circumstances is held in some doubt.[15] What with unanswered prayer, and the diminished possibilities of prayer, the author believes humans hold little sway with God. While some Old Testament texts may retain something of this jealous and particular deity, in general the Old Testament softens these edges and introduces much more positive and hopeful images.

Jacob and the Prophets – Costly Prayer

One of the common features we may observe in a number of 'prayer encounters' is a cost exacted from the pray-er. In Genesis we read of a mysterious, wordless encounter. Jacob 'wrestled' with God until daybreak (though the text of 32:24–32 actually reads that he wrestled with a man, there seems little doubt amongst scholars about this). He received a blessing for his trouble, yet he also bore an infirmity for the rest of his life because of the meeting. Alongside the story of Abraham bargaining for Sodom and Gomorrah (Gen. 18:16–33, see below), these two passages from the Bible's opening book show something of the scope of prayer, and its 'results'. They both try to tell us something about the action of God, though in vague terms of 'blessing' and 'judgement'. Both also involve an exploration of God by the pray-er. Abraham's questions are designed to probe the divine mercy and intent; Jacob engages in the most intimate of personal exchanges. Jacob paid a price for his prayer: he was changed by it. The cost to both may have been exhaustion! These consequences of prayer ('consequences' seems a more helpful word than 'results' here) may be illuminating: some suggest that

---

[14] Dale Ralph Davis, *2 Samuel* (Fearn: Christian Focus, 1999), p. 262.
[15] See Klein, *1 Samuel*, pp. 25f.

when we engage in intercession it is we ourselves who are changed, rather than God. This element of costly personal transformation of the pray-er is an important aspect of prayer.

Jeremiah's prayers bear a certain resemblance to Jacob's nocturnal struggle. In Jeremiah 15:10–18 and 18:19–23, for instance, the prophet's prayer is an agonised striving. Highly personal in nature, he throws himself on to God's support, though not without venting his anguish. His prayers include petitions, often about the fate of his opponents, but they have the feel of prayers through which a man is coming to terms with his mission, his God and himself. This also may be a useful insight into prayer.

The prophets in general are more noteworthy for their pronouncements on the abuse of prayer and religious practices as a whole. Their stand against mere outward form anticipates some of the harsh words that Jesus is reported to have used in the gospels against those whose prayer is a form of affectation, who aim to win status in the eyes of others.[16] There is a difference in emphasis here, however. Amos and Hosea, and also Isaiah, protest against the complacent offering of religious devotion that is detached from other moral and spiritual considerations (Is. 1:11a,14–17). This more socio-economic, prophetic perspective on prayer is a reminder that true prayer can never be 'privatised'. Prayer and the whole of life must be indissolubly linked if we are to retain integrity in prayer. Thus prayer will also lead us into spheres of moral and social justice.

The Corporate and the Personal

In the Old Testament we observe prayer as a corporate activity, and as individual piety. Sometimes the line

---

[16] cf. Christopher R. Seitz, 'Prayer in the Old Testament or Hebrew Bible' in Richard N. Longenecker (ed.), *Into God's Presence* (Grand Rapids: Eerdmans, 2001), ch. 1.

between the two is hard to draw: Isaiah's remonstrations are decidedly corporate in their address, while carrying immense individual responsibility. A figure such as Nehemiah, one of the founders of 'Judaism', illustrates how a more personal devotion begins to emerge from the predominantly corporate background. His prayers, as he toils in the rebuilding of the city, are highly personal but petition for corporate ends. He offers a penitential prayer in which he knows himself to be implicated in the shared sin of the people (Neh. 1:6ff.).

The Old Testament on the whole has often been thought to yield a corporate devotion, though this may be a matter of genre – a consequence of the types of prayers that are recorded. This creative tension between the corporate and the personal is evident in the Psalms. Form critical study of the Psalms helped scholars to understand their setting in the community life of the nation and the temple, but it would be overstating the case to suggest that they reflect only slightly the emergence of individual piety from corporate devotion.[17] It is truer to observe that corporate and individual elements may be found alongside one another and that they refine and inform one another[18] – just as they do in church life. While the traditional view that saw David as the author of the Psalter made of them a very individualistic collection, it is also too sweeping to describe them all as 'just' communal songs,[19] and when Psalms are more individualistic, they are very much songs of individuals-in-community. They scale the heights and plumb the depths of a people's experience, and embody many of their aspirations and concerns. Some Psalms certainly do seem to have been individualistic in origin (for

---

[17] C. W. F. Smith, 'Prayer' in G. A. Buttrick (ed.) et al, *Interpreter's Dictionary of the Bible*, vol. 3 (Nashville: Abingdon, 1976), p. 861.
[18] See Frederick J. Gaiser, 'Individual and Corporate Prayer in Old Testament Perspective' in Paul R. Sponheim (ed.), *A Primer on Prayer* (Philadelphia: Fortress, 1998), pp. 16ff.
[19] cf. James L. Mays, *Psalms* (Louisville: Westminster John Knox Press, 1994), pp. 9ff.

example, 3, 17, 26), but some of those in turn are more properly understood as 'royal' Psalms in which the King 'speaks' in a representative role on behalf of the whole people, or indeed is spoken to as the representative of the people (for example, 28, 2).

Balentine remarks that the Psalter is the most 'concentrated resource for biblical prayer'[20] but also notes that scholars have fallen into the trap of concentrating their discussions of prayer too much on the Psalter at the expense of the rest of the Hebrew Bible.[21] However, as James Mays points out, it may be possible to discern within certain Psalms not only a microcosm of the Psalter's 'theology of prayer' but an Old Testament 'theology of prayer' in miniature. Thus, in Psalm 86, says Mays, we perceive that prayer is (1) the cry of a servant to his or her God, (2) in confidence that God will respond, (3) and can help. Furthermore, prayer is 'the utterance of an identity that is lived out',[22] and through prayer the individual prayer seeks to be shaped by the God to whom he or she prays.[23]

All of this underscores the very strong corporate elements in prayer that we do well to consider when we are thinking of the nature of Christian prayer. One of the balances that has to be achieved is that between personal and corporate elements. Which should be considered primary? It would appear from the Old Testament that the corporate dimension is primary, but there is also enough evidence of personal devotion to make that by no means insignificant. The fact that individuals often pray 'on behalf of' others, or that they offer penitence as part of a larger whole (Dan. 9:4–19 is another fine example of this), gives us a clue as to the proper relation between individual and corporate prayer. To act as representative of the people is a

---

[20] Balentine, *Prayer*, p. 16.

[21] Ibid., pp. 236ff.

[22] Mays, *Psalms*, pp. 279ff.

[23] For a discussion of the way in which the Psalms may deepen the prayer life of our contemporaries, see 'A School of Prayer' in K. Schaefer, *Psalms* (Collegeville: Liturgical Press, 2001), pp. xxv–xxxii.

priestly role, and the New Testament affirms that all Christians are priests (1 Pet. 2:5). The primary prayer is perhaps that prayer made by the church; personal prayer is the exercising by each of us of our priestly role, as we pray with and on behalf of the church. Barth will have something valuable to say on this.

'Prayer Changes Things': an Old Testament Perspective

A cliché has it that 'prayer changes things'. But what things, and how? And anyway, does prayer really have such an effect? The Old Testament has some light to shed on such questions, and its insights will go with us into a fuller discussion of these issues later in our study.

In Genesis 18:16–33 we seem to eavesdrop on Abraham bargaining with God. I was once asked to lead a Bible study on the passage under the title 'Does God change his mind?' A participant ventured that the Almighty seems prevaricating or even malleable when faced with intercession in this story. But such a negative judgement rests on an implicit assumption: that changing one's mind is not a good thing to do, or is a sign of weakness – a recognition, if you like, that we were wrong before and need to alter our position. But is this necessarily what might be meant by suggesting that God 'changes his mind' in response to prayer?

There is quite a literature developing that discusses the Old Testament passages that seem to suggest that God may indeed 'change his mind', or as it is more usually (and perhaps more biblically) put, that God sometimes 'repents'.[24] Without wishing to prejudge the matter, we do have to ask whether the tradition of Christian theology established in the earliest days may have led us to read scripture through the lens of a particular philosophical

---

[24] This is most clearly focused in the discussions of 'Open Theism' in American publications. See, e.g., Gregory A. Boyd, *God of the Possible: A Biblical Introduction to the Open View of God* (Grand Rapids: Baker, 2000) and Bruce A. Ware, *God's Lesser Glory: A Critique of Open Theism* (Leicester: Apollos, 2001), esp. pp. 41–100.

tradition. Many will be alarmed to be told that, whereas they thought they were reading the Bible in such a way as to honour its unique authority, in fact they have seriously misjudged certain texts because they have not allowed scripture to speak with its own authentic voice. It is something like this that Karl Barth had in mind when he complained that we should attend to revelation to discover who God is. If God is revealed in Jesus to be other than what our other assumptions suggest ('absolute in contrast to all that is relative, exalted in contrast to all that is lowly, active in contrast to all suffering, inviolable in contrast to all temptation, transcendent in contrast to all immanence, and therefore divine in contrast to everything human') such other beliefs are shown to be 'quite untenable, corrupt, and pagan, by the fact that God does in fact be and do this in Jesus Christ'.[25]

John Sanders thus duly concludes that in their explanations of texts of 'divine repentance' writers such as Paul Helm, Norman Geisler and Bruce Ware make their judgements on the basis of external (i.e. non-biblical) philosophical assumptions.[26] Geisler is the most straightforward here, explicitly deducing God's immutability and unconditioned nature from 'extra biblical propositions',[27] but Sanders judges that something similar is going on in the other writers too. It is a serious question whether anyone can read the Bible without any 'lens' derived from his or her cultural, philosophical or religious baggage, but awareness of that fact does seem to be an important principle. But what does the Old Testament say?

The Old Testament does not give an *absolutely* clear lead one way or the other: some texts seem to suggest that God does 'change his mind' (e.g. Ex. 32 – 33 and 2 Kgs 20),

---

[25] Barth, *C.D.* IV/1, p. 186.

[26] John Sanders, *God Who Risks: A Theology of Providence* (Downers Grove: IVP, 1998), pp. 66–70.

[27] Norman Geisler, *Creating God in the Image of Man?: The New Open View of God – Neotheism's Dangerous Drift* (Minneapolis: Bethany House, 1997), pp. 90, 108, quoted in Sanders, *God Who Risks*, p. 67.

others that God does not (e.g. Num. 23:19 and 1 Sam. 15:29).[28] However, there are so many texts that imply some kind of divine change of heart (Sanders claims at least thirty-five),[29] and from so great a variety of Old Testament traditions and genres[30] that they do have to be taken very seriously. Are they mere accommodations to human weakness of understanding, as Calvin suggested, just anthropomorphisms, or are they – within the context of the Old Testament's view of God as relational and covenantal – direct pointers to a vital truth about who God is?

It will be useful here to focus on a particular passage: Exodus 32, one that Sanders deals with in some detail. Following the manufacture of the golden calf Moses and God have what Sanders describes as a 'heated and tense exchange'[31] during which God appears to disown the Israelites (God describes them as *'your* people' in 32:7) and inform Moses of a new plan in which he (Moses) becomes the focus of the promise previously given to Abraham (God says 'Now let me alone, so that my wrath may burn against them and I may consume them; and of you I will make a great nation', 32:10). But Moses does not let God alone, instead he contests this decision ('But Moses implored God, saying . . .' [32:11]). The text says 'implored', but 'argued' would fit just as well with what follows. Moses now speaks to God of *'your* people', turning around the previous divine statement (32:11); he warns God that the Egyptians will misconstrue God's motives in delivering the slaves if God turns his wrath on the Israelites now (32:11ff.); and he reminds God of the promise to Abraham which God now threatens to set aside ('how you swore by your own self' [32:13]). Exodus 32:14 says baldy: 'And the Lord changed his mind about the disaster that he planned

---

[28] cf. Richard Rice, 'Biblical Support' in Clark Pinnock, Richard Rice, John Sanders, William Hasker and David Basinger, *The Openness of God* (Carlisle: Paternoster, 1995), pp. 32f.

[29] Sanders, *God Who Risks*, p. 72.

[30] Ibid., p. 73.

[31] Ibid., p. 63.

to bring on his people.' Sanders observes that God is willing to be changed by the intercession of one with whom God stands in relationship. 'God is willing to allow [Moses] to influence the path he will take. God permits human input into the divine future. *One of the most remarkable features of the Old Testament is that people can argue with God and win.*'[32] If this is so, it is an important insight into the nature of prayer; if it is argued that the passage does not mean what it appears to say we have to ask on what grounds such a judgement is made.

But if 'people can argue with God and win' such victories are not guaranteed in the relational interaction of prayer. If the pray-er could always guarantee a 'result' as long as he or she followed a particular process or technique, we would have strayed from relationship-based prayer into magic and manipulation. But that is clearly not what the Old Testament in general, nor this passage in particular, would have us believe. For at 31:31–34 Moses does not 'win'. Here Moses pleads for the transgressors before God ('if you will only forgive their sin' [32:32]), but his success is at best limited ('whoever has sinned against me I will blot out of my book' [32:33]). Divine approval of requests, even from such as Moses, is not guaranteed. If we are right to see here a suggestion that God sometimes may respond to human requests, we would be equally right to notice that this is no foregone conclusion, and we might speculate on why sometimes the answer seems to be 'yes' and why sometimes 'no'.

When we come to the New Testament material we will see that it is often suggested that the Gethsemane prayer of Jesus should be considered as the model of prayer. Moses is not pictured in Exodus 32 as meekly uttering 'your will be done', but perhaps Jesus' prayer was not so meek either?[33]

---

[32] Ibid., p. 64, italics mine.

[33] 'His petition is not empty rhetoric but a serious effort to determine the will of God . . . he does not believe that everything must happen according to a predetermined plan . . . Together they determine what the will of God is for this historical situation.' Ibid., p. 100.

Maybe in the contrasting outcomes to Moses' intercessions in this chapter we can discern that sometimes God can 'make room' for human requests while still pursuing his purposes, while at other times – for reasons hidden in the mystery of the divine will or even in the exigencies of creaturely situations – such divine acquiescence is not possible. If this is what Exodus 32 and similar Old Testament passages tell us, it could be a very important insight indeed into the nature of prayer – and the identity of God. But the Gethsemane prayer understood as a model of meek submission will not illuminate Exodus 32 very satisfactorily. The request declined in 32:33 *may* have been declined because it was not in accord with God's will – the usual understanding of the Gethsemane prayer. But when we look at the interchange in the earlier part of the chapter we discover that God's 'change of mind' in 32:14 came about because of Moses' intercession: in other words, God's will changed in response to the intercession. Oscar Cullmann, as we shall see, argues that this possibility must underlie any correct reading of Jesus' prayer in Gethsemane.

Jesus and the Synoptic Gospels
The Prayer Life of Jesus: Abba

It often seems important for Christians to have an insight into the prayer life of Jesus himself, as well as learning from Jesus *about* prayer: we want to copy his practice.[34] Is it possible to reconstruct Jesus' own prayer life, or to claim authenticity for Gospel teaching on prayer? There was a time, a generation or so ago, when these questions would have had to have been answered rather tentatively. However, contemporary scholars seem to suggest strongly that we are not at the mercy of complete historical scepticism, and that we are now able to transcend it and make positive

---

[34] Perhaps even, as N. T. Wright suggests, to share his prayer life, and thus the life of God: 'The Lord's Prayer as a Paradigm of Christian Prayer' in Longenecker (ed.), *Into God's Presence*, p. 132.

and reliable assertions from gospel data – always bearing in mind, of course, that we are not dealing with historical accounts of the same sort as modern-day reports of events.[35]

We know that the regular pattern for prayer in the time of Jesus[36] was a thrice-daily one, with prayer offered at sunrise, mid-afternoon and sunset. The first and last of these 'offices' would include the recital of the *shema* – a semi-creedal doxology – and there would be space for spontaneous prayer also. In corporate worship this free prayer tended to become more and more set. Petitions were included on weekdays between the benedictions. Each petition was of a particular character – beginning and ending in praise. Jesus was brought up in a devout home (Lk. 2, 4:16) and almost certainly absorbed and made his own the customary religious practices of his day, though scholars differ somewhat in their view of the extent to which this was the case.

Jeremias boldly states that 'with all probability . . . no day in the life of Jesus passed without the three times of prayer' and that we can 'sense from this something of the hidden inner life of Jesus, something of the source from which he daily drew strength'.[37] James Dunn probably captures more of the contemporary consensus though when he says that here, as on other matters, Jeremias' judgement in *The Prayers of Jesus* has gone beyond the evidence. Many of the recorded instances of Jesus' going to the synagogue in the Gospels seem to illustrate an ulterior motive to do with his own ministry (e.g. Mk. 1:21ff.; Mt. 9:35; Lk. 4:15ff., 13:10). And, as Dunn points out, Jesus is so critical of the tradition in general terms that without more evidence on any particular it is difficult to be certain.[38]

---

[35] cf. James D. G. Dunn, *Jesus and the Spirit* (London: SCM, 1975), pp. 12ff; see also Dunn's *The Evidence for Jesus* (London: SCM, 1985).

[36] See Asher Finkel, 'Prayer in Jewish Life' in Longenecker (ed.), *Into God's Presence*, and Luke T. Johnson, *The Writings of the New Testament: An Interpretation* (London: SCM, 1992), pp. 133ff.

[37] Joachim Jeremias, *The Prayers of Jesus* (London: SCM, 1967), p. 75.

[38] Dunn, *Jesus and the Spirit*, p. 16; cf. Jeremias, *Prayers*, p. 75.

Be that as it may, Jeremias makes three points about the prayers of Jesus which with some qualification still demand a central place in any account.

(1) He draws attention to what seems to be a firmly established tradition about Jesus praying in solitude, sometimes at night (e.g. Mk. 1:35, 6:46,48, 14:32-42; Lk. 6:12).[39] Others would add that this custom of lone prayer seems particularly to be used in emergencies, before great decisions and in 'retirement'.[40]

(2) In contrast to the *shema* and *tephilla*, in daily use, the prayer that Jesus taught his disciples appears to have been given in Aramaic. The invocation of God as *Abba* is also Aramaic. Jesus prayed, and taught his disciples to pray in such a way that he removed 'prayer from the liturgical sphere of sacred language and places it right in the midst of everyday life'.[41] This ties in closely with his next point, perhaps the most important of all.

(3) When the disciples approached Jesus with the request 'Teach us to pray' they were given a model prayer which functioned not only as devotional guidance but also as a clue to the characteristic spirituality of Jesus' disciples.[42] Jeremias argues that the giving of any new prayer indicates some dissatisfaction with forms currently in use, but goes on to discuss the distinctive element in this prayer – the mode of address to God. All the prayers of Jesus address God as 'Father'[43] (with the exception of the cry of dereliction on the cross, where Psalm 22 is being quoted: Mk. 15:34, cf. Mk. 14:36). Jeremias concludes that Jesus always used the form *Abba* given here, a colloquialism

---

[39] Jeremias, *Prayers*, p. 76.
[40] Smith, 'Prayer', p. 862. cf. I. H. Marshall, 'Jesus – Example and Teacher of Prayer in the Synoptic Gospels' in Longenecker (ed.), *Into God's Presence*, pp. 116ff.
[41] Jeremias, *Prayers*, p. 76.
[42] cf. G. M. Soares-Prabhu, 'Speaking to "Abba": Prayer as Petition and Thanksgiving in the Teaching of Jesus' in Christian Duquoc and Casiano Florestan (eds), *Asking & Thanking* (London: SCM, 1990), pp. 31–43.
[43] See Marshall, 'Jesus – Example and Teacher', pp. 127–9.

originating in the language of children, and that it is his most characteristic mode of speech, being a profound expression of his authority and mission. With this filial intimacy 'a new way of praying is born', and in the thankful spirit of this model prayer God's reign is made real here and now.[44]

Jeremias has almost certainly overstated his case in arguing for the complete uniqueness of Jesus' *Abba*, but it is widely acknowledged that his regular use of it was most unusual, and most unusually intimate, for his day.[45] The evidence for Jesus' use of the term is not massive in quantity, but it is unanimous. Dunn remarks that 'when we "listen in" on Jesus' prayers the distinctive word we hear is *Abba*!'[46] Neither should we linger too long on its childish connotations.[47] It came to have a more extended use, even though it is true that 'family intimacy' remains a major connotation. 'Obviously it was precisely because of this note of intimacy that *Abba* was so little used by Jesus' contemporaries in addressing God'[48] and, conversely, because of this intimacy why it was used so consistently by Jesus.

This use of *Abba* is one of the characteristics of Jesus' personal prayer that was taken up with consistency and enthusiasm by the early church.[49] It is a sign of an important element in Christian prayer, namely that of an intimacy which derives from a filial relationship to God. This suggests security, but a mutual responsibility of the Father to the children (security), and of the children to the Father (vocation). Christian prayer is intensely personal in nature, and Jesus' use of *Abba* is a significant factor in this development.

---

[44] Jeremias, *Prayers*, p. 78.

[45] Dunn, *Jesus and the Spirit*, p. 23.

[46] Ibid., p. 21: italics Dunn's. cf. Cullmann, *Prayer in the New Testament*, p. 41, who shares Dunn's judgement on Jeremias.

[47] James Barr, 'Abba isn't Daddy', *Journal of Theological Studies* 39 (1988), pp. 28–47.

[48] Dunn, *Jesus and the Spirit*, p. 23

[49] cf. Romans 8:15; Galatians 4:6.

The personal nature of prayer is evident throughout scripture. Such prayer is seen as an interchange between persons, each party retaining integrity, and the characteristics of personhood. But when prayer is seen in such a light, this insight also prepares us for some of the particular problems associated with intercession.[50] For persons are free beings, with rights over their own futures, rights to choose even the wrong options. Human beings are persons; God is personal. What bearing does the personal nature of intercession have upon our understanding of it?

The Synoptic Gospels: Matthew, Mark and Luke

We now turn to the way the writers of the synoptic Gospels present Jesus' life of prayer and teaching on prayer. It is Luke who shows a particular interest in the subject, often adding his own material or making editorial alteration to common traditions which underline the theme of prayer. But each of the synoptics contains significant material. Apart from the exclamatory prayers in the passion narrative, we have only two personal prayers of Jesus in the synoptics – Matthew 11:25ff. and Mark 14:36. There are more references to Jesus praying: Mark 1:35, 6:46; Matthew 14:23; Luke 3:21, 5:16, 6:12, 9:18 and 28ff. Luke 22:31ff. contain a reference on Jesus' lips to his own prayer, and other texts seem to show Jesus quoting from traditional prayers of his day (e.g. Lk. 10:26 and Mk 12:26). From such details is the overview of Jesus' prayer life built up.

We consider now three elements in Jesus' prayer: his own prayer in Gethsemane; the prayer he taught his disciples; and the various teachings on prayer recorded.

Jesus in Gethsemane

Jesus' prayer in Gethsemane on the night of his arrest is direct and telling: 'Father, for you all things are possible; remove this cup from me; yet not what I want, but what

---

[50] cf. Clements, *The Prayers of the Bible*, p. 11.

you want' (Mk 14:36). Here we would seem to have strong testimony to Jesus' own reliance on prayer in this most fraught moment.[51]

'Yet not what I want, but what you want' expresses a trust in God which fits well with the *Abba* address, and is consonant with much of Jesus' teaching (e.g. Mt. 6:25–34). Smith expressed the traditional judgement that 'The crux of all prayer in the Bible is the prayer of Jesus in Gethsemane, where surrender is yet addressed to God as Father.'[52] If this is so then prayer is to be understood as a means of surrendering to the will of God, as a way of coming into line with it, of learning to bear it. Prayer becomes a means of asking God to be God; of doing as God wills. This is a profound insight, though not to be practised uncritically. How do we know what God's will is? Is it simply to be identified with what happens to us? How do we know when we have truly learnt to succumb to it and bear it? If prayer *were* reduced simply to this it would make some of the problems of prayer vanish. That may be too simple a move, but we might expect this 'model' prayer in Gethsemane to figure strongly in a Christian understanding of prayer.

A bolder interpretation of this prayer is called for. Perhaps in what appears as 'resignation' to the Father's will we should more properly see disappointment at Jesus' own unanswered prayer? Or, as Cullmann and Sanders[53] suggest, we should detect a greater degree of 'negotiation' here than our hindsightful knowledge of the story allows? Says Cullmann, to the question of the legitimacy of prayers of intercession and petition:

> the Gethsemane prayer gives a positive answer here, since Jesus includes the readiness to bow to God's will whether or not it corresponds to his wish, in the petition 'let this cup pass from me' . . . It is part of God's loving will that his creatures should also

---

[51] For discussion of the issues of historicity in this prayer, see Dunn, *Jesus and the Spirit*, pp. 17–21.
[52] Smith, 'Prayer', p. 862.
[53] Sanders, *God Who Risks*, p. 100.

present their wishes to him, whether he can grant them or not, just as parents want their children to ask them trustingly for a gift, even if they are not certain of getting it. *The words 'if it is possible' in fact presuppose that God can not only reject but also fulfil a request . . .*[54]

Cullmann is significant among New Testament scholars in his willingness to pursue the larger theological questions raised by his exegesis: his observation here, that the Gethsemane prayer is not simply one of 'submission' but of exploration and perhaps negotiation ('if it is possible' suggesting it may *be* possible for an alternative outcome), is significant.

The Lord's Prayer

The Lord's Prayer is given in two different versions by Matthew and Luke. Matthew inserts his version into the Sermon on the Mount (6:9–13), while Luke places his in a more open context (11:2–4). The Lukan context is thought more likely original, as is Luke's shorter and less formal version,[55] though some maintain that they are two separate traditions each traceable back to Jesus. I want to draw out just two issues.

The prayer begins with the *Abba* address, and then craves the hallowing of God's name. The next petition defines and extends this, and immediately points forward to that Gethsemane prayer: 'may your kingdom come, your will be done', and once again it is the first call on the Christian's prayer that God's will be done 'on earth, as in heaven'. T. W. Manson detected a 'realized eschatology' in noting that 'there is a sense in which the kingdom comes whenever and wherever God's will is acknowledged and obeyed on earth',[56] but that should not allow us to screen out the highly future-eschatological tone of this petition and of the whole prayer. The Kingdom is breaking in but is

---

[54] Cullmann, *Prayer in the New Testament*, p. 34, italics mine.
[55] cf. David Hill, *The Gospel of Matthew* (London: Marshall, Morgan & Scott, 1972), pp. 134ff; also Cullmann, *Prayer in the New Testament*, p. 40.
[56] T. W. Manson, *The Sayings of Jesus* (London: SCM, 1950), p. 169.

not yet fully actual. We pray between the 'now' and the 'not yet': we pray for the Kingdom.

There is considerable discussion amongst scholars on the exact meaning and significance of Matthew's phrase translated into English as 'Give us today our daily bread.' Is this a prayer for today's meals, or the bread of the Messianic banquet? The Greek *epiousion* (usually rendered 'daily') is uncertain and, indeed, unique.[57] Hill follows Jeremias in rendering it as 'that which is coming', denoting bread for the coming day (tomorrow, or the rest of today), *and also* the eschatological bread of the Kingdom.[58] Harrington agrees, recalling the Eucharistic interpretation of the Latin Church Fathers.[59]

Schweizer is unimpressed by such arguments, believing that bread is not particularly characteristic of the Messianic banquet, and that Jesus shows a concern for mundane matters, which well fits with a more ordinary interpretation. 'The petition probably means: grant that we may lie down to sleep, not with a sense of abundance or surety against hard times, but simply without despair; knowing the coming day has been provided for.'[60] In a context where Jesus has been speaking of going without provisions, Johnson takes the term to have an immediate connotation – 'the bread we need', and Luke's wording seems to emphasise the ongoing nature of this need for bread, 'day by day'.[61]

The question is not whether this 'everyday' meaning is correct, but whether it is the whole story – is there a deliberate eschatological 'double meaning' here?[62] Jesus seems to be instructing his followers to pray for what Augustine was

[57] Luke T. Johnson, *The Gospel of Luke* (Collegeville: Liturgical Press, 1991), p. 177.

[58] Hill, *The Gospel of Matthew*, pp. 137ff.; Jeremias, *Prayers*, p. 102. Cullmann takes a similar view, *Prayer in the New Testament*, pp. 52–4.

[59] See Daniel J. Harrington, *The Gospel of Matthew* (Collegeville: Liturgical Press, 1991), p. 95.

[60] Eduard Schweizer, *The Good News According to Matthew* (London: SPCK, 1976), p. 154.

[61] Johnson, *The Gospel of Luke*, pp. 177ff.

[62] cf. Wright, 'The Lord's Prayer', pp. 136, 142ff.

later to call 'temporal competence' – enough, though not an extravagance, of the things we need to live day by day. But knowing that Jesus' teaching is so thoroughly eschatological, can we easily dismiss Jeremias' option? Schweizer himself can say that the Lord's Prayer provides a way of learning to live in the perspective of the future.[63] If we allow the double meaning,[64] it reinforces the eschatological nature of Christian prayer. There is a very strong case for saying that, in the model Christian prayer, both everyday goods and eschatological perspective are present.

Jesus' teaching on prayer
The teaching of Jesus on prayer falls into two categories – the parables and other sayings and teaching.

Luke records parables in which the prayer theme is prominent at 11:5–8 and 18:1–8 and 9–14. The latter of these three, the Pharisee and the Tax Collector, teaches of proper and improper attitudes to God – including, but not exclusively, in prayer. But the other two parables have as a common theme what we might call importunity in prayer – 'keeping at it'. At 11:5–8, a man disturbs his friend in the night to borrow three loaves of bread in order to entertain an unexpected nocturnal visitor of his own. Reluctantly, the friend agrees. 'Even though he will not get up and give him anything because he is his friend, at least because of his persistence he will get up and give him whatever he needs' (v. 8). God's character is thus contrasted with the unwilling friend, and the believer is encouraged to pray persistently: 'God responds graciously to the needs of his children.'[65] The following passage (vv. 9–17) goes on to stress the certainty of God's answering prayer. Despite any contrary appearances, persevere in prayer, as 'God wants those who pray to be persistent.'[66]

---

[63] Schweizer, *Matthew*, p. 158
[64] As Joel B. Green does: *The Gospel of Luke* (Grand Rapids: Eerdmans, 1997), pp. 442ff.
[65] I. H. Marshall, *The Gospel of Luke* (Exeter: Paternoster, 1978), p. 462.
[66] Cullmann, *Prayer*, p. 20. See also Green, *The Gospel of Luke*, p. 449.

The message of 18:1–8 is similar, though the context is of teaching on the Son of Man and the parousia.[67] An old widow nags away at a judge to secure her rights – finally, he succumbs. But the parable has a sting in its tail. For Jesus turns it on to his audience to ask whether they will be as persistent and faithful as the heroine of the story – 'when the Son of Man comes, will he find faith on earth?' (v. 8b). Endurance is the desirable quality portrayed here, and it is to be a trait of the believer's praying. God's people will be vindicated more certainly than the unjust judge acted for the widow. (Does this element of ultimate vindication indicate that prayer for the future Kingdom is what is in mind here?) And, unlike the judge, God will respond soon. Verse 7b seems to have been inserted to deal with the perceived delay in God's action – 'Will he delay long in helping them?' Marshall comments that 'to the elect it may seem to be a long time until he answers, but afterwards they will realise that it was in fact short'.[68] This text is quite significant if it can be taken as an early indication, perhaps dating back to Jesus himself, of wrestling with prayer that apparently remains unanswered, or has a delayed answer. We will encounter other ways in which the church may have grappled with this, especially in the epistles.

The second category of teaching is the series of sayings on prayer and related matters. This brings us to Matthew 7:7–11 and its Lukan parallel at 11:9–13, texts that at first may seem to promise intercessory blank cheques. Harrington remarks that 'the emphasis throughout is on the almost automatic efficacy of the prayer of petition'.[69] But the background to these terms may indicate otherwise. 'Seeking' and 'finding' are terms used at Qumran for the quest for God's hidden wisdom (see Jas 1:5, below). The image of 'knocking' is used by the rabbis for gaining

---

[67] Marshall believes that the prayer theme is more original than the current context. *The Gospel of Luke*, p. 670.

[68] Ibid., p. 676.

[69] Harrington, *The Gospel of Matthew*, p. 105, and Johnson similarly on the parallel, *The Gospel of Luke*, p. 179. See Hill, *The Gospel of Matthew*, p. 148.

correct interpretation of the law, and for prayer for God's mercy. These background usages may suggest a limitation upon what is to be asked for, which severely limits any 'blank cheque'. Beare articulates this admirably:

> These are not general truths. They do not apply to human requests of one another, and they do not apply to all our prayers to God. Other people do not always give us what we ask, and all of us have known the disappointment, sometimes the bitterness, of unanswered prayer. If we recall that the theme of the whole sermon is the kingdom of heaven, and the way of winning admission to it, we may apply the words specifically to petitions for entrance. Of this primarily we have the assurance that everyone who asks receives, that everyone who seeks finds, and that everyone who knocks at the gate is admitted. It is God who grants the most precious of all gifts, who is found by all who seek, and who opens to all who knock at the gates of his mercy.[70]

Taken in such a way, Matthew 6:33f. becomes a summary of Jesus' attitude to prayer, though it may not have that as its primary theme: 'But strive first for the kingdom of God and his righteousness, and all these things will be given to you as well.'[71]

About this asking, seeking, knocking, there is no unfailing magic ritual. 'The fact that the seeker is promised to find in no way means he can coerce God.'[72] Jesus is concerned with the importance and joy of prayer – not with its misuse.

Verses 9–10 stress the father–child context of prayer and bring out elements of trust and dependence. Matthew and Luke differ in both contexts and wording for the whole passage. Matthew's wording is often preferred, but Luke's context thought more original. However, the very last

---

[70] F. W. Beare, *The Gospel According to Matthew* (Oxford: Blackwell, 1981), pp. 191ff.

[71] On the inclusion of 'God's saving justice', see section on 1 John. Beare's position is perhaps slightly overstated as it stands. cf. Marshall, 'Jesus – Example and Teacher', p. 129, and, on the parallel, Green, *The Gospel of Luke*, p. 449.

[72] Schweizer, *Matthew*, p. 172.

words raise an interesting issue. Matthew reads (v. 11b)
'how much more will your Father in heaven give good
things to those who ask him!' Luke substitutes 'the Holy
Spirit' (Lk. 11:13) for 'good things'. If Matthew's words are
more 'original', what would account for Luke's editing? It
is true that the Spirit is a characteristic Lukan theme, but
could there be another reason – more to do with the
grappling over unanswered prayer, and the ready counter
to this at hand in narrowing the contents of that prayer?
Could a prayer for the Holy Spirit seem easier to account
for than one that asks for 'good things' in general?
Dibelius, for one, thinks this could be the case, and the
argument has a certain appeal.[73]

Matthew 6:8b ought to be noted: 'your father knows
what you need before you ask him'. This might seem to
undermine the very effort of prayer, yet does not seem to
have curtailed Jesus' own praying. What is its meaning?
Perhaps it is the father–child context that will once more
illuminate the text for us. Just as a father knows his family's
needs before they are put into words, and yet waits for
them to ask in confidence and trust, so God knows what
we want before we ask. It should not undermine effort so
much as reassure of God's interest and concern. Prayer is
not here envisaged as Seneca's 'wearying of the gods', or as
something which in great efforts wearies the believer.
Rather it is something given to the believer as a gift, and
not something performed 'to achieve a goal or support a
claim'.[74] Far from providing a disincentive to prayer, Jesus
tries to stress the certain access of the believer to God who
knows us through and through and is yet ready to hear us.
Cullmann observes that, though God does not need our
prayers, God does want them.[75] Of this we shall have more
to say later, for there are clearly still issues outstanding
here. Augustine, too, will shed light for us.

---

[73] Martin Dibelius, *A Commentary on the Epistle of James* (Minneapolis:
Fortress/Hermaneia, 1976), p. 219
[74] Schweizer, *Matthew*, p. 147.
[75] Cullmann, *Prayer*, pp. 19ff.

Before moving on we ought to say a word about Matthew 17:20 // Mark 11:22ff.: the saying about faith and the moving of mountains. The difficulty is that it seems to portray faith as a human accomplishment and effort. But the promise is made even to faith 'the size of a mustard seed'. And so we must see the stress here as being not on faith as some human work, but upon the believer's renouncing of his or her powers and opting to rely on God's. Thus the engine of prayer is confidence in God – as in Psalm 86.

The Gospel of John and 1 John

If the study of the synoptics suggests that teaching on prayer is closely associated with the language of the Kingdom of God, we have to recognise that the vocabulary of the Johannine literature is rather different. Here too though there is a subtle indication given that the petitioner works within certain limits. The distinctive Johannine phrase is 'in my [Jesus'] name'. This formula functions in a similar way here to the synoptic assumption that prayer should be offered in submission to God's will: it qualifies petitions.[76] If the Johannine language seems more extravagant at first in its promises ('whatever you ask in my name') this is actually because the expression 'in my name' signifies a state of union between the believer and Jesus, not a merely external association of name. 'It is as though the union with Christ in Johannine prayer was experienced so intensely that there was no problem in leaving all individual wishes out of account.'[77] Here, we might say, 'submission' is recast as 'union'.

The 'Farewell Discourses' of John's Gospel comprise chapters 13 – 16, and are perhaps best known for the

[76] Ibid., p. 106. See also Andrew T. Lincoln, 'God's Name, Jesus's Name, and Prayer in the Fourth Gospel' in Longenecker (ed.), *Into God's Presence*, pp. 155–83.

[77] Cullmann, *Prayer*, p. 106.

promise of the Holy Spirit that they contain, but the motif of prayer is also an important one, recurring like a refrain at 14:13f., 15:7,16 and 16:24ff. Chapter 17 then contains the High Priestly Prayer of Jesus, in which he intercedes on behalf of his disciples. The prayer-motif is established firmly in this important and unusual Gospel section. The refrain-like effect of this is underlined by the very similar wording used at each point: 'I will do whatever you ask in my name, so that the Father may be glorified in the Son. If in my name you ask me for anything, I will do it' (Jn 14:13f.).

These words recall Matthew 7:7–11, but their context seems to reveal a more thoroughly worked out theological approach. The promise of verse 12 was that the disciples will do 'greater' works than Jesus, and like the prayer theme, such a promise depends upon one of the controlling metaphors of the discourse, that of 'indwelling'. This metaphor runs alongside the prayer-motif through all of these chapters, 13 – 17 (e.g. 15:1–8, 17:21a). The disciples do Jesus' work, and Jesus does what the disciples ask: their activity is seamless.[78] Schnackenburg interprets this to mean that, far from having almost every possible petition in mind, the evangelist is thinking particularly of the tasks and attendant difficulties of proclaiming the gospel.[79]

It is valuable to see that the phrase 'in my name' is not simply Johannine code for 'praying for the Kingdom' or saying 'not my will but yours be done'. A case could be made out for this. It would begin by recalling the importance of the 'name' in Jewish thought, the way in which it was taken to sum a person's character and meaning. Thus, to pray 'in X's name' would be to pray according to the character, the mind, of X. This interpretation is not far off, of course. But the Fourth Gospel's insight is yet more profound. 'A Christian prays

---

[78] Rudolf Schnackenburg, *The Gospel According to St John*, vol. 3 (New York: Crossroads, 1968), p. 72.
[79] See Lincoln, 'God's Name, Jesus' Name', pp. 168–70.

in Jesus' name in the sense that he is in union with Jesus,' says Raymond E. Brown.[80] For the 'in the name of' does not simply mean 'tuning in' to the character or mind of Christ, or even imitating it. Rather, the 'in my name' continues and develops the indwelling motif. Brown observes that 'because the Christian is in unison with Jesus and Jesus is in unison with the Father, there can be no doubt that the Christian's requests will be granted'.[81] But Brown is also quick to point out that this context of union with Jesus means that the requests involved will not be petty ones, but rather are of such a sort that when granted the Father is glorified in the Son (v. 13). Along similar lines to Schnackenburg, Brown suggests that they 'are requests pertinent to the Christian life and to the continuation of the work by which Jesus glorified the Father during his ministry (17:4)'.[82]

Both commentators agree in confining the petitions to be granted to those associated with mission, or, on Brown's more generous reading, those things 'pertinent to the Christian life'. Their linking of 'in my name' to the indwelling theme makes best sense of the text, here and in chapters 15 and 16. But at first sight it seems that they are bringing over assumptions from the synoptics in the restricting of the subject matter of prayer – unless we may be given fairly wide scope to interpret proper items for prayer under the headings of 'the Christian life' and 'mission'? But as we consider other crucial texts the case for their interpretation accumulates.

The indwelling theme resurfaces at 15:7: 'If you abide in me, and my words abide in you, ask for whatever you wish, and it will be done for you.' Verse 8 goes on to talk of the disciples bearing fruit for the glory of the Father. If these verses are kept tied together, then the 'whatever you please' seems to point towards the 'bearing fruit', and

---

[80] R. E. Brown, *The Gospel According to John*, vol. II (New York: Anchor/Chapman, 1971), p. 636.
[81] Ibid.
[82] Ibid.

becoming disciples. Thus 'whatever you ask' is an asking towards bearing fruit, discipleship. Indeed, this 'ask for whatever you want' is the strongest affirmation in the Gospel of the 'power of prayer', but the assumption is that – on the basis of union and indwelling with Jesus – the believer will ask for that which will bear fruit for Jesus.

The beginning of 16:24 recalls the synoptic sayings perhaps more than any other Johannine text: 'Ask and you will receive.' But the thrust of verses 23–27 is to be found in the different modes of presence of the Jesus who says 'in my name'. 'Until now you have not asked anything in my name' (v. 24), says Jesus, but when Jesus goes back to the Father and the Paraclete is given, this changes:

> Very truly, I tell you, if you ask anything of the Father in my name, he will give it to you. Until now you have not asked for anything in my name. Ask and you will receive, so that your joy may be complete (Jn 16:23f.).

At 16:26f. the implication seems to be that the disciples' faith and love makes them one with Jesus and therefore beloved of the Father, as is the Son: the mediator combines in himself both of the parties to be mediated. The Son is united with the Father, and the believer becomes involved in this relationship; the presence of the Spirit enables and enriches it. Here we have a clear presentiment of a theme that will occupy us later: the open Trinity.

If Christian prayer is conceived of as 'in the name of Jesus', in what sense is it qualified, restricted, or indeed opened up by such prayer? The Johannine 'answer' is helpful and definitive. The union of the believer with Christ, and the assurance that prayer will be answered because asked 'in his name', recalls the pneumatological reading of prayer given in Romans 8:26ff., where the indwelling of the Spirit not only makes prayer possible, but actually directs the content of that prayer – albeit content impossible for us to articulate in human language. This way in which efficacious prayer begins with as well as ends in God is another important and enduring insight. It is the reverse of the view that says that 'We answer our own prayers' – this reverse says 'Our prayers are God answering God.'

An added nuance to this distinctive understanding is given in 1 John, and we will quickly turn to that now. The writer of 1 John varies the Gospel's motifs in a particular way that – though not at odds with the Gospel – underlines one of its themes especially. The epistle's contribution comes in the way it 'unpacks' what the indwelling of the believer in Christ involves in a more practical way. Thus 1 John 3:22–24:

> and we receive from him whatever we ask, because we obey his commandments and do what pleases him. And this is his commandment, that we should believe in the name of his Son Jesus Christ and love one another, just as he has commanded us. All who obey his commandments abide in him, and he abides in them. And by this we know that he abides in us, by the Spirit that he has given us.

These verses are interesting for a number of different reasons. First, we notice straight away that the familiar formula ('in his name') is missing. Second, the promise of answered prayer once more seems very broad ('whatever we ask'). Third, despite the absence of the formula, the Gospel's indwelling theme is very much in evidence, though in a different form from the Gospel. Here the believer 'remains in God', and the proof of this inter-penetration of the Father is the presence of the Spirit. The epistle seems to have a less Christocentric orientation than the Gospel on this matter, and the writer of the epistle may not think so decisively of Jesus as the intermediary between Father and believer.[83]

---

[83] See David Rensberger, *1 John, 2 John, 3 John* (Nashville: Abingdon Press, 1997), p. 105.

But once more the granting of petitions is made conditional, not this time upon the formula 'in the name of Jesus' but 'because we obey his commandments and do what pleases him' (v. 22b). The keeping of commandments is then defined as (1) belief 'in the name' of the Son, and (2) mutual love, as commanded by the Son. If Christ is removed from the indwelling theme, he is very much present here as the ground of the believer's relationship to the Father.

Brown is probably right to see a covenant theology undergirding this. He says:

> We may situate the issue in the relationship of a covenanted people to its God. Part of the covenant is that the people of God live up to His commandants (words), not because they are an imposition or a test, but because they give expression to God's very nature as a just and loving God. In turn the people who live according to the commandments are brought close to the God whose justice and love they mirror in their lives, and the unity of wills brings the granting of their requests.[84]

This covenant interpretation points the way out of a possible dilemma. At first sight it may seem that the believer's lifestyle or even (more specifically) good deeds will be the condition for answered prayer (cf. Job 22:23–27) – not the granting of petitions dependent on what is asked for or the way it is asked for, but upon the good works of the ask-er. This dichotomy can be avoided: the pursuance of God's justice, for the author of 1 John, following in an honourable Jewish–Christian tradition, *unites the believer's will to God's* so that he or she always asks aright.

The verses at 1 John 5:14–16 contain nothing startling. The context here is prayer for fellow believers who have fallen into sin. The writer affirms that 'if we ask anything according to his will, he hears us'. The 'anything' here must be qualified by the context: 'If you see your brother or sister

---

[84] R. E. Brown, *The Epistles of John* (New York: Anchor/Chapman, 1983), p. 461. See Rensberger, *1 John, 2 John, 3 John*, pp. 107ff.

committing what is not a mortal sin . . . you will ask, and God will give life to such a one.' Verse 15 contains what must be taken as a very strong statement of the efficacy of such prayer – it is so certain that the believer will be answered that it is as if he or she has received his or her request even before he or she has offered it. 'And if we know that he hears us in whatever we ask, we know that we have obtained the requests made of him.'

Through these Johannine passages, then, we have seen apparently extravagant promises about prayer be thoroughly qualified by recurring motifs. The most prominent in the Gospel was that of mutual indwelling. We saw there that the use of the formula 'in my name' was very closely allied to that. In the epistle there is a less 'mystical' feel. Here the successful petitions are grounded in the believer's keeping of the commandments, and of asking in line with the will of God. The Gospel may well limit the appropriate requests to matters pertaining to the mission of the Christian community, or, more broadly, to the Christian life. That latter option may not be much of a limit! The epistle has one passage in which the nature of the petitions is very particular, and another in which they seem genuinely more open ended.

More New Testament Voices
Paul

> In Paul we see a Christian at prayer and the Christian practice of prayer in its fullness. In the letters his concern for his people and their problems is lifted up to God . . . all [letters] except Galatians and 2 Corinthians begin with an expression of thanksgiving for his readers and an assurance of constant prayer on their behalf (Rom. 1:8f, 1 Cor. 1:4, Phil. 1:3f, Col. 1:3–5,9, 1 Thes. 1:2, 3:9, 2 Thes. 1:3, 2:13, Phm. 4–6).[85]

We have a fuller picture of Paul from the epistles than any other 'early' Christian (in our discussion we cannot engage

---

[85] Smith, 'Prayer', p. 864.

questions of authorship, or make fine distinctions about the material in Acts), so we would expect to find a number of allusions to, teaching about, and indications of the practice of prayer.

We read of his petitions and his thanksgivings, and we have several substantial pieces of prayer material in his writings.[86] His praying is rooted in the revelation of God in Christ, it is borne up by the presence of the Spirit,[87] and it is noteworthy for our study that his intercessions are primarily for the spiritual needs of others rather than their 'everyday' ones.[88] He prays for their growth in grace and sanctification; he prays for, and requests prayers concerning his missionary tasks; he prays that Christians will live together in peace, and that their witness will enhance their proclamation of the gospel; in words probably derived from an early (Aramaic) liturgy, he prays for the final coming of the Kingdom in the parousia. Says Longenecker:

> Prayer in the Pauline epistles is never understood as something initiated by humans in order to awaken a sleeping or reluctant deity. Nor is it understood as negotiating or bargaining with God. Rather, it is always an acknowledgement of dependance on God, a response to what God has done in both creation and redemption, and a declaration of God's goodness in inviting people to present their praise and petitions before him.[89]

There are two passages in particular I want to examine: one deals, in part, with the role of the Spirit in prayer; the other touches on the question of 'unanswered' prayer – or rather, prayer that receives a different answer from the one requested.

---

[86] e.g., Rom. 15:5f., 13; Phil. 1:9–11; Col. 1:9–12; 1 Thes. 3:11–13, 5:23; 2 Thes. 1:11f., 2:16f.
[87] See Cullmann, *Prayer*, p. 71.
[88] See Richard N. Longenecker, 'Prayer in the Pauline Letters' in Longenecker (ed.), *Into God's Presence*, p. 225.
[89] Ibid., pp. 223ff.

The 'thorn in the flesh'
We begin with 2 Corinthians 12:7–10:

> Therefore, to keep me from being too elated, a thorn was given to
> me in the flesh, a messenger of Satan to torment me, to keep me
> from being too elated. Three times I appealed to the Lord about this,
> that it would leave me, but he said to me, 'My grace is sufficient for
> you, for power is made perfect in weakness.' So, I will boast all the
> more gladly of my weaknesses, so that the power of Christ may
> dwell in me. Therefore I am content with weaknesses, insults,
> hardships, persecutions, and calamities for the sake of Christ; for
> whenever I am weak, then I am strong.

This is a remarkable passage, showing as it does Paul's *via
crucis*, indicating his strong sense of suffering for and with
Christ. It exhibits one of those memorable and profound
Pauline paradoxes: not only is the divine foolishness wiser
than the wisdom of humanity, but the divine power is most
fully effective in human weakness. Quite apart from its
value as a commentary on the cross of Christ, Paul's 'thorn
in the flesh' has implications for a number of aspects of
Christian living, not the least of them being prayer.

Three times the apostle 'pleaded' with the Lord that his
affliction should be removed. Each time the answer was
'no', though Paul came to see that it was not a wholly
negative 'no'. For just as Paul is left to endure he is also
promised grace sufficient for his need and shown that this
is the way it must be for God's power to be most effective,
most powerful. Charles Elliott suggests that the first step
for Christians who feel powerless in the face of the world's
crisis today is actually to own up to that powerlessness and
look to the power which comes to perfection in our
weakness.[90]

This displays a theological and pastoral nuance not
always evident in our discussions of prayer, especially
when the impression seems to be that requests for healing

---

[90] Charles Elliott, *Praying the Kingdom* (London: DLT, 1985), ch. 1.

offered properly will *always* he heard. Paul's petition does not receive the hoped-for answer, but this is turned to good effect and into a spiritually beneficial experience. God is here acknowledged to be the best judge of these things! Augustine captures the mood of Paul well:

> We know not what to pray for as we ought in regard to tribulations, which may do us good or harm; and yet, because they are hard and painful, and against the natural feelings of our weak nature, we pray, with a desire which is common to mankind, that they may be removed from us. But we ought to exercise such submission to the will of the Lord our God, that if He does not remove those vexations we do not suppose ourselves to be neglected by Him, but rather, in patient endurance of evil, hope to be made partakers of greater good, for so His strength is perfected in our weakness.[91]

The Spirit's help

The theme of Romans 8 is the majestic one of life in the Spirit, and life lived in Christian hope. Paul speaks about the gift of the Spirit as the first fruits of God's deliverance, and speaks of the way in which creation joins with us in eager longing for final liberation. The Spirit's aid in this waiting and anticipation is vital. But the Spirit helps us in other ways too.

> Likewise the Spirit helps us in our weakness; for we do not know how to pray as we ought, but that very Spirit intercedes with sighs too deep for words. And God, who searches the heart, knows what is the mind of the Spirit, because the Spirit intercedes for the saints according to the will of God (Rom. 8:26f.).

The theme of 'weakness' is common with 2 Corinthians 12:7–10, and once more it is a weakness in which God

---

[91] Augustine, 'To Proba' in Marcus Dods (ed.), *The Works of Aurelius Augustine*, vol. 13, J. G. Cunningham (tr.) (Edinburgh: T & T Clark, 1875), XIV/25, p. 147ff. or http://www.newadvent.org/fathers/1102130.htm.

himself comes to help the believer with divine strength. Not here the strength to endure, or to exhibit or channel the power of God, but simply the strength to pray.

Karl Barth sees in this passage an admission that, as a human activity, prayer is a doomed enterprise: 'but because we wait upon God, our waiting is not in vain'.[92] It seems likely that, for Paul, this hopelessness is caused by our being caught in a sort of in-between state, the 'not yet'. The hope we entertain is for 'unseen things', and only the Spirit is able to anticipate these things in prayer. It is as if we are on a journey but are unaware of the destination. Leon Morris sees the widest possible application here:

> It is not only the case that we do not pray very well; it is also the case that, while we often think we know what we need, we are not always good judges of that either . . . Our horizon is always limited, and we do not know what is best.[93]

What Paul presents here is an eschatological understanding of prayer, and an eschatological analysis of the dilemmas of prayer. That is, prayer is not simply difficult because we have an imperfect understanding of ourselves, God and our world, nor because we have imperfect faith. Rather these difficulties are themselves rooted in the fact that we are in between times, and are awaiting that final deliverance of which we have but a foretaste. Prayer thus becomes an eschatological act – a yearning in hope, albeit with a reliance on God's Spirit to give voice to such hope because it is beyond our articulation. Says Ziesler: 'Whether the words are unspoken or unspeakable, unformulated or unable to be formulated, God understands the thoughts that are implicit. Only God understands God and it is God through his Spirit who is at work in these inarticulate prayers.'[94] God uses the

---

[92] Karl Barth, *The Epistle to the Romans* (Oxford: OUP, 1933), p. 317.
[93] Leon Morris, *The Epistle to the Romans* (Grand Rapids: Eerdmans, 1988), p. 327.
[94] J. Ziesler, *Paul's Letter to the Romans* (London: SCM, 1989), p. 223.

believer's weakness to make prayer more effective, more effective than it would be if we were not reduced to such helpless reliance on the Spirit – again an echo of 2 Corinthians 12:

> It is not simply that words fail believers who know all along what they want to pray for but cannot express it. The measure of their confusion and frustration as belonging to both epochs is that they do not know what God's will for them and their social context is . . . but the Spirit itself intercedes . . . This is precisely the wonder and the poignancy of the eschatological tension: the Spirit does not eliminate or transform believers' total inability to maintain the proper dialogue between God and man; rather the Spirit works in and through that inability.[95]

Paul's engagement with the subject of prayer is profound and illuminating. We have seen him make a genuinely creative attempt to deal with the question of unanswered prayer, and we have seen him construe prayer as an eschatological exercise. This immediately recalls the 'praying for the Kingdom' of the synoptics, and we must assume that eschatological prayer was a characteristic of the earliest church (see Rev. 22:20). This will need to figure in our constructive thinking on prayer.

Hebrews

One of the writings with which one associates the term 'intercession' in the New Testament is the Epistle to the Hebrews. The most obvious text is 7:25, and it may also serve to illustrate that a particular sort of intercession is denoted: 'his power to save those who come to God through him is absolute, since he lives for ever to intercede for them'. Jesus' intercessory and mediatory roles are both depicted here.

The reader of the epistle will already have seen (4:15f.) that it is Jesus' particular ability to sympathise with human

---

[95] James D. G. Dunn, *Romans 1–8* (Waco: Word, 1988), p. 477.

difficulties which makes him so able to represent them, and which makes him (and through him, God) so approachable. In 7:25 the role of intercession is underlined, and it is believed to have been part of the earliest confessions of faith (cf. Is. 53:12). Just as Jesus interceded for Peter (Lk. 22:32), and more generally for the other disciples (Jn 17), so now he intercedes for all who come to God through him. This intercession should not be envisaged as a desperate pleading with the reluctant Father to spare believers. Jesus' ministry is priestly but also royal. He should be pictured, suggests Swete, 'as a throned priest-King, asking what He wills from a Father who always hears and grants His request'.[96]

But what form does this intercession take? What is its purpose? The characteristic emphasis of the epistle on approach, and by implication, on acceptability to God, seems to lead in the direction of limiting the scope of Christ's intercession to obtaining forgiveness for the believer. However, the context here is somewhat more open than this. As Montefiore points out,[97] while intercession for help and forgiveness are not identical, they do overlap, and either could be in the writer's mind here.

Hebrews provides little more than a statement about prayer, if intercessory prayer in the general sense is what is meant in the sections on intercession, though it does also give an interpretation of intercession as mediated by Christ. Indeed, in the writer's eyes, the intercession is Christ's. Of course, while such a view may not have an exact likeness elsewhere in the New Testament, it is not without familiar echoes. It is not so far from the thought of Romans 8, where the Spirit prays in believers. It is also not so far removed from the Johannine understanding in which the believer and Christ are united, 'indwell' one another, in prayer as in other aspects of life. However, none of these

---

[96] H. B. Swete, *The Ascended Christ* (London: Macmillan, 1910), p. 95.
[97] Hugh Montefiore, *The Epistle to the Hebrews* (London: A & C Black, 1964), p. 129.

pictures have quite the same 'feel' as the one from Hebrews, coloured as it is by priestly images, of Christ interceding on behalf of believers. Perhaps the most to be said, in search of common themes, is that once more God (in this case the Son) seems to be playing a significant, perhaps even initiatory role, in offering prayer, not just receiving it: in some sense, prayer begins as well as ends with God.

James

If one looks for signs of wrestling with some of the more philosophical problems associated with prayer, and perhaps for some accommodation to those problems, the Epistle to James provides interesting material. It has a strong emphasis on the practical matters of Christian living and morals (Luther dubbed it the 'epistle of straw' because of what he saw as an improper importance given to 'good works'). But it also contains three references to prayer that demand our attention.

The writer begins by encouraging his readers in times of trial, and goes on to make these comments on prayer:

> If any of you is lacking in wisdom, ask God, who gives to all generously and ungrudgingly, and it will be given you. But ask in faith, never doubting, for the one who doubts is like a wave of the sea, driven and tossed by the wind; for the doubter, being double-minded and unstable in every way, must not expect to receive anything from the Lord (1:5–8).

This admonition is interesting firstly for what is considered the true subject matter of prayer – wisdom – but also for the implication that the reason for such a prayer being granted lies in the petitioner.[98] In Philippians 3:15 Paul suggests that God has more wisdom to reveal to those who

---

[98] Patrick J. Hartin, *James* (Collegeville: Liturgical Press, 2003), pp. 36, 59, 273.

are not yet mature, and the author of James may have something similar in mind when he counsels those who through afflictions are maturing toward moral perfection to pray for wisdom – to attain to a proper perspective on their circumstances. It is possible that disappointment over unanswered prayer in the Christian community also shows itself here in the way in which the request is rather limited in scope. This passage would hardly be enough to base such a theory upon, but when taken in conjunction with others the cumulative case for such an interpretation increases. Furthermore, if wisdom is not granted, the writer seems to suggest that rather than holding God responsible for the 'failure' we would do better to examine ourselves.

The usefulness of James as a reliable indicator to the contemporary understanding of these matters is shown by comparison to a slightly later document, *The Shepherd of Hermas*. In *Hermas* 9 we have advice that corresponds quite closely with these verses. While *Hermas* urges prayer and petition it also instructs its readers to 'purify your heart from all vanities of this world', which may limit the possible subjects of our petition to properly 'spiritual' ones. These of course (as with wisdom in Jas 1:5) are much more subjective in the way they are recognised and perceived. It is sometimes difficult to say whether someone has been granted wisdom or not: I might think my prayer has been answered; you might not! James and *Hermas* both insist on faith before requests will be granted. In this they follow a line which runs back through Paul (1 Cor. 12:9, for example) to Jesus himself (Mk 11:23f.).

James 4:3 says 'It is because you do not pray that you do not receive; when you do pray and do not receive, it is because you prayed wrongly, wanting to indulge your passions.' This verse (which again recalls *Hermas* 9:4) is set in the context of a discussion about disunity, and about 'befriending the world'. There seems a prima-facie case for a contradiction with Matthew 7:7, which we looked at earlier. This exercised the minds of the earliest Christian commentators somewhat, and it was often solved by analogy with a teacher. If a teacher promises her pupils that she will teach them a subject, she cannot be held responsible if a poor student fails to learn because of his own lack of ability. In the same way, thought the Fathers, answer to prayer must be understood to be linked with the manner in which one prays: one who prays for the Spirit, or wisdom, and yet does not receive them, they argued, prayed with frivolous motives.

Martin Dibelius, however, was convinced that this verse possesses great historical significance. He wrote:

> No doubt the enthusiastic certainty in the answer to prayer was widespread in the earliest communities due to particular experiences . . . Disappointments were inevitable, and they necessarily led to the qualification of the promise, so that answer to prayer became dependent either upon the disposition of the petitioner or upon the type of petition.[99]

If this is so, and it is impossible to prove it incontrovertibly from the text, the letter would represent one of the earliest efforts to come to terms with – perhaps even rationalise – unanswered prayer. Faced with prayers that apparently receive no answer, it is possible that James suggests two parallel strategies: finding fault in the pray-er; and petitioning for a narrower range of benefits (e.g. wisdom, rather than something more tangible).

The final passage of significance is found at James 5:14–16. After exhorting all 'in trouble' to pray, James has some words about prayers of healing for the sick. A rite evidently already established in the primitive Christian community is described, whereby the church elders anoint the sufferer with oil and pray over them. Verse 15 states, unequivocally, that 'The prayer of faith will save the sick, and the Lord will raise them up' – it goes on, 'and anyone who has committed sins will be forgiven.' This last phrase

---

[99] Dibelius, *James*, p. 219.

would appear to reflect the belief of illness caused by sin. While we would not generally feel comfortable with such a view today, we also know how human beings behave as psychosomatic unities, and understand something of how physical disorders may arise from the disjunction of relationships and inner harmonies. In such circumstances as James describes, both the cause and the effect may be removed by the power of prayer.

But does not the confidence with which the writer states 'the prayer of faith will save the sick' jar somewhat with what we have said about accommodation to disappointments, and the softening of such absolute promises? In fact the writer may be being subtler than he appears to be at first sight. The healing depends upon a *charisma*, a gift of the Spirit. This means that any disappointments could be explained as resulting from the lack of, or departure of, the *charisma* in the first place.

Further evidence for the encountering of disappointments over prayer may be present in verse 16, with its urging to mutual confession, and then its remarks about the prayer of the 'righteous' man. The need for confession before intercession clearly implies that some things need to be dealt with before the prayer might be heard: if these are not dealt with, perhaps not all (or any?) of the prayer will be heard. Similarly, the expression 'the righteous' is not meant to convey the image of some super-spiritual giant of the faith. It is the designation for any devout person in the traditional Jewish sense (cf. Ps. 34:15,17; Prov. 15:29), and is probably meant to include every believer. Nevertheless, the adjectival 'righteous' does provide some sort of qualification.

The Epistle of James, then, may provide us with real evidence that the early church had to wrestle with some of the problems of prayer. They seem to have coped with them, in so far as they did, by insisting on a proper attitude on behalf of the petitioner, and by narrowing the subject matter of prayer somewhat. The second restriction may be a considerable one; the first could give *carte blanche* to explain anything in prayer that does not turn out as we might have hoped. It is also, more sinisterly, a potentially brutal weapon to wield against fellow believers, impugning their faith and purity, and a potential source of abuse among believers. None of this is a necessary consequence from James: it is an abuse, however, that may be observed through the Christian centuries.

Conclusion

In conclusion, we must gather up the insights gained from our biblical study for our future investigations. To avoid delaying or pre-empting future discussion, I will list them briefly in summary form.

(1) Generally from the Old Testament we saw something of the variety of prayer, personal and corporate, and read some difficult texts. We also began to see how prayer involved exploration of God, could be costly to the pray-er, and involved the whole of our lives – including the socio-economic spheres. Any contemporary exercise in prayer may be similarly costly to the pray-ers, but perhaps so might a study of it.[100] In the Psalms, a scholar suggested, we see a microcosm of the Old Testament's theology of prayer: (i) is the cry of a servant to his or her God, (ii) in confidence that God will respond, (iii) and can help.

(2) We saw how notions of prayer and 'images' of God were closely related. We observed that the Old Testament seemed to offer an image of God as One who is 'personal, accessible, loving, powerful, and compassionate', and who seeks a relationship of partnership with humankind.

---

[100] 'Are we in the church prepared to risk questions that compel us to understand God differently from our ancestors . . .? Are we willing to rethink God's power, God's compassion, God's justice?' Balentine, *Prayer*, p. 294.

(3) World view is an issue that will never be far away from our conversation about intercession. The Old Testament seems to suggest a view of the world where God is active and present in all and to all.

(4) Most controversially, perhaps, some accounts of prayer suggest that our prayers can affect God's will and change events: 'One of the most remarkable features of the Old Testament is that people can *argue with God and win.*'[101]

(5) In the synoptics we observed the important part prayer played in the life of Jesus, and examined his distinctive mode of prayer – especially the intimate form of address, *Abba*, and thus Christian prayer's highly personal nature.

(6) The prayer in Gethsemane, that God's will be done, was presented as at the heart of Jesus', and the Christian's, prayers, though we also saw that it should not be read (as often it is) as simply a prayer of submission.

(7) The Lord's Prayer was seen to exhibit concern for everyday needs *and* yearning for the 'eschatological day'. Prayer for the coming Kingdom was central.

(8) This prayer for the Kingdom may have also been in mind in much other teaching about prayer, even when it appeared at first to be more wide ranging. Thus 'Seek first the Kingdom of God' could serve as a good motto for Christian prayer.

(9) We may have detected the first signs, in Luke's editorial work, of a grappling with unanswered prayer that led to a development in the thinking of the community. Jesus may have touched upon this problem himself; the community was to return to it, perhaps most overtly in the Epistle of James.

(10) Jesus called for persistence, confidence and trust in prayer.

---

[101] Sanders, *God Who Risks*, p. 64, italics mine.

(11) The Fourth Gospel portrayed the life of prayer more mystically, as being part of the mutual indwelling of believer and Jesus. Together with what Paul says about the Spirit's role in our prayer, we see the beginnings of a Trinitarian theology of intercession here. Because of this mutual indwelling, prayer 'in the name of Jesus' (understood as prayer for Jesus' purposes) would surely be answered. 1 John has a similar notion, expressed in the covenant theology of God's commandments.

(12) In the Johannine writings, and especially in Paul, we see that prayer both begins and ends in God. In Hebrews, Jesus' role as 'intercessor' in the believers' prayers reflects this. Alongside texts that speak of the Spirit aiding us in our prayers, 'interceding with sighs too deep for words', this points to the deep mystery that our prayers may be initiated by God in us.

(13) Paul also shows a creative way of dealing with unanswered prayer, and speaks of God's power through human weakness.

The struggle to comprehend prayer, and the temptation to limit its scope, continued as the Christian faith continued to develop. We now turn to see how questions like 'For what should we pray?' have been answered through the Christian centuries.

2

Beginning a History of Intercession

The God who is Free to Answer

Two strands from our examination of scripture need to be borne in mind as we contemplate our next step: a historical enquiry into the way intercession has been theologically configured. One is the way in which the earliest Christians grappled with the idea of some sort of proper limit on the content of petitions – understanding 'ask and you will receive' in a more or less narrow way. Another may be linked to this, may be its cause – it is the difficulty encountered when prayer appears to remain unanswered. In these strands we see a prefiguring of much of the debate about prayer that has taken place among theologians and philosophers in the following centuries.

But we will also see a new element. A third strand evident in scripture suggested that (sometimes) humans can 'argue with God and win', but subsequent theologians of prayer have been much more cautious with such claims. God's 'knowing best' is a scriptural position too, but it seems to become less flexible and pliant under the influence of ideas from elsewhere. Prayer is still thought to make a difference, but in a way that may seem less convincing. Part of this debate we will now try to touch upon. We cannot attempt a thorough review of every development and writer. Instead we will offer a brief account and critical analysis of a cluster of major treatments, attempting to set up a debate between major historical figures and our own concerns. The writers chosen have not been selected in an entirely arbitrary way; indeed the list resembles something like a roster of the 'giants' of theological history. They have been chosen because of their general importance, and because they have written significantly on prayer. They also represent various theological epochs and approaches. They are Origen, Augustine, Thomas Aquinas, John Calvin, Friedrich Schleiermacher and Karl Barth, and the order of treatment will not be chronological, but more thematic.

Augustine

It may well be claimed for Augustine of Hippo (354–430) that he stands as the most influential thinker from Patristic times. Augustine's theology is always overlaid with concerns for pastoral matters and Christian spirituality, even though he also turns his hand readily to polemic. But his treatment of prayer in the letter *To Proba* is certainly both pastoral and deeply spiritual. It was written in 412 to the wealthy widow of a Roman nobleman who had fled to Carthage and established a religious community there, following the sack of Rome in 410. She became a friend of Augustine, and often turned to him for help and counsel. One of the subjects upon which she turned to him was prayer, and, judging by Augustine's letter, many of her concerns and questions were very 'contemporary'.

Augustine advises Proba to cultivate detachment to her wealth and possessions. Before one can properly devote oneself to prayer a certain 'desolation' is required.[1] 'Detachment' is an interesting concept in the theology of prayer. Perhaps it begins in the Gospels when Jesus urges his disciples not to worry about their material needs, but instead to set their hearts on the Kingdom of God (Mt. 6:33). The idea reaches some sort of climax in Meister

---

[1] Augustine, 'To Proba', III/7, p. 147ff. or http://www.newadvent.org/fathers/1102130.htm.

Eckhart, writing in the thirteenth century.[2] For him, the one who would draw near to God in prayer must first become detached from outward and inward distractions. Gerard Hughes uses the similar notion of 'indifference' in his *God of Surprises*, a book that owes a great deal to a different historic tradition of prayer, the Ignatian.[3] The doctrine is neither as austere nor as world denying as it might at first appear, though it can too easily become what Schleiermacher calls 'resignation'.[4] Here, detachment becomes the inability to prefer one possible course of events rather than another, and suggests a God who is totally deterministic. Indeed, Augustine's God seems to tend that way, as one might expect from a champion of predestination. Augustine can say that:

> if anything is ordered in a way contrary to our prayer, we ought, patiently bearing the disappointment, and in everything giving thanks to God, to entertain no doubt whatever that it was right that the will of God and not our will should be done.[5]

Benignly, this quite properly asserts that God's will cannot be forced or overpowered in prayer. More sinisterly, such a strong notion of the divine will might immediately qualify any ideas of petition and intercession.

What to pray for, and the problem of prayer being unanswered, are linked at this point in Augustine's thought. The topics for prayer coincide with those of the Lord's Prayer.[6] Augustine does, it is true, interpret this fairly magnanimously. He tells Proba that 'a short solution of your difficulty [over what to pray for] may be given

---

[2] For an account of Eckhart with particular reference to this 'detachment', see Terry Tastard, *The Spark in the Soul* (London: DLT, 1989), pp. 38–67.

[3] Gerard Hughes, *God of Surprises* (London: DLT, 1987), p. 185.

[4] See the discussion of Schleiermacher below, and then Barth's comments.

[5] Augustine, ' To Proba', XIV/26, p. 161.

[6] Ibid., XII/22, p. 158.

thus: "Pray for a happy life."[7] Even this happiness is qualified by propriety: 'He . . . is truly happy who has all that he wishes to have, and wishes to have nothing which he ought not to wish.'[8]

The legitimate wishes of men and women do, however, encompass some fairly mundane items. They may quite properly wish (and, therefore, pray) for marriage and children. They may also wish for honour and power for themselves so long as they want to use these qualities to promote the interests of those who may become dependent upon them.[9] Prayer for financial gain is not disqualified either, though a certain equilibrium of wealth is best: neither too rich, nor too poor – Proverbs 30:8 is quoted, 'give me neither poverty nor riches'.[10] Prayer can petition for friendship. Of these things and more Augustine can say 'For all these things . . . it becomes us to pray: if we have them, that we keep them; if we have them not, that we may get them.' But such mundane needs do not get to the heart of true happiness, for:

> we know that both the competency of things necessary, and the well-being of ourselves and of our friends, so long as these concern this present world alone, are to be cast aside as dross in comparison with the obtaining of eternal life.[11]

Augustine places prayers for the 'unseen' above prayers for the 'seen'. These terms are quite useful for referring to a range of prayer topics that we will encounter, and indeed that we have already come across in the scriptures: prayers for the Holy Spirit, for eternal life, and even for the Kingdom, may seem to be for realities beyond our normal vision, even if they are experienced with extraordinary intimacy, or if their effects may be perceived by the human eye.

---

[7] Ibid., IV/9, p. 149.
[8] Ibid., V/11, p. 150.
[9] Ibid., VI/12, p. 150.
[10] Ibid., VI/12, p. 151.
[11] Ibid., VII/14, p. 152.

We may have seen a shift taking place in the New Testament where, as time passed, the stress seemed to be more on prayer for 'unseen' things and less on mundane things. A possible motivation for such a development, it was suggested, was that problems had been experienced in having prayers for more 'tangible' things answered. If worldly goods are not forthcoming – prayer remains 'unanswered' – then it may be 'safer' to proscribe the topics for prayer to things less easily perceived. This is an understandable, though dubious move. It is dubious because it 'gives up' on prayer for things that affect our everyday lives. In our discussion of the Lord's Prayer we saw a double meaning to the petition for daily bread – not just the bread of the coming Kingdom, but also the bread we need to live today and tomorrow: the 'competency of things necessary', in Augustine's terms. Even if Jesus told his disciples to put the Kingdom first and not worry about material things, he also assured them that God is concerned about such things and will provide them.

But there is a further problem in that it now seems more difficult to account for unanswered prayer for such unseen qualities. While the 'narrowing' of petition to such things as 'wisdom' (as in James), or 'eternal life', or other such 'unseen' commodities may seem helpful because it decreases the problems of intervention, or the matter of disappointment, in other ways it actually increases the problematic paradox of petition. If I petition God for wisdom but still seem unwise then it may appear that the fault must lie in myself – my disposition is not ready, or perhaps the time is not right. But can it ever *not* be the right time for wisdom? And why would God wait for me to pray before giving 'all good things', before giving wisdom to me?

These questions may not be totally insoluble. Indeed, Augustine himself hints at some answers. But the switch from 'seen' to 'unseen' by no means cuts the knot of petition and intercession. Augustine addresses head on the question of praying to a God who knows our needs better than we do ourselves:

Why this [encouragement to pray] should be done by Him who 'before we ask Him knoweth what things we have need of', might perplex our minds, if we did not understand that the Lord our God requires us to ask not that thereby our wish may be intimated to Him, for to Him it cannot be unknown, but in order that by prayer there may be exercised in us by supplication that desire by which we may receive what he prepares to bestow. His gifts are very great, but we are small and straitened in our capacity of receiving . . .[12]

So Augustine suggests that, far from informing God, or even properly asking God for this or that, our prayers serve to make us ready to receive what God has decided to give us. God wills wisdom for all: when we pray earnestly and properly for wisdom, we make ourselves fit to receive it. Our hearts, as it were, are prepared for the divine wisdom as soil might be prepared for the seed. Presumably, when I ask for some worldly good, God similarly sees this as a preparation of the heart to receive God's gifts in the proper spirit.

Three points can be made immediately about this argument. The first is that Augustine seems to have moved the praying goalposts: *petition* has become *preparation*. We ask not to receive, but to be ready.

The second point is that, if God withholds wisdom until that moment when, by prayer, we make ourselves ready to receive it, how does this differ materially from the cruder perception? In one, we pray for 'z', and God answers by giving 'z' to us. In Augustine's refined explanation: God wills to give us 'z' but withholds it until we properly prepare ourselves by praying for 'z'. The end result is the same, and in both our prayer has, so to speak, 'triggered' the divine gift. What is different is in the suggestion that *God only gives that which he has always determined to give*. When petition becomes preparation the pray-er cannot 'argue with God' about the 'what' but only the 'when'. The third point is that Augustine can only make such a

---

[12] Ibid., VIII/19, p. 155.

suggestion because of his strongly predestinarian approach: God's will is deterministic, specifically, it is *pre-*deterministic. The 'solution' which his divine determinism offers him is only required because of the particular views which Augustine, like so many who wrote before and after him, holds about the omnipotence, omniscience and immutability of God – questions to which we will return later. If God has always determined to give 'z', and this is understood within a framework where everything is pre-determined, then we may assume that the prayer and the answer is also pre-determined.

The use of words in prayer performs a similar function, according to Augustine. His remarks suggest that when we externalise our prayers in words we can more easily observe them and so gauge our progress in prayer, and appropriate and internalise them. 'To us, therefore, words are necessary, that by them we may be assisted in considering and observing what we ask, not as means by which we expect that God is to be either informed or moved to compliance.'[13] Augustine gives an example here:

> When we say: 'Thy kingdom come', which shall certainly come whether we wish it or not, we do by these words stir up our own desires for that kingdom, that it may come to us, and that we may be found worthy to reign in it.[14]

Augustine's position on prayer is shot through with ambiguity, then. He encourages us to pray for things worldly and 'spiritual', the seen as well as the unseen. But he seems to classify one type as more worthy than the other. He also says that in asking for this or that we are not persuading God to give it, but preparing ourselves to receive it – though we have noted that there are similarities between some of the questions raised by these positions. All this is stated against a background of a highly

---

[13] Ibid., IX/18, p. 155; XI/121, p. 157.
[14] Ibid., XI/21, p. 157.

deterministic deity, who has decided in advance what will and will not be given, a position that might be thought to undermine prayer of any sort.

Immanuel Kant and Friedrich Schleiermacher

Augustine's position finds echoes in what may seem unexpected places as the history of the theology of prayer unfolds: in Kant (1724–1804) and in Schleiermacher (1768–1834), both associated with liberal theology, to name but two. The combination of ideas discovered in Augustine leaves the reader with the impression that prayer in no way affects God, or alters the way things will go; rather prayer is an act which may affect the pray-er, and the way he or she goes. On moral grounds, Kant propounded a similar theory of prayer. He felt that any attempt to influence the deity with our requests was undesirable superstition. In his *Religion Within the Limits of Reason Alone* he argues that the purpose of private prayer is 'firmly to establish goodness in ourselves, and repeatedly to awaken the disposition of goodness in the heart'.[15] Kant believes that God's wise plan cannot (and should not) be diverted by our prayers, and that 'we cannot hold that any prayer which is for a non-moral object is sure to be heard'.[16] Kant construes corporate prayer in a similar vein. Prayer in church is not a 'means of grace', but a 'moral ceremony'.[17]

Kant's writings have been enormously influential for theology. His work, representing the full flower of the Enlightenment, brings together two highly significant cultural and intellectual developments. One is the scientific world view, which was based upon the work of Newton and others. While it is true that Kant wanted to limit the scientific epistemology so as to make room for the insights and truth of religion, morality and art, he also accepted (as

[15] Immanuel Kant, *Religion Within the Limits of Reason Alone* (New York: Harper Torchbooks, 1960), p. 181.
[16] Ibid., p. 184.
[17] Ibid., p. 185.

an 'Enlightenment fact') the closed universe that science described. Direct divine action was not to be considered. The highly mechanistic conception of natural regularity made it impossible for those working with such a framework to conceive of God's influence on the world as anything other than a 'suspension' of the prevailing order. The second development was the autonomy of the human individual. Our modern ideas of individuality began to emerge in recognisable forms during this period, and Kant's individual was one who desired to live his or her own life, making his or her own moral decisions, without the well-meaning interference of any god. These factors go some way towards explaining Kant's highly moralistic account of prayer.

Schleiermacher is usually spoken of as the most influential theologian of the nineteenth century. He was influenced by German pietism and the Romantic movement. His work also reflects the impact of Kant, and the developments we have mentioned.

Schleiermacher's major work, *The Christian Faith*, was published in 1829, thirty-six years after *Religion Within the Limits of Reason Alone*. In *The Christian Faith* he argues most strongly that 'the religious self-consciousness . . . coincides entirely with the view that all . . . things are conditioned and determined by the interdependence of nature'[18] and that 'it can never be necessary in the interest of religion so to interpret a fact that its dependence on God absolutely excludes its being conditioned by the system of Nature'.[19] As stated above, this mechanistic understanding of nature could not conceive of divine influence being exerted without a breakdown or suspension of this 'system'. Thus Schleiermacher stresses that prayer and its fulfilment or refusal must be seen as part of the original divine plan (rather than *ad hoc* adjustments to it) 'and consequently the

---

[18] Friedrich Schleiermacher, *The Christian Faith*, H. R. Mackintosh (tr.) (Edinburgh: T & T Clark, 1928), p. 170.
[19] Ibid., p. 178.

idea that otherwise something else might have happened [i.e. prayer changing the course of events] is wholly meaningless'.[20]

Here we see Schleiermacher's Newtonian view of the world. Everything is 'conditioned and determined by nature'. But this Newtonian view has become wedded to the ancient Christian notion of predestination: 'our statement places prayer, too, under the divine preservation, so that prayer and its fulfilment or refusal are only part of the original divine plan'.[21] In Schleiermacher, Augustine and the Enlightenment meet!

As Schleiermacher continues he once more shows his debts to the past: like Kant, he claims the moral high ground in prayer, and shows further evidence of how thoroughly Newtonian his view is; like Augustine, from a base of predestination, he goes on to discuss what we should pray for and how we may still expect answers, in a way which is paradoxical or contradictory, depending on one's assessment.

His debt to Kant (and to Newton) comes through in answering his own question of whether the 'hearing' of prayer is a delusion. Any belief that we exert real influence on God's will and purposes, and deflect them, 'conflicts with our primary and basal presuppositions that there can be no relation of interaction between creature and creator'.[22] This seems an extraordinary assertion: is Schleiermacher discounting any interactions between God and the world? Or is he claiming that the world cannot affect God (a doctrine with a long pedigree in Christian tradition)? For Schleiermacher, any theory of prayer that makes such assumptions about influencing God can only be described as a 'lapse into magic'.[23] Thus, on 'scientific' (or, more properly, metaphysical) and moral grounds he shuns the view that 'prayer changes things'.

---

[20] Ibid., p. 180.
[21] Ibid.
[22] Ibid., p. 673.
[23] Ibid.

However, he can still go on – in a very Augustinian style – to ask questions about the right mode of praying in order for the prayer to be answered, and what such an answer might be. With reference to the Fourth Gospel, he argues that only prayer in the name of Jesus, and that means both reflecting his concern and made in his spirit, will be heard.[24] This goal, of prayer in the name of Jesus, is more likely to be attained by the corporate prayer of the church, where less is left to the idiosyncrasies of individuals. Indeed, prayer offered in Jesus' name 'in view of the power received by the Son from the Father . . . cannot but be fulfilled'.[25] But what can it mean for prayer to be 'heard', bearing in mind what Schleiermacher has already said about the impossibility and undesirability of 'deflecting' God's purposes?

Prayer offered in the name, in the spirit, with the concerns of Jesus, is prayer which follows the normative pattern for prayer, that is, prayer for the Kingdom of God.

> But between prayer and its fulfilment there exists a connexion due to the fact that both things have one and the same foundation, namely, the nature of the Kingdom of God. In that Kingdom the two are one – prayer as Christian presentiment growing out of the whole action and influence of the divine Spirit, and fulfilment as experience of Christ's ruling activity in relation to the same object. Seen thus, fulfilment would not have come had there been no prayer: for then the point would not yet have arrived in the development of the Kingdom of God on which the fulfilment must follow. But fulfilment does not come because prayer is offered (as though prayer could here be regarded isolatedly as a cause in itself), but because the right prayer can have no other object than what is in line with the divine good pleasure. Neither would it have come, in virtue of the divine decree, even had there been no prayer (as though the divine decree bore upon particulars apart from their natural nexus): it comes because the inward state that gives rise to

---

[24] Ibid., p. 671.
[25] Ibid.

prayer itself forms part of the conditions under which it was possible for the result eventually to emerge.[26]

This is a telling extract, and shows just how thoroughly Schleiermacher has worked the Augustinian position into his scheme, and how he has integrated it into the Newtonian world view. On the one hand, he still (like Augustine) wants to say that prayers are answered – the right prayers, for the right things, at the right moments, of course. He is able to dovetail this with his predestinarian/ scientific deterministic position by asserting that (1) the 'right' prayer is itself part of the divine plan ('prayer growing out of the whole action and influence of the divine Spirit'), and (2) similarly, the 'answer' is also part of the pre-ordained programme. Like Augustine, then, Schleiermacher suggests that our prayer is really the method by which we prepare ourselves for that which God has already determined to give. His further qualifications, however, serve to weaken the link between prayer and fulfilment that he has laboured to establish. He weakens this link is two ways.

First, and quite reasonably, he argues that for prayer to be answered it must be 'in line with the divine good pleasure'. It is when he considers the obverse, whether the answer would have come without the prayer, that the real difficulty arises. He wants to say that it would not, that the state of affairs obtained because of the prayer is linked to the prayer in a direct way. He has already said that the prayer must not be considered a cause. But at the conclusion of the above extract he states that the answer and the prayer are alike embedded in a particular stage of the development of the Kingdom (a phrase with an almost Hegelian ring). Unless the right moment has come for the prayer, the right moment will not have come for its answer: the fulfilment 'comes because the inward state that gives rise to prayer itself forms part of the conditions under

---

[26] Ibid., p. 673f.

which it was possible for the result eventually to emerge'. They are not related causally, but by their co-incidence in the progress of the Kingdom of God. But what if the right moment comes for the prayer, and more urgently for the 'fulfilment' of the right prayer? Are we to understand that the fulfilment is delayed, waiting for the prayer, so to speak – which would cast them back into a causal, or more sequential relationship? Or must we suppose, and this seems more akin to Schleiermacher's other arguments, that the prayer is inevitable because pre-ordained? If the latter is the case, then the link between prayer and fulfilment is shown to be truly tenuous: the prayer becoming a fiction, or illusion, planted by God in the worldly process, in order to anticipate that which will surely come.

This predestinarian interpretation is supported by Schleiermacher's use of the concept of 'resignation'. His sermon entitled 'The Power of Prayer in Relation to Outward Circumstances' takes as its text the prayer of Jesus in Gethsemane. Jesus' prayer to be delivered from the cross was not answered by deliverance. Instead Jesus learnt submission to the will of God. Thus Schleiermacher joins countless other writers and thinkers in seeing this prayer in Gethsemane as the prototype of all Christian prayer. Yet Schleiermacher claims that Christians have the privilege of laying before God the 'wishes about the more important concerns of [their] lives'.[27]

Schleiermacher goes on, 'But while I most sincerely encourage you to do this, I just as earnestly entreat you . . . by no means to feel sure that what you ask will of necessity take place because of your prayer.'[28] Far from bending God's will, in Jesus' case it merely served the opposite process. He:

---

[27] 'Selected Sermons of Schleiermacher' in Friedrich Schleiermacher and Keith W. Clements (ed.), *Friedrich Schleiermacher: Pioneer of Modern Theology* (London: Collins, 1987), pp. 185–94. This quotation from p. 186f.
[28] Schleiermacher, *The Christian Faith*, p. 187.

bent his own wish before the thought that the will of the Father might be something different. To reconcile himself to this, and willingly to consent to it, was now his chief object. There you see the effect that such a prayer ought to have.[29]

Prayer has as its chief purpose the aligning of our will to God's, and the seeking of courage to endure difficulty and hardship.[30] What other end can it have, given Schleiermacher's divine determinism? If we lay our wishes before God, he says, we are laying them before the unchangeable, 'in whose mind no new thought or purpose can arise since the day when he said, "all is very good". What was then decreed will take place; we must not lose sight of the indisputable certainty of this thought.'[31] Resignation to the divine will is the only option.[32] (See Barth's comments on 'resignation' below.)

So certain and convinced is Schleiermacher that God's will is all-determining, and that the human will is pretty worthless (perhaps here he is less a follower of the Enlightenment doctrine of autonomy and more one of the Reformation and Augustinian doctrine of total depravity), that he further undermines the suggestion that human prayers are woven into the divine purpose in advance: this is not, for Schleiermacher, a question of omniscience but of omnipotence; it is a matter of immutability, and of omni-competence and sole-competence, in the divine:

or is this your idea: it is true that the Eternal cannot change his purpose, but knowing all things beforehand, he knew when and what his pious and beloved children would ask from him, and has so arranged the chain of events that the issue shall accord with their wishes? That is at once to honour the wisdom of God and to flatter the childish fancies of men.[33]

---

[29] Ibid., p. 189.
[30] Ibid., pp. 189, 192.
[31] Ibid., pp. 189, 185
[32] Ibid., p. 670.
[33] Schleiermacher and Clements (ed.), *Friedrich Schleiermacher*, p. 188.

In this matter, Schleiermacher goes further than Augustine.

In putting the conformation of human will to the divine will at the centre of his theology of prayer, Schleiermacher is reflecting a central insight of the Christian tradition. But there seems little left of his other assertions about the value and purpose of prayer once they have been scrutinised except this conformation of the human will to the divine. The double determinism he has inherited from Augustine and Newton forbids otherwise. Indeed, his position serves not only to narrow down the contents of prayer to that of mere resignation to the divine purpose (a narrowing even beyond the most extreme form which may be seen in the New Testament), it also contrives to lock the believer (in fact, all creatures) into an hermetically sealed and divinely determined system with no place for the exercise of human free will and no interchange between God and those whom God has made.

This verdict on Schleiermacher would seem to lead us back to consider one who, in our popular theological stereotypes, may be particularly associated with predestinarian views – John Calvin. In fact, as I hope to show shortly, Calvin's treatment is rather more open than Schleiermacher's. But before we come to Calvin we will go back further, to the great doctor of medieval theology, Thomas Aquinas.

Thomas Aquinas

Aquinas' enquiry into prayer, like all other enquiries in the *Summa Theologiae*, is laid out in a logical series of objections and refutations under a series of questions and articles. The justification for the practice of prayer is necessary because 'it behoves us to account for the utility of prayer as neither to impose necessity on human affairs subject to Divine providence, nor to imply changeableness on the part of the Divine disposition'.[34] Aquinas' answer has a familiar ring:

---

[34] Thomas Aquinas, *Summa Theologiae* (London: Burns & Oates, 1922), 2/2, Q.83, http://www.newadvent.org/summa/308302.htm.

For we pray not that we may change the Divine disposition, but that we may impetrate that which God has disposed to be fulfilled by our prayers, in other words 'that by asking, men may deserve to receive what Almighty God from eternity has disposed to give,' as Gregory says (Dial. i, 8).[35]

Thus understood, Aquinas continues, we pray not to tell God of our needs and desires, for God already knows these. Instead, our prayers help us by reminding us of the 'necessity of having recourse to God's help in these matters'.[36] This is, presumably, not a question of the necessity of gaining some new input by God into the chain of events through our prayers – this chain is decided from eternity. Instead it must be the necessity of living lives open to God in a more general way, and open to divine strengthening grace. 'Our motive in praying', writes Aquinas, 'is not that we may change the Divine disposition, but that, by our prayers, we may obtain what God has appointed.'[37] Again: 'We ought not to endeavour to make God will what we will; on the contrary, we ought to strive to will what He wills',[38] for as Socrates says, 'when we pray we frequently ask for what it had been better for us not to obtain'.[39]

Aquinas (1225–1274) seems to occupy more than a chronological mid-point between Augustine (to whom he refers with great regularity) and Schleiermacher.[40] This is all the more interesting when one remembers Aquinas' seminal position in so much Roman Catholic theology. Like these two writers, especially Augustine, this basic starting point in the theology of prayer which seems to cut the

---

[35] Ibid., 2/2, Q.83, http://www.newadvent.org/summa/308302.htm.
[36] Ibid., 2/2, Q.83, http://www.newadvent.org/summa/308302.htm.
[37] Ibid., 2/2, Q.83, http://www.newadvent.org/summa/308302.htm.
[38] Ibid., 2/2, Q.83, http://www.newadvent.org/summa/308305.htm.
[39] Ibid., 2/2, Q.83, http://www.newadvent.org/summa/308305.htm.
[40] Terrance Tiessen reflects a similar judgement on Aquinas, though I take issue with him on how Calvin and Barth may be thought to figure in any 'line of descent': *Providence and Prayer* (Downers Grove: IVP, 2000), p. 179.

ground from under further debate does not stop Aquinas from pursuing other questions: should we pray for temporal things? for example. Aquinas answers this in the affirmative. We are to seek temporal gifts not in the first but in the second place. In saying that the Kingdom must be sought first, Jesus does not imply that temporal goods are not to be sought at all, but that they should be sought afterwards, 'not in time but in importance'.[41] More and more echoing Augustine, and perhaps going a little further than him here, Aquinas stipulates that we may ask for such temporal things in so far as they are 'expedient for salvation'.[42] Much nearer our own time, H. H. Farmer was to make similar assertions.[43] Farmer argued rather more positively than Aquinas for the propriety of temporal petitions, saying that only through such everyday things does the life of the spirit take on reality, thus perhaps implying that 'first and second place language' is out of place; he also suggests that the limitation upon this is provided by God's purposes – paralleling Aquinas' 'expedient for salvation'. Thus a businessman or woman may pray for his or her business, not so that he or she can make lots of money, but so that others will be benefited by its enterprise.

Praying for 'temporal' things extends to the 'necessities' of life. Aquinas suggests a limit here: the limit of God's greater knowledge of our needs. 'He who faithfully prays God for the necessaries of this life, is both mercifully heard, and mercifully not heard. For the physician knows better than the sick man what is good for the disease.'[44] There is a further qualification along these lines:

---

[41] Aquinas, *Summa Theologiae*, 2/2, Q.83, http://www.newadvent.org/summa/308306.htm.

[42] Ibid., 2/2, Q.83, http://www.newadvent.org/summa/308306.htm.

[43] H. H. Farmer, *The World and God* (London: Nisbet, 19362), pp. 262ff.

[44] Aquinas, *Summa Theologiae*, 2/2, Q.83, http://www.newadvent.org/summa/308315.htm.

without any doubt we receive what we ask for, yet when we ought to receive it: 'since certain things are not denied to us, but are deferred that they may be granted at a suitable time', according to Augustine . . . and again this may be hindered if we persevere not in asking for it.[45]

Yet through all this talk of what will be given, or deferred for the propitious moment, or 'mercifully not heard', Aquinas inserts a refrain which seems to undermine all this talk of asking and being heard: 'Prayer is offered up to God, not that we may bend Him, but that we may excite in ourselves the confidence to ask.'[46] What does asking mean and imply within such an understanding of God? Elsewhere in the *Summa* Aquinas shores up this somewhat deterministic position. 'We must therefore say that what happens here by accident, both in natural things and in human affairs, is reduced to a pre-ordaining cause, which is Divine Providence.'[47] He goes on in this section to quote Augustine that 'nothing happens at random in the world', but all by Divine providence. Alongside this 'foreordination' of events is foreknowledge of them, though technically for Aquinas God does not 'know things in advance' as the 'fore' suggests, because God is atemporal. For Aquinas it is likely that the notion of God's 'eternity' is the means by which he is able in some sense to reconcile divine determinism, divine knowledge and human freedom.[48] The relation of divine foreknowledge to ideas of divine determinism and human freedom is hotly contested, and we shall have to return to it.

In this omni-controlling providence, the causation of the natural world and of human beings functions as a system of secondary causes: 'God's immediate provision over everything does not exclude the action of secondary causes: which are the executors of His order.'[49] Aquinas

---

[45] Ibid., 2/2, Q.83, http://www.newadvent.org/summa/308315.htm.
[46] Ibid., 2/2, Q.83, http://www.newadvent.org/summa/308309.htm
[47] Ibid., 1/5, Q. 116, http://www.newadvent.org/summa/111601.htm.
[48] See Tiessen, *Providence*, p. 190.
[49] Aquinas, *Summa Theologiae*, 1/1, Q. 22, http://www.newadvent.org/summa/102203.htm.

does insist on creaturely free will exercised through these 'secondary causes', part of a terminology taken over from Aristotle. But even allowing for the technical sense in which Aquinas uses 'secondary cause' one is moved to ask whether it is not a fiction to use the term 'cause' at all if everything is predetermined 'behind the scenes'. Here we find ourselves faced with a position sometimes known as 'compatibilism', in which human free will and divine determinism are somehow asserted to be concurrent – though when pushed most writers in such a position seem to favour the divine over the creaturely will.[50] In his section on the will of God Aquinas takes the paradox between divine determinism and 'natural causation' to almost unbearable lengths. 'The will of God must needs always be fulfilled', he says,[51] but goes on to suggest that the divine will does not impose necessity on all things: 'to some effects He has attached necessary causes, that cannot fail; but to others defectible and contingent causes, from which arise contingent effects'.[52] How this squares with 'nothing happens at random in the world' is not straightforward. He goes on, 'Hence it is not because the proximate causes are contingent that the effects willed by God happen contingently, but because God has prepared causes for them, it being His will that they should happen contingently.'[53] But what is the force of 'prepared' here? And does it undermine the argument? 'From the very fact that nothing resists the divine will, it follows that not only those things happen that God wills to happen, but that they happen necessarily or contingently according to His will.'[54] Even allowing for the distinction he proceeds to make between absolute and conditional necessities, this logic seems to take us to the brink of theological non-sense

---

[50] See Tiessen, *Providence*, pp. 184–93, et al.

[51] Aquinas, *Summa Theologiae*, 1/1, Q. 19, http://www.newadvent.org/summa/101906.htm.

[52] Ibid., 1/1, Q. 19, http://www.newadvent.org/summa/101906.htm.

[53] Ibid., 1/1, Q. 19, http://www.newadvent.org/summa/101908.htm.

[54] Ibid., 1/1, Q. 19, http://www.newadvent.org/summa/101908.htm.

– or perhaps, more positively, profound paradox. In what way do these counter-assertions qualify one another? How does 'conditional necessity' qualify the statement that 'nothing happens at random'? How can God *determine* that some occurrences happen *contingently*?

Aquinas' position seems similar to Augustine's in its determinism, and in the contention that in prayer we ask for those things that God has already determined to give. He resembles Augustine also in the way that prayer is portrayed as an activity that affects us rather than God. His debt to Augustine is apparent from the many references to him. If his system seems more rigid than Augustine's it may be because of the structure of the *Summa* and the more thoroughly pressed version of the arguments. If his position seems to reach similar conclusions while showing evidence of less ambiguity, it may be that Aquinas is a victim of his own method. Against the background of Aquinas' thought Calvin's may seem similar, and yet more nuanced, more paradoxical in a genuine sense, more personal, and provide more of a spur to prayer.

John Calvin

For Calvin (1509–1564) prayer is 'the chief exercise of faith, and [that] by which we daily receive God's benefits'.[55] We find two great paradoxes in Calvin's thought on prayer. The first is this: on the one hand we find the freedom and sovereignty of God plainly asserted, but on the other hand enough assertion of the freedom of the believer to undercut any simplistic predestinarian stereotype. The second concerns anthropomorphic language used of God freely, with a simultaneous recognition of the inadequate and highly provisional nature of such language – a qualification made so strongly that one wonders what is left of the content of the language.

---

[55] John Calvin, *Institutes of the Christian Religion*, J. T. McNeill (ed.), F. L. Battles (tr.) (London: SCM, 1961), 3/20/1, p. 850.

One side of the first paradox is illustrated by the 'question and answer' pattern of the Geneva Catechism. Of prayer, and in particular the Lord's Prayer, the question is asked: 'When you ask that God's will be done, what is your meaning?' The answer given is: 'That all creatures be subdued to his obedience, and so dependent on his nod that nothing be done but by his will.' The question then probes further: 'Do you think then that anything can be done against his will?' The answer is: 'We pray not only that what he has in his own counsel decreed come to pass, but also that, all contumacy being overcome and subdued, he may subject the wills of his own and direct them to obedience.'[56] Clearly we have here a God who has to overcome creation's 'contumacy' rather than simply direct everything from all eternity: does Calvin suggest that the overcoming of this 'contumacy' is not a foregone conclusion? Calvin goes on to speak of the need to 'yield up our wills' to God through prayer, so that we may come to desire only what God desires.[57]

Calvin speaks much of the Spirit's aid to us in forming our prayers, or of the intercession of Christ in us.[58] But he also labours the point that we are free – indeed, under obligation – to bring our prayers to God. We must at all times be 'encouraged to pray by a sure hope that our prayer will be answered',[59] and we should 'take refuge in God, not at all doubting he is ready to extend his helping hand'.[60]

The other side of this paradox is expressed in Calvin's commentary on Psalm 17:1. Of this, Ronald S. Wallace comments that 'it would defraud God of his honour did we not refer every cause and every situation in which we are

---

[56] John Calvin, 'Catechism of the Church of Geneva' in *Calvin: Theological Treatises* vol. XXII, J. K. S. Reid (tr.) (London: SCM, 1954), p. 125.

[57] Ibid.

[58] Calvin, *Institutes*, 3/20/5, p. 855; 'Catechism', p. 122.

[59] Calvin, *Institutes*, 3/20/11, p. 862.

[60] Ibid., 3/20/11, p. 863.

involved to Him and leave Him to determine the issue'.[61] Such a statement fits in far better with what we might expect from one known in popular thought as a champion of predestination. God's sovereignty is well known as one of Calvin's most prominent themes, but there is much material from his work on prayer which seems to lead the other way – into talk of the freedom of creation within the freedom of God.

This assurance of prayer's answer seems to indicate a responsive God, whose freedom is more significant than his fore-ordination. But the assurance of an answer to prayer is qualified in three ways. First, by the statement that prayer is, in fact, 'not so much for his own sake, as for ours'.[62] This comment is made against the objection that prayer is futile because God already knows our troubles and needs. Calvin gives six reasons for continuing to pray. These six points are to do with the believer's aligning his or her will to God's and purifying his or her desire, and cultivating a thankful spirit amidst God's 'present help'. Part of this, it must be admitted, involves embracing with greater delight 'those things which we acknowledge to have been obtained by prayers',[63] but the general tenor of the six points stresses our receptivity rather than God's responsiveness and open-handedness.

The second sort of qualification to the frequent assurances that prayer will be answered comes by way of dealing with apparently unanswered prayer. The word 'apparently' becomes very important in the sort of treatment that Calvin gives the subject. His answer to the problem is rather different from the method that sets out to limit the possible options for prayer – though he has something to say about that also (see below). An extended quotation from the *Institutes* will make the point, and also show how skilfully Calvin makes it:

---

[61] Ronald S. Wallace, *Calvin's Doctrine of the Christian Life* (Edinburgh: Oliver & Boyd, 1959), p. 280. I am indebted to Wallace's work for help in navigating Calvin's commentaries.
[62] Calvin, *Institutes*, 3/20/3, p. 851.
[63] Ibid.

But if finally even after long waiting our senses cannot learn the benefit received from prayer, or perceive any fruit from it, still our faith will make us sure of what cannot be perceived by sense, that we have obtained what was expedient.

Besides, even if God grants our prayer, he does not always respond to the exact form of our request but, seeming to hold us in suspense, he yet, in a marvellous manner, shows us our prayers have not been in vain. This is what John's words mean: 'If we know that he hears us whenever we ask anything of him, we know that we have obtained the requests we asked of him' (I Jn. 5:15). This seems a diffuse superfluity of words, but the declaration is especially useful because God, even when he does not comply with our wishes, is still attentive and kindly to our prayers, so that hope relying upon his word will never disappoint us. But believers need to be sustained by this patience, since they would not long stand unless they relied upon it.[64]

This extract is significant not only for Calvin's recognition that his proposal may seem rather obscure and verbose ('diffuse superfluity of words') rather than genuinely subtle, but also for the two answers it contains. Calvin suggests that God may seem not to answer our prayers whereas in fact (1) God may answer by giving something other than what we asked for – 'what is expedient',[65] and (2) that God may delay answer until the time is propitious – 'seeming to hold us in suspense'.[66] He is prepared to say things about God in this regard, and about God's purpose in keeping us in suspense, which seem bold, or even unhelpful to modern ears. 'For the Lord proves his people by no light trials, and does not softly exercise them, but often drives them to extremity and allows them to lie a long time in the mire before he gives them any taste of his

---

[64] Ibid., 3/20/52, p. 919.

[65] cf. John Calvin, *Commentaries*, W. Pringle, J. Anderson et al (trs) (Edinburgh: Calvin Translation Society, 1845–1853), on 2 Cor. 12:8. Also on line at http://www.ccel.org/c/calvin/comment3/comm_index.htm.

[66] cf. Calvin, *Commentaries*, on Ps. 10:17.

sweetness.'[67] Elsewhere he speaks of prayers that do not 'immediately penetrate into heaven',[68] and which require perseverance, and/or a more lively faith.

The third sort of qualification to the assurance that our prayer will be answered relates to the question of the content of prayer, with which we have already become familiar. Calvin, like Augustine, distinguishes two strands within our petition. He says: 'In asking, we lay before God the desires of our heart, seeking from his goodness, first, the things which serve his glory alone, and then the things which also minister to our profit.'[69] This recalls Augustine's distinction between petitions for what I called the 'seen' and 'unseen'. Calvin follows in according a secondary place to the mundane petitions. Of course, Calvin's more generalised language begs many questions. One could argue that it is precisely in and through the reception and use of mundane blessings that God's glory is served. Could it not be that the dichotomy suggested between 'God's glory' and 'our profit' is a thoroughly false one – at least some of the time?

Calvin is scornful of those who treat prayer as a form of self-indulgence, and speaks of the need to ask aright:

> We have noted another point: not to ask any more than God allows. For even though he bids us pour out our hearts before him (Ps. 62:8; cf. Ps. 145:19), he still does not indiscriminately slacken the reins to stupid and wicked emotions; and while he promises that he will act according to the will of the godly, his gentleness does not go so far that he yields to their wilfulness. Yet in both, men commonly sin gravely; for many rashly, shamelessly, and irreverently dare importune God with their improprieties and impudently present before his throne whatever in dreams has struck their fancy. But such dullness or stupidity grips them that they dare thrust upon

---

[67] Calvin, *Institutes*, 3/20/52, p. 919.
[68] Calvin, *Commentaries*, on Ps. 89:47–48, p. 455.
[69] John Calvin, *Opera Selecta*, vol. 1, Peter Barth and Wilhelm Niesel (eds) (Monachii: Kaiser, 1926), p. 101, cited in T. H. L. Parker, *John Calvin* (London: Dent, 1975), p. 41.

God all their vilest desires, which they would be deeply ashamed to acknowledge to men . . . Yet, God does not allow his gentle dealing to be thus mocked but, claiming his own right, he subjects our wishes to his power and bridles them. For this reason, we must hold fast to John's statement: 'This is the confidence we have in him, that if we ask anything according to his will, he hears us' (I Jn. 5:14).[70]

There is an interesting distinction contained here. Calvin believes that God indeed will act 'according to the will of the godly' – this is as plain an assertion of the worthwhileness of prayer as one could hope to find. But Calvin is clear that while God acts according to the will of the godly, God will not act according to the 'wilfulness' of any.

The other point of note is the use of a typically vivid image. It occurs in two slightly different forms: he speaks of 'not slackening the reins to stupid and wicked emotions' and 'he subjects our wishes to his own power and bridles them'. Drawn from the everyday life of his time, Calvin uses this picture to speak of the way that God deals with inappropriate petitions, and 'purifies' them. He uses the image frequently, and in the Catechism employs it in a powerful statement of the same point:

It would be a very preposterous method of praying to indulge our own desires and the judgement of the flesh. For we are too foolish to be able to judge what is expedient for us, and we labour under this intemperance of desire which has necessarily to be bridled.[71]

This statement is much stronger in its implication that our own freedom in petitioning is undermined by our own lack of insight and purity of heart than many of Calvin's pronouncements.

In his commentary on Matthew 17:19 Calvin seems to come closer to those thinkers who narrow down the content of prayer, and the responsiveness of God, and

---

[70] Calvin, *Institutes*, 3/20/5, p. 855.
[71] Calvin, 'Catechism', p. 122.

therefore the freedom in praying and living of the believer. He says: 'As nothing is more at variance with faith than the foolish and irregular desires of the flesh, it follows that those in whom faith reigns do not desire everything without discrimination, but only that which the Lord promises to give.'[72]

As Wendel summarises Calvin's doctrine in his celebrated study, 'as soon as prayer relies upon the divine promises its object must necessarily be the content of those promises'.[73] Certainly Calvin says that our prayers must be in accord with God's will, and that our desires in no way bind God,[74] and that our prayers are always a response to divine initiative, and as such should 'sum up' God's promises.[75]

And yet Calvin gives such a 'high profile' to the ministry of intercession, suggesting that it is a genuinely effective activity. As Wallace observes, 'it is the presence in the midst of the Church of every age of those who come before God to make intercession that continually saves the Church in each generation from perishing through the coldness and indifference of the rest of its members'.[76]

We began by speaking of two paradoxes in Calvin's thought on prayer, the second to do with Calvin's use of language. He notes that scripture gives authority for the believer to speak to God in prayer as if he or she can in some way prevail upon God to do things he would not otherwise have done unless we had prayed. Calvin can ask 'Who is man that God should show compliance to his will? . . . Yet he voluntarily condescends to these terms' so that he can comply with our desires.[77] God's generosity and responsiveness is underlined: 'Faith will succeed in

---

[72] John Calvin, *Commentary on a Harmony of the Gospels*, W. Pringle, J. Anderson et al (trs) (Edinburgh, Calvin Translation Society, 1845-1853), on Mt., p. 320f.
[73] François Wendel, *Calvin* (London: Collins, 1953), p. 254.
[74] Calvin, *Commentaries*, on Rom. 8:27, p. 178.
[75] Wallace, *Calvin's Doctrine*, p. 292, citing sermon on Deut. 26:16–19.
[76] Ibid., pp. 288f.
[77] Calvin, *Commentaries*, on Ps. 145:19, p. 282.

obtaining anything from the Lord because he values it so much that he is always ready to gratify our desires as far as is good for us.'[78] The last few words do qualify the assurance, of course, and make this statement contain the whole conundrum – 'anything . . . as far as is good for us'! Most shockingly, Calvin suggests that believers 'ought importunately to harass God the Father till at length they wrest from him what he would otherwise appear unwilling to give'.[79] Admittedly, this advice to 'harass' comes in a commentary on the parable of the Unjust Judge and the Persistent Widow in Luke 18, but even allowing for the way in which the form of that story would influence Calvin's words, his language seems strong. One could suppose that the word 'appear' might be another qualification smuggled in to dampen the effect, but it is unlikely that too much should be made of that. In fact Calvin goes on, in the same commentary, to say that 'God wills to be, as it were, wearied out by prayers'!

As it were, wearied out by prayers. For Calvin this vivid and anthropomorphic language cannot be the last word. God, he says, does not vary in purpose, nor is he subject to changes in his passions and attitudes. As Wallace comments, God 'does not go back on what he has previously decided. In using such language, then, [God] is humiliating Himself to speak in our way. [Calvin] wants us to understand that.'[80] Calvin says, revealingly, that God 'has made a pact with us that when we shall require it he will accomplish all that we ask so that we can always feel that he has willed to accord to our will and desire'.[81] Despite this, we must not believe that through prayer 'we gain a victory over God and bend him slowly and reluctantly to compassion'.[82] We are led back then, to a restriction on prayer. We do not bend God's will to

[78] Calvin, *Commentary on a Harmony of the Gospels*, on Mt. 15:28, p. 269.
[79] Calvin, *Commentaries*, on Lk. 18:1–8.
[80] Wallace, *Calvin's Doctrine*, p. 291.
[81] Calvin, sermon on Deut. 9:13-14 – see Wallace, *Calvin's Doctrine*, p. 291.
[82] Calvin, *Commentary on a Harmony of the Gospels*, on Lk. 18:1–8, p. 198.

compassion; our prayers, if they are to be answered, must be for those things which God has already determined – they must be 'according to his will'. The assessment we make of such language will be significant for our theology of intercession. To consider it as mere accommodation, with Calvin, is at once to undermine the suggestion that such texts might illuminate the way God 'really' relates to creation.

What do we make of Calvin? To be sure, in his work we find similar material to that which we have found difficult in other writers: opposing statements allowed to stand alongside one another without an exact explanation of how the dialectic between them is to be understood. On the one hand, God never deviates from his purpose; on the other, we are called to prayer believing God will act 'according to the will of the godly'. Are we to understand the latter as a concession to the human need to speak anthropomorphically? Do the comments on the paradoxical use of language effectively remove the other paradox with which we were concerned, between the fore-ordained purpose of God, and the freedom of God to respond to humankind?

Even if this were the case, Calvin would have made no small contribution to the theology of prayer. For we would have seen a possible interpretation of a great deal of biblical and post-biblical writing on prayer, and of the Christian experience of prayer, in these terms. However, we may suspect that while Calvin's remarks about the nature of theological language here must be taken with great seriousness and seen to have a real bearing on this matter, it would be a mistake to assume that Calvin wishes them to bear the weight of a total explanation. For he also pursues with some vigour the theme of the freedom of God. After all the qualifications have been made about the assurance that prayer will be answered – qualifications of content, purpose and propriety – there is that thread weaving in and out of his thought perhaps best instanced in our quotation from the commentary on Psalm 145:19, that God 'voluntarily subjects himself' to our petitions 'so that he can comply with our desires'.

This line we shall see taken up and pursued by Barth, though still with accompanying qualifications and paradoxes. It may be helpful now to see two theological routes running from Augustine. One runs from Augustine through Aquinas to Schleiermacher; the other goes from Augustine through Calvin to Barth, and it is to him that we now turn.

Karl Barth

The resemblances on the subject of prayer between Karl Barth (1886–1968) and John Calvin are striking. While losing nothing of the subtly of Calvin's thought, Barth develops particular motifs from Calvin. A Barth 'reader' is subtitled 'theologian of freedom',[83] and it is his treatment of the freedom of God which is crucial to an understanding of his contribution to the theology of prayer.

Barth deals with prayer in a significant way several times during the course of his massive *Church Dogmatics*. As with other subjects that get similar treatment, he never refers back to previous references, nor does he indicate any consciousness that his views may be developing. This is a real frustration, for it must be borne in mind that the work was written over more than thirty-five years, and one volume that concerns us is the final one, which remained in incomplete and unrevised form on his death. Because the discussions of prayer occur in different contexts, the best that can be said is that Barth's treatment is somewhat akin to a spiral-form, where he speaks about some of the same issues again in later volumes, but also introduces new themes. Though he gives no indication that he is consciously developing his thought, it seems that his thinking on prayer may have changed at least in emphasis. For Barth, prayer is the proper work of the Christian, within which is contained all that is demanded of him or her as a

---

[83] Karl Barth, *Karl Barth: Theologian of Freedom*, Clifford Green (ed.) (London: Collins, 1989).

Christian.[84] As for Calvin, prayer is an act of obedience: 'We
owe it to the command of God to pray . . . we should and
must pray if we are to be Christians.'[85] Petitioning God
implies no impudence or presumption:

> On the contrary, [the Christian, in petitioning] is doing that which
> corresponds and answers to the situation in which he finds himself
> placed by the Word of God. He does that which he is not merely
> permitted but commanded to do in this situation . . .
>
> The true worship of God is that man is ready to take and actually
> does take where God Himself gives, that he seeks and knocks in
> order that he may really receive.[86]

In *Church Dogmatics* III/3 Barth treats prayer as one of the
prime and distinctive Christian acts, alongside obedience
and faith – each of the three 'contains' the other two and
yet has its own distinctive elements.[87] Prayer consists of
various elements: praise and thanksgiving, confession and
penitence, petition and intercession. As is suggested by the
derivation of 'prayer' in most languages, the centre of
prayer is to be found in petition.[88] Thus Barth parts
company with perhaps the majority of theological thinkers
and writers on the spiritual life, who have tended to see
petition (as Schleiermacher did) as a sign of human
weakness and egocentricity. Our prayers ought always to
include petition and intercession (and Barth will specify
the sorts of petitions and intercessions in due course) to be
authentic prayer – an interesting comment on the trend in
many non-liturgical congregations now to omit the

---

[84] Barth, *C. D.*, III/3, pp. 264ff.
[85] Ibid., IV/4, p. 44; cf. III/4, p. 97.
[86] Ibid., III/3, p. 270.
[87] 'In obedience the Christian is the servant, in faith he is the child, but
in prayer, as the servant and the child, he is the friend of God, called to
the side of God and at the side of God, living and ruling and reigning
with Him.' Ibid., III/3, p. 286. The theme of 'the friendship of God' is
not insignificant for our subject: see Jas 4:1ff. and Jürgen Moltmann,
The Church in the Power of the Spirit (London: SCM, 1977), pp. 114–21.
[88] Barth, *C.D.* III/3, pp. 265–8.

outward-looking intercession and turn in upon itself with the warm glow of praise. Granted the central place accorded to petition, then, how does Barth deal with some of the accompanying problems?

Early on, in I/2, Barth says that 'praying, asking of God, can consist only in receiving what God has already prepared for us, before and apart from stretching out our hands for it'.[89] This already strong sense of prayer being for our sake, as similar to the 'preparation' we found in Augustine, is strengthened further by frequent statements about the divine sovereignty found throughout his work. For example, he asserts the sovereign Lord always accompanies the creature 'preserving, cooperating and overruling, in all that it does, and all that happens to it'[90] as the Lord of the creature's freedom,[91] and the one whose 'final purpose' is assured of completion.[92] But like other writers we have considered, Barth makes statements about the divine purpose and human freedom and cooperation with it which seem in acute tension with one another. Tiessen argues that Barth must be read in what we might call an Augustinian way, with the statements about sovereignty given greater weight, or the final word. However, Barth's account may not be so easily aligned with a deterministic reading.[93]

In volume II/1, he writes about the 'hearing of prayer' in the following terms:

---

[89] Ibid., I/2, p. 454.

[90] Ibid., III/3, p. 13, cited also by Tiessen, *Providence*, p. 208. Tiessen gives greater prominence to this language of sovereignty than I will want to give.

[91] Barth, *C.D.* III/3, p. 49.

[92] Ibid., III/3, p. 132, cited by Tiessen, *Providence*, p. 209.

[93] See Sanders, *God Who Risks*, p. 185 et al, and the discussion of Sanders in Tiessen, *Providence*, esp. pp. 227ff., but also throughout the chapter. Of unacknowledged importance here is Tiessen's own discussion of Barth's treatment of the Thomistic–Aristotelian concept of causality, with God as 'first cause' and creatures as 'second causes'. Barth warns that divine causation must not be conceived of in too scientific a sense, or as too much like human causation. Tiessen, *Providence*, pp. 214–16, citing Barth, *C.D.* III/3, pp. 95–109.

the prayers of those who can and will believe are heard; that God is and wills to be known as the One who will and does listen to the prayers of faith . . . We need not hesitate to say that 'on the basis of the freedom of God Himself God is conditioned by the prayer of faith.' The basis is His freedom. It is thus a form of His Sovereignty, and therefore of His immutable vitality that He is willing not merely to hear but to hearken to the prayer of faith . . .

The living and genuinely immutable God is not an irresistible fate before which man can only keep silence, passively awaiting and accepting the benefits or blows which it ordains. There is no such thing as a Christian resignation in which we either submit to a fate of this kind or come to terms with it. Resignation . . . is always the disconsolate consolation of unbelief. There is, of course, a Christian patience and submission, as there is also a Christian waiting upon God . . . [who wills to be] our God and therefore a Helper in our distress, allowing Himself to be moved by our entreaties.[94]

In such a way Barth begins to establish the freedom of God to be a God who responds to prayer. New definitions of God's 'immutability' and 'sovereignty' are hinted at, and Barth returns to these subjects later. The most striking language here is that with which Barth boldly claims that God is 'conditioned' by the prayer of faith. This seems irreconcilable with the earlier statement in I/2 that we may only receive through prayer that which has already been prepared for us. It is this 'later' position, based on the freedom of God, which Barth goes on to develop (and qualify).

If we had read on in the passage I have just quoted at some length we would come across the qualification that God's being 'conditioned' by the prayer of faith 'does not mean that God puts the reins of world government in the hands of believers or that believers may feel or act as sharers of His throne'.[95] But in III/3 he affirms that prayer allows believers a 'share in the universal lordship of God',

[94] Barth, C.D. II/1, pp. 510ff.
[95] Ibid., II/1, p. 511.

for God does not wish to 'preserve, accompany and rule' creation 'in such a way that He is not affected and moved by it'. Instead, Barth insists, God will 'converse' with creation, so that as God conditions all things, God is also 'determined by them'.[96]

While III/3 may not contradict II/1, there is some shift in stress. Barth wishes to emphasise the rapport between God and the world, and the freedom of a sovereign God expressed in the freedom to be responsive to the world. The earlier remark that God is 'conditioned' by the prayer of faith is now buttressed with an even stronger one – that God chooses to be 'determined' by his creatures. He goes on:

> God is not free and immutable in the sense that He is the prisoner of His own resolve and will and action, that He must always be alone as the Lord of all things and of all occurrence ... He is free and immutable as the living God, as the God who wills to converse with the creatures, and to allow Himself to be determined by it in this relationship. His sovereignty is so great that it embraces both the possibility, and, as it is exercised, the actuality, that the creature can actively be present and cooperate in His over-ruling. There is no creaturely freedom which can limit or compete with the sole sovereignty and efficacy of God. But permitted by God, and indeed willed and created by Him, there is the freedom of the friends of God concerning whom He has determined that without abandoning the helm for one moment He will still allow Himself to be determined by them.[97]

Barth thus begins a redefinition of divine immutability. By III/4 it has been further established. Here Barth suggests that the immutability which has often been predicated of the deity in theology befits only an idol, not the true and living God. 'God is certainly immutable', says Barth, but immutable in taking the side of God's creatures, through

---

[96] Ibid., III/3, p. 285.
[97] Ibid.

his grace and mercy. *'The glory of His omnipotence and sovereignty consists in the fact that He can give to the requests of this creature a place in His will.'*[98] In this way Barth is able to suggest, with great daring, that God allows humanity to 'participate in His omnipotence and work'.[99]

Even in the earlier *Dogmatics* this question is approached positively. God does not alter when in revealing God's self as the One who listens to prayer, says Barth. God is, and remains, the Lord of Creation. This listening to prayer (what we have called 'responsiveness') does not lessen God's Lordship over creation by becoming more changeable: on the contrary it demonstrates that Lordship in a way that nothing else could. When God is manifested as the one who listens to, is conditioned by, prayer, 'what else can be revealed . . . but that He is Creator and Lord of all things?'[100]

It is through prayer that this share in the divine omnipotence becomes real. When we speak of God 'hearing' our prayer, according to Barth we mean the way in which a human request is received and adopted into the divine purpose, and that the divine action then corresponds with the human request. Our petition 'is not only received by Him but infallibly passes over into His plan and will and cannot lack the corresponding divine speaking and doing'.[101] 'Infallibly' is a very strong word, and because of this confidence Barth echoes the theme of the need for 'assurance' in prayer, a theme we noticed in the New Testament, and which was a favourite of Luther and Calvin, amongst others.[102]

If the notion of obedience plays a central role in Barth's treatment of prayer, it must also be said that his interpretation is characteristically Christocentric. For all our needs there is one gift; to all our asking there is one

---

[98] Ibid., III/4, p. 109, italics mine.
[99] Ibid.
[100] Ibid., II/1, p. 512.
[101] Ibid., III/4, p. 106.
[102] Ibid., III/4, p. 107.

answer – Jesus Christ.[103] In his Son, his Word of Salvation, God controls, upholds, accompanies and rules all things, and provides for all creation's needs.[104] Christian petition can thus be described as 'simply the taking and receiving of the divine gift and answer as it is already present and near to hand in Jesus Christ'.[105]

As Barth goes on to talk of Jesus Christ as the answer to all petitions, he does so within the context of the covenant relationship between God and humanity. It is within the covenant that the Christian receives that which God is and does for him or her. Barth says, with a turn of phrase which has an Augustinian ring once more, that what God offers the believer 'is destined for him',[106] but that the believer can only take and receive it by asking for it. The creature's only status before God is thus as 'the one who asks', so underlining total dependence upon God. Whereas for Calvin, coming 'empty-handed' in prayer is primarily a mark of human sinfulness, [107] for Barth it is also a sign of our asking for all our needs, of our total dependence.[108]

The Christocentricity of prayer is underlined by the place of Christ as the 'first and proper suppliant'.[109] Jesus lived by grace, obedience and trust. He is the pioneer and exemplar of Christian prayer. As Barth establishes Jesus' position in this way, he introduces notions of 'solidarity'. With Jesus, his asking and receiving was not for himself alone, but for the world. When the church prays, then, it asks 'with' Jesus,[110] in his name and by the gift and work of the Holy Spirit. The church 'will not allow its Lord to be alone in prayer, but it will be at His side with its own asking, however imperfect and perverted and impotent

---

[103] Ibid., III/3, p. 271

[104] Ibid., III/3, p. 271.

[105] Ibid., III/3, p. 274.

[106] Ibid.

[107] e.g. Calvin, *Institutes*, 3/20/9, p. 860.

[108] e.g. Barth, *C.D.* III/3, p. 268, cf. *C.D.* III/4, p 97.

[109] Ibid., III/3, p. 274.

[110] Ibid., III/3, p. 277.

this may be compared with His'.[111] The church will pray that it may truly be the community of Jesus, asking for his love, his word, his witness, and so on, so that it may be real and effective as his community. But just as Jesus' petition was petition for and on behalf of the world, so the church's petitions (and those of individual Christians when they pray alone – though still, primarily, as part of the church)[112] are also intercessions for others. Furthermore, 'the asking community stands together with its Lord before God on behalf of all creation . . . The asking of the community anticipates as it were that of creation as a whole. It gives voice and expression to the groaning of creation.'[113] Our only advantage over the world is that we know God is our Lord and theirs too. So, 'we' believe in the midst of others who do not. ' "We" thus do so provisionally in their place . . . Hence, "we" also pray in anticipation with them and for them as we pray with and for one another and ourselves.'[114]

While Barth develops the theme present *sotto voce* in Calvin of the 'freedom of God' in relation to prayer, at the same time not wholly destroying the dialectic or paradox, he still asserts the sovereignty and foreknowledge of God. As we have seen, Barth begins to re-interpret God's sovereignty, but nevertheless, when it is coupled with God's foreknowledge it retains some of its more sinister, prayer-cramping, aspects. One of the ways in which the other side of the paradox is maintained is through discussion of Jesus' prayer in Gethsemane.

While Barth is able to say that the Christian should draw near to God and ask for 'all that is necessary to his situation',[115] it is still the prayer of Gethsemane which Barth

---

[111] Ibid.
[112] Ibid., III/3, p. 280.
[113] Ibid., III/3, p. 278.
[114] Ibid., III/4, pp. 102ff.
[115] Ibid., III/3, p. 269: even though 'necessary' may de-limit somewhat the possible content of prayer, it cannot be understood to rule out all temporal blessings.

invokes, early on in the *Dogmatics* at least, as a paradigm for prayer. Though prayer should, as the Lukan parables suggest, be persistent and insistent, 'the prayer of faith has also the characteristic of the prayer in Gethsemane, in which the will of God is resolutely and finally set above the will of men' – only this kind of prayer will definitely be heard.[116]

It is difficult to know what weight must be given to this 'Gethsemane motif' in Barth's thought. It is not as prominent as in some thinkers, and when it does recur,[117] it is set up as a model for prayer, only to be demolished again as one that offers final adequacy (see below). We have already noted Barth's comments in criticism of any kind of bogus 'resignation', and this also must be taken into account – not least because they occur on the same page of text as the Gethsemane reference! This suggests that Barth would not want to reduce prayer, even after the many qualifications, to seeking God's will and aligning with it and accepting it. Of course, prayer seeks to be about God's will; God will never do anything 'against' his will. But what Barth calls the 'status' of the believer as defined by his being 'one who asks' suggests a more fluid understanding of the prayer 'interchange'.

Other features of Barth's work on prayer add shades of meaning to such a 'Gethsemane motif'. He suggests in his last volume that prayer for the Kingdom is the 'purest' form of prayer, because it rests entirely with God, looking beyond all that humanity can do. It also alone carries the unreserved expectation of being heard.[118] But he goes on from this to make a point more 'activist' than 'resigned'. Praying for the Kingdom, he says, claims Christians in working for righteousness in the world. These two things, 'pure prayer' and socio-political activism, go hand in hand.[119]

---

[116] Ibid., II/1, p. 511.
[117] Ibid., III/4, p. 92.
[118] Ibid., IV/4, p. 245.
[119] Ibid., IV/4, pp. 261f.

Barth also rules out the interpretation of prayer as principally a subjective experience for the believer. To put Gethsemane at the core of one's theology of prayer may be to make it more a matter of 'us' than God, of submission rather than petition. While Barth admits that prayer does have a subjective effect,[120] this admission is in the context of an affirmation of God's command to the believer to pray, and God's promise to 'hear' – that is, prayer's 'objective' effect. All merely subjective interpretations of prayer are to be strongly rejected, says Barth.[121]

How then does Barth tackle some of the other questions that arise, even supposing one can make a case for the genuine responsiveness of God in prayer? For instance, God obviously will know our true needs better we do ourselves – so why pray? Does not that suggest that we are trying to influence God's will, which already has our best interests at heart?[122] The stories of Jacob at Peniel (Gen. 32:24ff.) and Jesus in Gethsemane (Mt. 26:36ff.) may seem to suggest that the submission of the will is the true and practical meaning of prayer, and establish the objection that any understanding of prayer which seeks to show it to be other than a 'devotional exercise for the inward development and deepening of the one who prays' is incorrect.[123] Some may feel that their requests are too trifling for God's attention.

But for Barth such an approach fundamentally misconstrues the basis of prayer, and also the doctrine of God. The real basis of prayer is human freedom before God alongside God's command that we pray: this is the proper expression of the divine–human relationship. 'God in his freedom wills man to pray that he may answer.'[124] Barth proceeds to sweep aside objections to prayer:

---

[120] Ibid., III/3, p. 286.
[121] Ibid., III/3, p. 287.
[122] Ibid., III/4, p. 91.
[123] Ibid., III/4, p. 92.
[124] Ibid., III/4, pp. 92ff.

There can be no place for all the pious and impious arguments against the permissibility and possibility of asking in prayer. What does it matter that God is all-knowing and all-wise, and what reason have we for the luxury of humility which will cross the path of God's counsel and will with human asking, when it is the all-knowing and all-wise God Himself who commands us to come to Him with our requests?[125]

Here Barth again turns to his theme that God chooses to be God *with us* and that God wills to share the divine Lordship. His question is that, granted that this is the nature of the God to whom we pray, 'what use is the objection that we can only pray that His will should be done apart from and in opposition to ours?' These arguments against prayer are 'dispersed to the wind' by the nature of the God of the Covenant.[126]

Linked to this question (or, as Barth would have it, non-question!) of whether God does not already know better than we what is good for us, is the similar one of what we should pray for – what should the content of prayer-as-petition be? We have already observed that the church's prayer should on the one hand be for itself, to be more really the community of Jesus, and on the other hand it should be for and on behalf of all creation.[127] The prayer of the individual Christian might be modelled on the Lord's Prayer.[128] It begins with petitions for everything 'necessary to his situation',[129] but must become intercession for and on behalf of creation.

As soon as one leaves the narrower guidelines of the Lord's Prayer and begins to pray for 'everything necessary', the possibility of distortion and inappropriate prayer becomes evident. Into our prayers may flow all that is wrong and fallen in our natures ('the whole of human

---

[125] Ibid., III/4, p. 96.
[126] Ibid.
[127] See above, and ibid., III/3, pp. 271–80.
[128] Ibid., III/3, p. 280.
[129] Ibid., III/3, p. 269.

short-sightedness, unreasonableness and stupidity'), like pollution flowing into the Rhine.[130]

Here Barth reminds us that while petition is the heart of prayer, it is not the whole of prayer. Prayer's other components (thanksgiving, repentance, worship) need to be present and purify our petitioning and desire. Inevitably, our prayers sometimes will be 'impure', but we must come to God as we are, and God knows well what we are. Because of the 'intervention' of Christ and the Spirit in our prayers, we are to understand prayer as a cyclical movement which comes from, and returns to, God. Thus God accepts our request as it is and gives to it that purified meaning that it did not have when we offered it up. While we must ask fearlessly, commending ourselves to God's grace, we have to realise that hardly any request we make will remain 'untouched' by divine cleansing and purifying reception of it.[131]

Clearly this account of our prayers has an advantage and a disadvantage – and we cannot easily have the one without the other! On the one hand, we are assured here that our poor prayers are acceptable even though they are distortions of the best that we should pray for. Indeed, God in 'hearing' them makes them the best. However, on the other hand, one wonders what is left of our prayers by the time they have been cleansed in this way by God. Does this not in fact suggest that the repeated assurances that God wishes to share his Lordship with us through prayer, and wants to respond to his creation, and commands us to pray – does this not suggest that all of this has little 'cash value' if in fact *our prayers* are altered and changed beyond recognition by their divine reception?

Barth returns to the subject of prayer in the next and final volume of *Dogmatics*. We see there the same notion of 'divine purification' of prayer, but also a more positive evaluation of human prayer in itself. Our prayers will

---

[130] Ibid., III/3, p. 100ff.
[131] Ibid., III/3, p. 101.

inevitably express our own assessment of what is best for ourselves and others, of what God ought to be doing for us! All our petitions are fulfilled, says Barth, but first they need to be fulfilled in the sense of being corrected and amended, transformed, for God alone really knows how things are and what is for the best. We might fervently hope that our prayers are close to God's will, and so might be heard, but we have no right to demand or expect it.[132]

The concession that what we pray may be close to the divine will is only dealt with briefly as a qualification to the more laboured point of 'divine purification', or, in this volume, 'divine transformation' of our prayers.

We may now make some concluding – if provisional – remarks about Barth's theology of intercession. Karl Barth sets out to establish the freedom of God in relation to the prayers of the believer: God is the God who is free to answer prayer, the responsive God. In this sphere, as in so many other theological spheres, Barth turns defence into attack – coming at an issue in entirely the opposite direction from many who have written before him. Far from undermining God's Lordship, it's only as the one who answers prayer that God is, and is seen to be, Lord. Barth convincingly begins to re-interpret divine sovereignty and immutability in this context. We are given a God who, while remaining true to God's self, is now free, as it were, to 'change his mind'! However, it is not clear what is left of this responsive God after this freedom to answer our prayers has been put alongside the inevitability of God's 'purifying' or 'transforming' them. In what sense are 'our' prayers the ones God is free to answer?

To some extent the questions shift in Barth's account away from those associated with immutability and omniscience to other more philosophical ones. If God can answer prayer, why is prayer (apparently) not more effective? Barth may want to invoke the motif of the 'hiddenness' of God here, but would that finally satisfy us?

---

[132] Ibid., IV/4, p. 107.

Why does God seem to answer some prayers and not others? Is this simply a question of the inscrutability of the divine will, or must we look for other explanations and criteria? Once one has successfully established the fact that God can and does answer prayer, new problems come into view. Many of these concern the nature of God's relationship to the world in more general terms: how is the 'rapport' of prayer related to God's general 'rapport' with his creation? Of course, Barth may not wish to admit to the validity of these questions, bearing in mind his particular theological ground-rules. However, to the present writer they seem inescapable.

Origen

In closing this chapter I want briefly to discuss one other figure, chosen as an early representative of a major (perhaps the major) way in which intercession has been understood theologically within the Christian tradition: Origen of Alexandria (185–254). It may seem odd to leave the earliest writer chronologically until the end, but in this way I want to highlight this early and persistent understanding of intercession, which is reflected also in several of the other writers we have considered. When such a trajectory is established so early and remains so persistent there are two possible explanations: either it is basically sound and fruitful; or it represents an early and unfortunate distortion of the biblical tradition. I do not want to join the ranks of those theologians, especially prominent in the nineteenth century, who judged the early Fathers to have 'sold out' biblical faith in favour of Greek metaphysical systems.[133] The early Fathers of the church did what they had to do in order to facilitate the missionary endeavours of the church, and so that their faith could seek understanding. However, it does now seem to many of our contemporaries that in translation of the gospel into early

---

[133] e.g. Adolf von Harnack, *History of Dogma*, vol. 1 (London: Williams & Norgate, 1894), pp. 45ff.

Greek thought forms something was lost in that translation. For all the Fathers' massive achievement, not least in Christological and Trinitarian discussion, helping their contemporaries and subsequent generations name the Christian God, in some respects their formulations were problematic. Origen's thought is plainly shaped by his philosophical milieu and assumptions, and it is partly the philosophical framework within which he works which allows him to be as creative as he is.

Origen wrote *On Prayer* in around 235 to encourage his friend and patron, Ambrose, and the presbyter Protoctetus, who were both in prison. Origen shows his subordinationist tendencies, suggesting that we should not pray to Jesus (one who himself prays) but to the Father alone,[134] and he seems to go further than Augustine in suggesting that we should pray only for the 'principal and truly great and heavenly things'[135] rather than material and physical things.[136] For there is no comparison between material and spiritual riches, between 'health of flesh and bone' and 'health of mind, strength of soul, and consistency of thought'. But why pray at all if God already knows what we want, and if God *does* know, can our prayers be effectual?

Origen begins by encouragingly referring to scripture passages where Jesus tells his disciples that they are now friends not servants (Jn 15:15), and where Paul speaks of the interceding Spirit (Rom. 8:26f.):[137] despite first appearances, prayer is not hopeless. Origen poses the problem thus:

---

[134] Origen, *On Prayer*, William A Curtis (tr.), http://www.ccel.org/o/origen/prayer/prayer.htm, X. Also available in Origen, *An Exhortation to Martyrdom, Prayer, and Selected Works*, Greer, Rowan A. (tr.) (Mahwah: Paulist Press, 1979).

[135] Origen, *On Prayer*, XI. Consequently, in XVII we have a generally spiritualised reading of 'give us this day our daily bread'.

[136] cf. Jay, Eric G. (ed. and tr.), 'Introduction' in Origen, *Treatise on Prayer* (London: SPCK, 1954), p. 71.

[137] Origen, *On Prayer*, I.

It is self-evidently absurd, God being unchangeable and having pre-comprehended all things and adhering to His pre-arrangements, to pray in the belief that through prayer one will change His purpose, or as though He had not already prearranged but awaited each individual's prayer, to make intercession that He may arrange what suits the supplicant by reason of his prayer, there and then appointing what He approves as reasonable though He has previously not contemplated it.[138]

The combination of divine intransigence with the complete foreknowledge produces this absurdity – the very thought that we might actually 'argue with God and win'. But while Origen has a strong sense of God's 'pre-comprehending' and 'prearrangement', he also believes in the freedom of human persons. These polarities are overcome by God who foresees what we will in our free will choose – and, indeed, pray – and so God takes account of them. In this way Origen attempts to get around the problems caused by divine omniscience by suggesting that human decisions are genuinely free, but that God foreknows from all eternity our free decisions and builds our prayers and his answers to them into his eternal plan. God's 'pre-comprehending' of all things includes pre-comprehension of our decisions and our prayers. God knows I will pray petition X at time T from eternity, and so builds in the appropriate divine response to X at time T+1.

If, therefore, our individual free wills have been known by Him, and if in His providence He has on that account been careful to make due arrangement for each one, it is reasonable to believe that He has also pre-comprehended what a particular man is to pray in that faith, what his disposition, and what his desire.[139]

God decides in advance which prayers will be answered and how, so that these prayers and their answers may be 'built in' to God's purposes. While Origen goes on to

---

[138] Ibid., III.
[139] Ibid., IV.

suggest that God decides that some things will only be given in response to freely offered prayer[140] there must remain a number of questions about his treatment. We have had cause to question, from scripture and elsewhere, whether it is appropriate to think of God as unchanging in this way, and the understanding of time which Origen reflects must also be considered carefully – in particular we will ask whether it makes sense to say that God can know a not-yet-actual future. Can God know something that *is not*? But also of concern is the indication that, despite a stress on human free will, God seems to dominate the future and all possibility. God pre-comprehends and pre-arranges. The question might be asked then: if I petition for X at time T, God will decide in advance to give X at T+1 in response to my prayer. But notwithstanding the claim that certain gifts are given only in response to prayer, suppose that God decides that X is to happen anyway, whether or not I pray for it? My prayer becomes redundant, the answer to it interpreted as a genuine response is really only an illusion. Intercessions may add interest and variety in such a scheme, but they do little to affect the way things go: that, God has already pre-comprehended and pre-arranged.

Would God do this? Who is the God who answers prayer? To this question we must now turn.

---

[140] Ibid., V.

3

The Answering God

Prayer and the Doctrine of God

The Identity of God and the Possibility of Prayer

One of the themes that we have encountered in reviewing both biblical and historical material is the link between our doctrine or image of God and an understanding of prayer. Who is the God to whom we pray? In this chapter we will consider various perspectives on this question.

Calvin identified God as 'the One who hears prayer',[1] and the Old Testament suggested an image of God as personal, accessible, dialogical; Jesus prayed to 'Abba', and Paul prayed not to 'God in general', but to the God and Father of our Lord Jesus Christ.[2] Forgetting this point has unduly hamstrung much talk on prayer, especially in regard to some of its more perplexing philosophical or theological problems. Christians may be identified as 'people who pray', but we do not just pray in general to any sort of 'god': we pray to the God and Father of our Lord Jesus Christ.[3]

---

[1] Calvin, *Commentaries*, on Ps. 65:2.
[2] e.g. 2 Cor. 1:3.
[3] For the importance of our images of God in Christian spirituality, see, e.g., Hughes, *God of Surprises*, pp. 34–6, and Stephen Verney, *The Dance of Love* (London: HarperCollins, 1989), pp. 84–7.

In surveying scriptural evidence a complex and diffuse picture emerged, of course. Instead of attempting to 'level out' this variation we should rather recognise and affirm the richness that scripture offers us when it speaks to and about God for us. The relative weight we give to different images and texts will affect how we speak of God, and God's relation to the world, in innumerable ways. We should not underestimate the difficulty or indeed the provisionality of this task. However, one consistent Christian insight is that in scripture and in prayer we encounter the God and Father of our Lord Jesus Christ, the 'Christlike God'.

The 'Christlike', Triune God

'To whom then will you liken God, or what likeness compare with him?' (Is. 40:18). God is *sui generis*; God is a 'one-off'. Any generalisations and likenesses immediately run into 'issues'. No wonder Augustine lamented that 'human language labours altogether under great poverty of speech'.[4] Philosophers and theologians here tend to work from somewhat different access points. Whereas the philosopher *qua* philosopher might work from general principles, the Christian theologian will often want to begin somewhere else. Christian theology, and the Christian doctrine of God, begins with Jesus Christ. To paraphrase 1 John 1:5, and to borrow from the title of a book by John V. Taylor, 'God is Christlike – and in him there is no unChristlikeness at all.'[5] It is in the person of Jesus that God is supremely revealed and known: 'in him the fullness of God was pleased to dwell' (Col. 1:19). Christians came to see that – whatever experience or knowledge of God they previously had, the encounter with Jesus gave this new and *normative* content. After the

---

[4] Augustine, *On the Trinity*, 5/10, p. 92, on line at http://www.ccel.org/fathers2/NPNF1-03/npnf1-03-11.htm#P1061_426002
[5] John V. Taylor, *The Christlike God* (London: SCM, 1992), p. 100.

encounter with Jesus, his followers found that the question 'Who is God?' suddenly had a somewhat different answer. The new answer to the question 'Who is God?' was revealed in their reflection on Jesus' authority, his forgiveness of sin, his implicit or explicit Messianic claims, his ministry of teaching and healing, his declaration that in him the Kingdom is at hand, and more. We might also recall the Johannine witness to the intimacy of Jesus with his heavenly Father, and the synoptic record of Jesus' practice in addressing his prayers to *Abba*, a practice into which he invites his disciples, saying 'When you pray, say "Abba, Father . . ."'

While I would want to stress the central importance of the resurrection of Jesus for Christological thinking, we should also note that it is the cross that has dominated Christian theology, academic and popular, and has been the focus of much liturgical and artistic imagination. The cross: a symbol of suffering and powerlessness; a challenging central symbol for Christians wanting to think about the identity of God and God's relation to the world. At the least we would seem to have to say that there is something profoundly paradoxical about the cross, where the victim is Lord. Divine power made perfect in weakness, as Paul discovered.

But the task of re-envisioning God had, in a sense, only begun for Christians when they made the leap to the Christlikeness of God.[6] The further tasks of 're-envisaging' God also related to other experience and thought. In particular, their experience of, and thinking about, God's Spirit also becomes important and determinative. In the Old Testament the Spirit of God was sometimes perceived as a physical force (1 Kgs 18:12), which enhanced a person's natural gifts (Gen. 41:38) or enabled a person for leadership (Judg. 3:10). The Spirit is active in creation (Gen. 1:2), but as well as this frequently overlooked role in God's

---

[6] See Rom. 1:3–4. This is an 'Easter leap': see C. F. D. Moule, *The Origin of Christology* (Cambridge: CUP, 1978).

beginning, God's Spirit also was understood to have a part in moving things towards God's end (Is. 44:3–5; Joel 2:28–29). The Spirit had an *eschatological* role, a role reinforced and developed in the New Testament's understanding.[7] We saw that prayer has an essential eschatological element. Prayer is, in some way, always a praying for the Kingdom to come, a longing for God's will to be done on earth as in heaven. It is no surprise when, in Romans 8, we encounter Paul speaking of the Spirit's part in our prayers that God's beginning and end are also part of the subject matter. The whole of creation groans in travail waiting with eager longing for deliverance, for God's end. The Spirit who brooded over the face of the waters at the beginning broods still over travailing creation as it (we) long for God's end in our prayers, and the Spirit gives voice to those prayers within us.

Whereas in the Old Testament, the Spirit was usually viewed as being bestowed upon particular individuals and/or for particular tasks, the future hope expressed in Joel 2 was that the Spirit would be given to all God's people in an ongoing way. This is the promise fulfilled at Pentecost. In John's Gospel the Spirit's coming unites the believer to the Father on Jesus' departure, thus drawing believers into the life of God. The Spirit will lead the disciples into all truth, and facilitate the believers' communication with the Father and the Son, even – somewhat eschatologically – the Spirit 'will declare to you *the things that are to come*' (Jn 16:13). In the context of the Farewell Discourse, this is as likely to be help given in and for prayer as for anything else. The Son teaches his disciples to pray, and the Spirit is experienced (Rom. 8) as God's own help in prayer as we cry out to the Father. The question 'Who is God?' is about to take on a new and remarkable answer, to which we may give the shorthand label, 'Trinity'.

---

[7] See C. K. Barrett, *The Epistle to the Romans* (London: A & C Black, 1957), pp. 159–60.

The new experience was of a constant inspiring and equipping presence that did indeed belong to those who knew and confessed the *risenness* of Jesus. The New Testament is wonderfully unsystematic about this: we have tantalising clues about the Son who is exalted alongside the Father, and of a Spirit who bestows gifts; moreover, a Spirit who initiates the prayer we cannot begin, and so is God praying to God through us using sighs too deep for words. But soon, as mission led abroad and the practice of worship, initiation and mission required reflection, a more systematic account would be necessary.

'The One who Hears' – Praying to and in the Triune God

'Go therefore and make disciples of all nations, baptizing them in the name of the Father and of the Son and of the Holy Spirit . . .' (Mt. 28:19). Leaving aside any scholars' questions about this text, it's a good point at which to pause in our discussion. It is the most, perhaps the only, explicit reference to the Trinity in the New Testament. It also suggests that the doctrine of the Trinity has an intimate relation to: (1) worship in general – the context of this passage is the disciples' worship of Jesus; (2) baptism and the experience of initiation into the Way of Jesus; (3) mission, the making of disciples. The Trinity, then, belongs not in some abstract debate in the academy but at the heart of the experience and life of the first Christians – in worship, initiation and mission. It is the relation of the Trinity to worship, specifically to prayer, that concerns us here. James B. Torrance suggests that, in contrast to defective understandings of worship that have fundamentally Unitarian assumptions, a proper view of worship sees it as 'the gift of participating through the Spirit in the incarnate Son's communion with the Father'.[8]

Christian doctrine did not develop simply because a coherent intellectual statement of the faith was required,

---

[8] James B. Torrance, *Worship, Community, and the Triune God of Grace* (Carlisle: Paternoster, 1996), p. 18.

but also because the dynamic of Christian worship and devotion acted as an engine in doctrinal development. Maurice Wiles gave a coherent account of this development by describing the *lex orandi, lex credendi* ('the rule of prayer is the rule of belief'),[9] and Christopher Cocksworth is particularly interested in these factors in his more recent study of worship and the Trinity.[10] Cocksworth's liturgist's perspective enables him to offer insights into 'Trinitarian texts' that might otherwise be missed. In Hebrews, for instance, he looks beyond 1:2.[11] References to the Spirit are few, but significant: the witnessing Spirit who speaks through the scriptures about Christ (3:7, 9:8); the eschatological Spirit who brings us a foretaste of the life to come (6:4); more significantly, we are told that Christ offers himself to God 'through the eternal Spirit' (9:14).

> Now if the way Christ offered himself to the Father on the cross was by the Spirit, we can safely assume that the way he goes on offering our worship to the Father is by the same Spirit. So we have here an indication that Christian worship does not just take place *in* God's presence but, in some sense, *within* God's presence, for we are taken into the dynamic between the Father, the Son he begets as his exact image and the Spirit who exists eternally.[12]

Similarly, he describes Revelation as a book which is 'deeply and richly Trinitarian',[13] though the Trinitarian references are themselves complex and sometimes opaque – but, importantly, the whole is seen through the lens of the *worship* of heaven. Revelation 22:17 envisages the Spirit and the Bride issuing the invitation: God calls us back to

---

[9] Maurice Wiles, *The Making of Christian Doctrine* (Cambridge: CUP, 1967).
[10] Christopher Cocksworth, *Holy, Holy, Holy – Worshipping the Trinitarian God* (London: DLT, 1997).
[11] Ibid., p. 75.
[12] Ibid., p. 77; italics mine.
[13] Ibid., p. 80.

God, and once more we have this sense of worship being caught up into the very presence of God.

The themes of worship, Trinity and prayer converge on the Eucharist, or Lord's Supper. In 'free' traditions such as my own, the Great Prayer of Thanksgiving is often not prescribed, and can in practice take on different forms, some of them rather anaemic. But a cursory glance at Eucharistic history reveals what Christians have considered the essential content of this thanksgiving since the earliest times. The Eucharistic prayer thanks the Father for sending the Son, and invokes the Spirit who will make real the presence of the risen Christ: the Eucharist only makes sense in Trinitarian terms. And in eschatological terms, for the feast of the Lord's Supper is a foretaste of the feast of heaven itself: 'until he comes'.[14]

The meal recalls the past – the Father takes on the suffering and sin of the world through the offering of the Son in the Spirit; this is made a present reality in the lives of those who take bread and wine; this present reality is a foretaste of the future in which the Spirit brings to consummation the Kingdom entrusted to the Son, and all return to the fellowship of the Father. The Eucharist, when God's Spirit is invoked and indeed present, is part of – and an anticipation of – the way God gathers us up into the open fellowship of the Triune God.[15] But we are now anticipating themes yet to be explored.

What the doctrine of the Trinity articulates and discloses is the profound truth of Romans 8:26: that prayer is God praying to God through God. We might go so far as to suggest that all prayer and worship is an anticipation of the eternal-time when the open Trinity gathers us up into the divine community.

C. S. Lewis reflected upon this Trinitarian view of prayer, conceding that speculation on the Trinity for its own sake is

---

[14] 1 Cor. 11:27.
[15] See Jürgen Moltmann, *History and the Triune God* (London: SCM, 1991) and Paul S. Fiddes, *Participating in God* (London: DLT, 2000), pp. 71ff.

a pretty fruitless exercise. However, the point of 'Trinity-talk' is to enable us to understand something of the dynamics of the Christian life. And more important than talking about the Trinity is being *drawn into* the Triune life of God:

> An ordinary simple Christian kneels down to say his prayers. He is trying to get into touch with God. But if he is a Christian he knows that what is prompting him to pray is also God; God is, so to speak, inside him. But he also knows that all his real knowledge of God comes through Christ, the Man who was God – that Christ is standing beside him, helping him to pray, praying for him. You see what is happening. God is the thing to which he is praying – the goal he is trying to reach. God is also the thing inside him which is pushing him on – the motive power. God is also the road or bridge along which he is being pushed to that goal. So that the whole threefold life of the three-personal being is actually going on in that ordinary little bedroom where an ordinary man is saying his prayers. The man is being caught up into the [life of God].[16]

This rather homely illustration[17] is a useful reminder of the Trinitarian basis of the Christian experience of worship and prayer.

The Triune God – God in Relationship

We have sought to indicate the way in which the Christian understanding of God as Trinity emerged as an articulation of the experience of worshipping God: Father, Son and Holy Spirit. Much more could be said about this development, but we must turn now to consider the doctrine of the Trinity in another way, in particular, to consider what might be meant by expressions such as 'the Triune Life of God', and why that may be significant for our thinking about prayer.

---

[16] C. S. Lewis, *Mere Christianity* (Glasgow: Fount, 1977), pp. 138f.
[17] Torrance tells a similar story: *Worship*, pp. 32ff.

Far from being a disposable or speculative luxury, the doctrine of the Trinity may be said to be *the* Christian doctrine of God in an important way. It is, in Walter Kasper's words, 'the Christian form of speaking about God'.[18] He says:

> The church does not hold on to the unity of God despite the doctrine of the Trinity. Rather, in the doctrine of the Trinity it is precisely holding fast to Christian monotheism. It even maintains that the doctrine of the Trinity is the only possible and consistent form of monotheism and the only tenable answer to modern atheism.[19]

The Trinity is the only viable form of monotheism: in part, this is because the Trinity involves a statement of 'otherness' within the Deity. God is already, as it were, not solitary. The relationship of the Trinitarian persons is, as required by ancient and contemporary understandings of personhood, one of reciprocation and mutuality. This will prove significant when we come to consider God's relation to the 'others' of creation.

In the early development of the doctrine, it fell to Tertullian to coin the vocabulary of Trinitarianism. He first used the term *trinitas*, and his formula of 'one substance, three persons'[20] has proved remarkably durable. Tertullian's opponents wanted to promote a strong sense of the *unity* of God, which they expressed in terms of 'monarchy'. Tertullian boldly set out to defend the unity while at the same time championing the 'Trinitarian' position.

All three, Father, Son and Spirit, are 'persons', and the Godhead is a 'trinity'. This did not undermine the unity of God, which was characteristically expressed by saying that

---

[18] Walter Kasper, *The God of Jesus Christ* (London: SCM, 1984), p. 233.
[19] Ibid., p. 295; cf. David Cunningham, *These Three are One* (Oxford: Blackwell, 1998), p. 8.
[20] Tertullian, *Against Praxeas* in A. Roberts, J. Donaldson and A. C. Coxe (eds), *The Ante-Nicene Fathers*, vol. 3 (Grand Rapids: Eerdmans, 1985), ch. 2, p. 598. On line at http://www.ccel.org/fathers2/ANF-03/anf03-43.htm#P10374_2906966.

Father/Son/Spirit were one in 'substance'. The Latin *persona* and its Greek equivalent *prosopon* were useful for expressing the independent subsistence of the Three. They seem to have originally meant 'face' or 'mask' (as an actor might have worn in ancient drama), and came to mean 'expression' or 'role'. *Persona* came to mean 'individual', the stress usually being on the external aspect or manifestation.[21]

The main contributors in later debate were Augustine and the 'Cappadocian Fathers'.[22] Tertullian and many others had used analogies for the Trinity drawn from nature, such as the root, shoot and fruit.[23] These analogies convey relations, and same-substance, but do so without conveying the *personal* nature of the reality of God. Augustine and the Cappadocians, while still using such images, used two rather different sorts of images that may clarify for us one of the key areas in Trinitarian debate.

Augustine is mindful of the difficulties of saying anything at all about God. The language of 'three persons' is employed, he says, not because it is adequate, but because we have to say something.[24] Augustine developed a number of analogies for speaking of the Trinity, which have their root – or so it will seem to us – in human psychology. Augustine looked to human psychology for his Trinitarian analogies since humanity was made in the image of God and must therefore have the imprint (*vestigium*) of the Trinity. His examples of *vestigia Trinitatis* include being, knowing and willing; the mind, its self-knowing and its self-love; memory, understanding and will; and the mind remembering, understanding and loving God. Augustine, like all the Western tradition of theology that followed him, emphasised the unity of the

---

[21] J. N. D. Kelly, *Early Christian Doctrines* (London: A & C Black, 19684), p. 115.
[22] Basil the Great, Gregory of Nyssa and Gregory of Nazianzus.
[23] See Kelly, *Doctrines*, p. 111, and Tertullian, *Against Praxeas*, ch. 8, p. 603. David Cunningham suggests a similar one: *These Three*, pp. 72ff.
[24] Augustine, *On the Trinity*, 5/10, p. 92; http://www.ccel.org/fathers2/NPNF1-03/npnf1-03-11.htm#P1061_426002.

Triune God. It seems no coincidence, therefore, that his illustrations come from within the 'unity of one person', so to speak.

By contrast the Cappadocians embody the Eastern tradition on the Trinity, which stresses the Triunity as much as, or before, the unity. Their most well-known image for the trinity is drawn not from 'internal' human psychology, but from *interpersonal* relationships: they spoke of the Trinity not just as memory, understanding and will, but as like the relationship between Peter, James and John.[25] This rather shocking 'social analogy', as it is called, needs to be tempered with an important piece of background information. The Cappadocians, like all the Fathers, expressed their theology in part through the vehicle of philosophical vocabulary (just as, in rather different ways, we must also inevitably do). Their particular form of Platonism understood that, when speaking of human persons, the underlying 'humanity' which three individuals shared was more 'real' than the individual humanity peculiar to each individual. So when they used their social analogy of Peter, James and John, the humanity which they shared and in which they participated was more real, more substantial than their individuality (their Peter-ness, James-ness and John-ness, if you like).

The Cappadocians were aware of the insufficiency of this 'social analogy' and its potential dangers, but there is no denying that even allowing for this, the social analogy gives a very different feel to talking about God as Trinity than those analogies which use impersonal images or those drawn from human psychology. It suggests a greater diversity within God than the former – more Western – images, which always seem to tend towards a sort of modalism. This more social, Eastern, view of the Trinity has become much more widely embraced in the West in the last few decades – and, partly as a result of this, Trinitarian theology has had a renaissance.[26]

---

[25] Basil the Great, *Letter 38/2*, on line at http://www.ccel.org/fathers2/NPNF2-08/Npnf2-08-56.htm#P3098_1005192.

[26] For a contrary view, Stephen Davis, Daniel Kendall and Gerald O'Collins (eds), *The Trinity* (Oxford: OUP, 1999).

Ironically, Karl Barth, who perhaps began this renewed interest in the Trinity, had a very Western approach. He began his *Church Dogmatics* with the Trinity, in a way that had become quite foreign and surprising. Liberal theology had either written off the Trinity altogether, as the result of fevered Greek speculation, or had given it a sort of 'epilogue' status – as a doctrine which helped summarise and hold together certain other statements about God in a more or less symbolic way.[27] Barth caused quite a stir – but when he comes to discussing vocabulary for the Trinity he deliberately turns his back on the traditional vocabulary of 'three persons' because, he says, it will convey entirely the wrong impression to a twentieth-century thinker. 'Person' is for us, he suggests, a separate individual, a separate centre of consciousness. He feels that this is not an appropriate way to speak of the Trinity and opts instead for the phrase 'modes of being'. God, he argues, subsists in three modes of being at once: as Father, Son and Spirit. Karl Rahner, the principal Roman Catholic theologian of the twentieth century, more or less a contemporary of Barth, had exactly the same reservations about the language of Trinitarian 'persons' – and he opted for similar language to Barth, speaking of 'modes of subsistence'.[28]

Jürgen Moltmann is among those associated in the West with a turn towards a more Eastern, social doctrine of the Trinity. He contrasts 'monarchical' conceptions of God (which may include a validation for oppressive forms of human relationship) with truly Trinitarian ones.[29] Moltmann insists that Trinitarian reflection must begin in the New Testament and specifically with what he calls 'the history of the Father, Son and Spirit'.[30] From the New Testament perspective we should not assume the unity and

---

[27] e.g. Schleiermacher, *Faith*, pp. 738–51.
[28] Karl Rahner, *The Trinity* (New York: Herder & Herder, 1970), pp. 109ff.
[29] See Moltmann, *History and the Triune God*, pp. 57ff., 125ff.; Jürgen Moltmann, *The Trinity and the Kingdom of God* (London: SCM, 1981), pp. 129–50.
[30] Moltmann, *Trinity and the Kingdom*, p. 16.

then try to come to terms with the Trinity: the New Testament gives us the Father, Son and Spirit – it is then up to us to understand how these three are one.

Just as we began this chapter by considering the identity of God as the Christlike God, so Moltmann suggests that the proper procedure is to use the passion of Christ as the 'hermeneutical key': the passion is the central event in the Trinitarian history of God.[31] A simple monotheism here would speak of God 'giving himself up' on the cross; but scripture speaks of 'God the Father giving up his Son'. On the cross, a death takes place in God. For the Son really dies, and the Father suffers the loss of the Son – the Father and the Son both suffer, but differently. The cross then becomes a Trinitarian event, and the Trinitarian trajectory leads to implications in many areas of life and Christian experience – worship, initiation, mission and beyond.

In order to see how this works out it is necessary to touch on the ancient notion of *perichoresis*. This Greek term was employed in the Patristic period (though rather late in use, the idea behind it was certainly present in the Cappadocians and Augustine) to denote the way in which the different persons of the Trinity *mutually indwell* one another. After their earliest discussions, the Fathers tended to resist distinguishing between the Persons by function – by what they *did*. After all, while we tend to associate creation with the first person of the Trinity, scripture tells us that the second (Col. 1:16; Jn 1:3) and the third (Gen. 1:2) persons were also associated with creation. The Cappadocians helpfully distinguished between the persons only in terms of their *relationships* rather than their *functions*, and Augustine gave ontological status to the concept of 'relations'.[32] The Father is thus distinguished by his Fatherhood, the Son by his generation, and so on. The relationships both distinguish them and yet also constitute them as 'persons'. The Cappadocians say most clearly,

---

[31] Ibid., ch. 2 and p. 183.
[32] See Paul S. Fiddes, *Participating*, pp. 16–19.

though Augustine says it too, that the *persons of the Trinity
are constituted by their relationship to one another.*[33] Each
person of the Trinity is present 'within' the others by
mutual indwelling.

Allied with the necessary doctrine of the mutual equality
of the persons (for no one person can be more or less God
than the others, but only equally God) these ideas point to
the Trinity as being a co-equal fellowship of persons who
subsist in mutuality and love. God is a 'community of
persons'. When God made humankind in God's image,
therefore, God did not make humankind to be solitary
individuals, but as interdependent, mutually indwelling
individuals who find their identity in community. To
understand humanity in this way is to understand it very
particularly as a sort of community – and one where forms
of domination and hierarchy are by definition out of order
and out of line with God's created purpose.[34]

By now some readers may be getting somewhat
impatient. What have some of the finer points of Trinitarian
thought to do with our thinking about prayer? Granted that
the development of Trinitarian thought owes much to the
experience of God as Father, Son and Spirit, and that it helps
us articulate profound truths about God being in some way
the source as well as the goal of our prayers, what further
can be gained by such discussion? The key to answering
that question lies alongside a further answer to the question
'Who is God?' The God and Father of our Lord Jesus Christ
is the Triune God, who is One and Three, who is three
persons in community. These persons are 'who' they are
because of their relationships. God is who God is because of
God's relationships, Father, Son and Holy Spirit: the
persons are constituted by and in their relationships.

---

[33] See Colin E. Gunton, *The Promise of Trinitarian Theology* (Edinburgh: T
& T Clark, 19972), pp. 93ff.

[34] Moltmann follows the implications of this through into areas such as
politics, the church, sexual politics and ecology. The Trinity becomes a
kind of hermeneutical tool for Christian discipleship. See, e.g., *Trinity
and the Kingdom*, ch. 6.

But to recall this idea that the persons of the Trinity are constituted by, and subsist in, relationship suggests that Rahner and Barth were too quick to discard the traditional language of Trinitarian discussion. A 'person' turns out to be not a solitary-individual-person, but an interpersonal-in-community-person, who exists in, for and because of relationships. It is not possible, given what we mean by person, to be one-person-in-isolation from others. This is precisely what the 'person' language of the Trinity may have been trying to suggest! Barth and Rahner seem to have been working with a very Enlightenment or 'modern' idea of person, the solitary individual who faces the world and alone seeks for truth. Instead, person is a profoundly *relational* term, and suggests not solitariness but community. And the three persons of the Trinity are not members of some closed and cosy divine club, but instead reach out to creatures in fellowship and love, drawing us into their shared life of personhood. Prayer is one way in which we are drawn into the life of the Trinity.

God is relational: can God be relational wholly satisfactorily 'within' the Trinity, or does God 'need' to relate to other creatures, other persons, outside of God's self? Such a 'need' is not an emotional need in the way that I might 'need company tonight'. It is, albeit I think in a rather weak sense, an ontological need. For God to be the God and Father of our Lord Jesus Christ, who is by nature relational both in terms of God's own Triune being and in terms of God's creativity, God 'needs' to be in relationship in order to be this sort of God – in order to be who God is. Those, like Moltmann and Fiddes, who argue for an 'open Trinity' believe that God does need to relate to others beyond God's self,[35] and we shall later hear a similar argument arising from the very nature of agency – considering God as One who acts in the world. The fundamentally 'relational' nature of God undermines any claims to God's lofty apartness from creation, and suggests immediately a

---

[35] Moltmann, *History and the Triune God*, p. 86.

God who will seek relationships with mutuality. This insight into who God is has profound implications for our understanding of prayer. The cover of the British edition of Fiddes' book on the Trinity, revealingly entitled *Participating in God*, illustrates the point. Matisse's painting of the dance has five figures, not three, as one might at first expect for a work on the Trinity. The two extra figures represent human persons drawn into the relational life of the Triune God more dynamically than Lewis' story of the ordinary man at prayer. Precisely because God is relational the relational Trinity into whose life we are drawn is the God who we know as the One who hears our prayers (Calvin).

God and the World

Closely related to the question of the identity of God is the related question of 'world view', which we have also touched upon several times, and a vital part of which is a consideration – in as precise a way as is possible for us – of *how we understand God and the world to relate to one another*. I say 'in as precise a way as possible for us' because absolute precision is beyond us. Scripture gives clues and hints; our God-given intellect explores and experiments with ideas, testing them against scripture and experience. The end may be a kind of model in our minds of how God and the world interact and relate, but it will remain a model.[36]

Some would have us believe that speculation on such matters is fruitless and even unfaithful. The biblicist may suggest that unless such models are suggested in scripture we should not attempt to construct or debate others: they are bound to be inadequate, perhaps even inherently doomed to mislead us. Such an objection founders on various counts. Scripture itself has a 'world view', or

---

[36] On models in theology, see Avery Dulles, *Models of Revelation* (Dublin: Gill & MacMillan, 1992); Ian G. Barbour, *Myths, Models and Paradigm* (London: SCM, 1974).

rather, shows evidence of various – often related – world views. These world views are expressed in models, such as the 'triple-decker universe', which to some extent integrate quasi-scientific understanding of the day, everyday common sense and theological perspectives.[37] To speak at all about the relation of God to the world draws us inevitably into discussing models of this relationship, and it is equally inevitable that if we are to be faithful disciples in *our* age that we will have to think like people of our age, at least to the extent of trying to use models of understanding which integrate 'scientific understanding, everyday common sense, and theological perspectives'. However, it *is* true to say that every and any model which we end up formulating and examining will be tested in some way against scripture and in dialogue with its interpreters through the Christian centuries.

Another kind of objection comes from those who believe for more general theological reasons that we should not attempt to describe and analyse the 'details' of God's relationship with the world. They might believe it irreverent, or just an impossible enterprise. Austin Farrer, for instance, suggested that we ought not to speculate on the nature of the 'causal joint' between God and the world.[38] While it is proper to recognise the sense that, in the end, all theological enquiry resolves itself into mystery, it is also true that there is some kind of imperative laid upon us by scripture and God's endowment of us with rational and enquiring minds to push things as far as we can. If we fail to probe the nature of the 'causal joint' as closely as we can we risk confusing mock piety with a failure of nerve.

Our next task, then, is to begin to think about how we might model the relation of God to the world. First we will look at the suggestions of a biblical scholar concerning models that may be discerned in scripture itself, and then

[37] See http://sol.sci.uop.edu/~jfalward/ThreeTieredUniverse.htm.
[38] Austin Farrer, *Faith and Speculation* (London: A & C Black, 1967), pp. 61ff.

we will examine a typology offered by a systematic theologian for examining and analysing such models.

An approach from biblical scholarship
In his book on divine suffering, Old Testament scholar Terence Fretheim proposes four ways of understanding the relationship of God and the world. The first two, the two extremes as he calls them, he dismisses immediately, but I want to pause over them for just a moment. They are (1) pantheism and (2) dualism.

A pantheistic understanding of the God–world relation identifies God with the world and the world with God. As the word suggests, all (*pan*) is God (*theos*), and God is all. There might seem to be a rather contemporary ring to such suggestions, but pantheism has been alive and well in every age, and may have been a religious option in some parts of the ancient near east just as it is now. But while divine immanence is a genuine Old Testament theme, it is very wide of the mark to think that scripture seriously suggests a pantheistic view of the God–world relation. Creation is not God, and sometimes stands sharply over against God, and God over against it. However, as I will suggest later, this particular extreme may not be so far from one of the often-espoused positions on this matter, a deterministic understanding – even one that seeks to stress the transcendence of God.

Similarly, dualistic perspectives on the world were not uncommon in the ancient world. Dualistic groups believed that the material world was evil, in direct opposition to the spiritual realm in general and God in particular. Outside of scripture's text, many of the first Christians were converted from such dualistic sects – Augustine himself was a convert from Manichaeism.[39] In dualism, God and the world are not simply 'independent of one another . . . [but] opposed to one another'.[40] Again, this is not a scriptural perspective,

---

[39] See the Hutchinson online encyclopaedia at http://www.tiscali.co.uk/reference/encyclopaedia/hutchinson/m0002193.html.
[40] Fretheim, *Suffering*, p. 34.

and in Genesis, when the task of creation is done, God pronounces the created order 'very good'.[41]

Fretheim goes on to suggest two models of the God–world relationship which fall clearly between these two extremes and which he claims can be seen in the Old Testament texts. He calls them (3) the 'monarchical' and (4) the 'organismic'. The monarchical model is, says Fretheim, 'the image that prevails in contemporary Old Testament interpretation',[42] and, we might add, in most popular Christian exegesis. As the label implies, the model suggests that God relates to the world as a monarch relates to his or her kingdom and subjects. There are connections here with some of the earlier discussion about the unity of God, with Tertullian on the 'monarchy', and with the more critical appraisal of Moltmann. There is a transcendence of order and rank implicit in the monarchical model, a difference between God and the world that amounts to a radical discontinuity. Few Christian theologians will feel very uncomfortable about this – the question is, have we located the discontinuity correctly? Fretheim sees this radical discontinuity expressing itself in terms of power and freedom (God has a monopoly on both) and also in God's being in control of his relationship with the world (creatures have no power to affect God who stands outside time, history and the created order). God stands apart from, outside, above, beyond, God's world.

But as the last paragraph wore on the reader may have begun to feel that such a view of 'God and the world' is somewhat problematic. For how can God be involved with persons if this relationship is entirely one way? What sort of relationship is it when one party holds every advantage, and indeed is entirely responsible for the shape and style of the relationship, and for what both parties must 'put into it'? More to our particular point: if God is not affected by

---

[41] Gen. 1:31, and the refrain 'God saw that it was good' in preceding verses.
[42] Fretheim, *Suffering*, p. 35.

the world, and indeed is not involved in history (and, therefore, time), what can it mean to say that God 'answers' our prayers of intercession? Any such answer may appear convoluted or disingenuous.

The earliest Christian theologians plied their trade in their own context. Theology was then, as it is now, in Anselm's celebrated phrase, 'faith seeking understanding'. Faith can only be understood in the thought forms available to the age in which thinking takes place, and for the earliest theologians this meant using the thoughts forms shaped by the ancient philosophies of Greece. Indeed, there was a missionary imperative also: for unless they could articulate their faith in a way that their contemporaries would find comprehensible, their work would be over before it had begun.

Many of the thought forms of scripture appear to have lost something in their translation into the vocabulary and thought forms of the ancient Greeks. It needed to be done, the risk needed to be taken: but we need also to recognise the cost of this enterprise. As an example that may be pertinent to our enquiry, we might consider the notion of God's 'faithfulness'. The faithfulness of Yahweh, a highly personal concept with its connotations of loyalty and fidelity, became a rather different concept when 'translated'. Personal loyalty became a metaphysical unchangingness: Yahweh's faithfulness became the 'reliability' of the Unmoved Mover, One who could not even respond to a beloved. It is this metaphysically unchanging deity which hovers about our biblical interpretation, as Fretheim points out.

By contrast, the organismic model of God–world relations configures many of these issues differently. Here, borrowing a phrase of Heschel, Fretheim suggests that there is a 'relationship of reciprocity' between God and the world.[43] This model, seldom reflected in scholarly exegesis, indicates a greater continuity between God and the world

---

[43] Ibid.

that amounts to an intimacy. God and the world are both now seen, *though in different ways*, as dependent on one another; it becomes as true to say now that God is affected by the world, as vice versa; God's sovereignty is qualified in various ways, mostly by creaturely freedom; God's knowledge is spoken of in ways closer to human knowledge. This reciprocity is not of an equal or equivalent kind: God and the world are not affected by one another in the same ways.[44] It is easy, and has been customary, to dismiss such perspectives as 'anthropomorphisms'. However, if one assumes that Christian talk about God begins by attending to the particularity of the scriptural witness, rather than to the generality of philosophical speculation, such easy dismissals are premature.

Fretheim's book, as its title indicates, seeks to offer an exploration of the 'organismic model' with the particular issues of divine suffering in mind, a very particular way in which God is affected by the world. This much is clear: whatever one model we formulate, it is unlikely to be straightforwardly congruent with every text in scripture. Honesty about this at the outset is essential.

An approach from systematic theology
Of the various writers referred to in this book, it is probably Terrance Tiessen who has attempted a project closest to my own.[45] His work is an engaging and impressive achievement, though his conclusions and mine are significantly different. He begins with the conundrum of the way people pray, and how that arises from, or indeed conflicts with, the views they hold about God's relationship with the world. He outlines not four but eleven different models of this relationship and he uses the device of a prayer group 'case study' to compare and contrast them throughout the book.[46] It is a helpful and grounded way to illustrate what is at stake.

---

[44] The much-maligned Process view of a dipolar God asserts just this.
[45] Tiessen, *Providence*.
[46] See pp. 26f., and then the conclusion of each exposition for the various 'model prayers'.

Tiessen places the models he identifies across a continuum, attempting to move from those that see God as being little involved in the historical process to those that see God as more and more the determining power in it. I will return in chapter 4 to a closer look at some of Tiessen's constructive suggestions. Here I want to focus on his analytical method: while I will dispute his conclusions, I believe that the tools he has used to forge them are well chosen and illuminating. In a table at the end of his book Tiessen lists the characteristics of the eleven models in relation to eight variables.[47] Each model is then construed as a particular combination of attitudes on these eight variables. I will list Tiessen's eight variables now because of the way in which they indicate some of the most important issues, and offer my own brief comments about the significance of them.

(1) *The nature of God's experience of time.* Praying about a particular state of affairs in our world is praying for an event or events, or a person or persons, *in time.* The nature of God's relationship to time is therefore of critical interest. Tiessen suggests that the models he identifies are divided between those that understand God to be related to time from within (God is temporal in some sense), and those that understand God to be related to time from without (God is eternal, in the sense of atemporal).

(2) *Whether God knows the 'actual future'.* God is usually described as 'omniscient' – all knowing. But what does that mean? This is a hotly debated matter, with a strong challenge emerging to the traditional view. Tiessen's use of 'actual' here differentiates the future that will in fact be actualised from those possible futures which are hypothetically possible but which will not in fact come to pass. These possible but unactualised futures are considered under the next variable . . .

---

[47] Tiessen, *Providence*, pp. 363f.

(3) *Whether God knows 'counter-factuals'.* This divine knowledge of hypothetical futures is sometimes termed 'middle knowledge', and Tiessen regards it as a valuable refinement on views of foreknowledge which exclude or ignore it.

(4) *Whether God takes a risk in creation.* Are we to regard God's purposes as assured? Are God's purposes certain to be achieved? However, Tiessen misses an important distinction in his discussion of this point. For some, and the position I will attempt to outline comes under such a category, there is a distinction to be made between 'penultimate' and 'ultimate' purposes. God's penultimate purposes may be 'at risk', but his final purposes may not be. Oscar Cullmann has a similar point in mind in some of his writings on New Testament theology,[48] and he sometimes uses the analogy of the decisive battle won with more battles before the final victory.[49] To refuse any idea of risk at all means, at the very least, that anything of any significance is 'bound' to occur in accordance with God's will; it could mean that 'everything' does so.

(5) *Whether God specifically permits all evils.* This question has a clear relationship to the previous one: in the first models considered by Tiessen, God gives creation freedom to err, but does not specifically permit any specific evils; in other models, God is conceived as choosing to permit just the evils which actually occur in our world in order to achieve his purposes. These are the evils 'against' which we sometimes pray. The question may be asked whether evils are really evils if God permits them for our higher good. Ethnic cleansing, child rape and countless other harsh examples of natural and moral evil stretch the credibility of such a position – but if creation has no risks, perhaps we are left with it?

---

[48] See, for instance, Cullmann, *Prayer in the New Testament*, pp. 138–41.
[49] Oscar Cullmann, *Christ and Time* (London: SCM, 1951), p. 84.

(6) *The sixth variable considers the nature of human freedom*, and it offers three alternative conceptions of it. Only in the fatalist model is human freedom illusory. In all the others human freedom is conceived of as either libertarian (in which one can make at least two different choices in each situation) or volitional (in which one acts according to one's will, even though the action taken may also be determined, in the terms of our discussion, by God). This question has a decisive impact on our understanding of prayer.

(7) *Whether prayer affects the outcome of events*. Rather startlingly, Tiessen claims that in all the models apart from two (with the least and the most divine control) prayer does affect the outcome. Again, to some of the issues raised in such discussion we will return, and I will want to argue that in most of Tiessen's models this affect is illusory or 'staged'.

(8) *Whether prayer changes God's mind*. It is helpful that Tiessen distinguishes between the seventh and eighth variables, as often they are collapsed together. It will surprise some readers, perhaps, that Tiessen suggests that in nearly all models 'prayer affects the outcome', yet in most of them prayer does not 'change God's mind'. What sort of effect does prayer have, then? I will want to argue later precisely that prayer does affect the outcome by (in part, and sometimes) 'changing God's mind' – though I am not sure that that is the language I would most want to use to describe what I believe happens, by God's grace.

One important issue of world view raised in Tiessen's identification of these variables is the relationship of God to time: it is again, in part, a question about who God is. To that we turn alongside a consideration of various problems in configuring God's relation to the world.

The Dialectics of Time, Knowledge and Power

In considering the nature of God's relationship to the world a number of interrelated ideas and concepts arise. Some of these perennial puzzles we will now consider: the question of God's relationship to time; the definition of God's 'omniscience'; and the nature of divine power and sovereignty. What will be suggested in each case is that a somewhat dialectical approach may prove to be helpful where a general affirmation of God's relationship to the world is qualified or tempered by a contrasting, dialectical affirmation.

God and Time

On a number of occasions during the foregoing discussion we have referred, directly or indirectly, to the nature of God's relationship to time; it featured quite explicitly as one of Tiessen's eight variables, and Origen's ancient and typical account of intercession assumed a very particular understanding of the matter. It is now appropriate and necessary to explore this relationship more directly. Indeed, any treatment of intercessory prayer is bound to consider this question at some point. If today I pray for my son's job interview next week, or for a friend to recover from illness, or for spiritual renewal in the church of which I am part, all these prayers relate to some future state. For me, none of these future states *are real* yet in any meaningful way. But what about God's relationship to such future possible states? Does God already experience the outcome of the interview, the resolution of the illness, the revived or moribund church? If God does already experience these outcomes, how might that affect my praying for them now? Very closely related to and overlapping with this subject is another to which we will come presently, that of God's omniscience (specifically, God's foreknowledge), and it is not always possible or desirable to keep the issues completely separated.

The eternity of God – timelessness, temporality, or eternal temporality?

God, it is routinely said, is 'eternal'. What might this mean? (1) That God stands outside time altogether and experiences everything, as it were, at once, atemporally. This we may call the traditional understanding of the eternity of God, and we may call it the absence or the negation of time. It is 'timeless time', without duration or 'seriality'. (2) Another possible definition of eternity does not make God atemporal, but defines eternity instead as being of unending duration. Some writers prefer the term 'everlasting' to 'eternity' to express this view, in which there remains duration and 'seriality'. What has been at stake here?[50]

One reason given to defend the 'timeless eternity' view has been what Paul Helm calls the 'basic theistic intuition that God's fullness is such that he possesses the whole of his life together'.[51] But it is not easy to see where this basic intuition comes from, or how it might be tested for authenticity.[52] One might assume that this intuition is smuggled in with certain philosophical assumptions, or perhaps reflects some psychological as much as theological requirement.[53] Another, related, reason given by advocates of this position is the linkage between time and change. Human experience of time is one often marked by regret and the fading of memory, by decline in powers, by the passing of experience: in summary, by loss.[54] Advocates of

---

[50] cf. Gregory E. Ganssle (ed.), *God and Time: Four Views* (Downers Grove: IVP, 2001), where Paul Helm, Alan D. Padgett, William Lane Craig and Nicholas Wolterstorff debate with one another as representatives of different positions. For a discussion of God and Time in relation to Process Theology and Jürgen Moltmann, see John O'Donnell's excellent study *Trinity and Temporality* (Oxford: OUP, 1983).

[51] Paul Helm, 'Divine Timeless Eternity' in Ganssle (ed.), *God and Time*, p. 30.

[52] See Nicholas Wolterstorff, 'Response to Paul Helm' in Ganssle (ed.), *God and Time*, p. 70.

[53] cf. John Macquarrie, *In Search of Deity: An Essay in Dialectical Theism* (London: SCM, 1984), pp. 181f.

[54] See Gregory E. Ganssle's 'Introduction' in Ganssle (ed.), *God and Time*, pp. 22f; Alfred North Whitehead, *Process and Reality* (New York: Macmillan, 1929), pp 318.

'timeless eternity' want to preserve the traditional doctrine of the immutability of God – arguing that God does not change in any respect. This idea is very ancient, but receives one of its classic formulations in Plato's *Republic*, where Plato says that God, being perfect, cannot change – not for the better, since 'perfect' means there can be no better; not for the worse, since that would betray an imperfection and rob God of perfection.[55] Because time and change are inevitably linked, Christian theologians who wanted to say that God was not vulnerable to this kind of loss tried to find a way of putting God outside time, a move which would also – it is often believed – save God's dignity. But how much does this naturally follow from the biblical witness? Is this not what Barth meant when he spoke of importing ideas of God from elsewhere rather than discovering who God is in God's revelation?

How might we reply to those who suggest that to place God within time makes God vulnerable to it in the same way we are: we for whom the past disappears from our view, and who may be surprised or overwhelmed by the future? We may propose that in God the past is perfectly retained, without loss. Some writers even suggest that the past is in some way 'redeemed' as God retains it.[56] The passing of time for God does not involve the loss of its value. As regards the future, Keith Ward suggests that it is not God's timelessness but omnipotence that gives God control over the future, that God is always able to cope with whatever time brings. If God has created a genuinely free creation, as opposed to one which is an extension of God's self, then creatures can make free decisions and God will have to take account of them in God's purposes: this is being 'changed' by them. But it does not follow that a creature is therefore greater than God. Only to overwhelm God would be to be 'greater' than God. Cullmann's D-Day analogy is once more pertinent.

[55] Plato, *The Republic*, Benjamin Jowett (tr.), bk 2, on line at http://classics.mit.edu/Plato/republic.html.
[56] e.g. Whitehead, *Process*, pp. 531–53.

Those who opt for 'temporal-eternity' have to make some adjustments to this strict doctrine of immutability, but their prime motive is often to do with a desire to show God to be involved in the world process. In particular, the nature of divine action, action that is responsive to worldly events, seems to require such an understanding.[57] Every act presupposes a before and an after, and action implies duration – but also preparation and 'consequation', what comes after it. Furthermore, action involves assessing and responding to other actions. Similarly, God's action seems to require temporality – before, during, and after. Those who argue for temporal-eternity do so, at least in part, because they want to preserve the involvement of God with temporal creatures. But something more is at stake than the reality of God's rapport with the world. If God's 'action' is conceived of as something which happens atemporally (in some way, from outside time), then it seems to many that it implies a view that God somehow has everything 'sorted' before anything happens, in every detail. *God's response is not so much a real response as an illusion which looks like a response*, built in to the system from the start. Thus the atemporal-eternal God might not only jeopardise the reality of divine action, but might also jeopardise the reality and freedom of the world itself. Free actions now appear to have been pre-programmed. Again eternity and immutability rub shoulders with omniscience and omnipotence.

The notion of immutability seems to derive from a Neoplatonic view of perfection. It is much more difficult to argue for such a view of metaphysical changelessness from the Bible alone. While mainstream Christian theology went down this path, some theologians and mystics offered other insights which seemed to suggest a temporally involved, suffering God which were never fully knitted into the theological tradition, but in the recent past they have come to seem more persuasive.

---

[57] cf. Nicholas Wolterstorff, 'Response to William Lane Craig' in Ganssle (ed.), *God and Time*, p. 171.

If we do start with the Bible, this second position of 'everlasting eternity' seems to have much to be said for it. A few texts are sometimes taken to support 'timeless eternity' but on examination the suspicion must arise that such a reading has to be made through the lens of the sort of philosophical assumptions we have just encountered. Psalm 90:1–4, for instance, actually speaks specifically of everlastingness rather than timelessness. Like John 8:58 ('Before Abraham was, I am') it really refers not to divine timelessness but to the rather different idea that God is present to every time and every moment. Other passages like James 1:17 and Malachi 3:6 are not testimony to metaphysical unchangingness but to constancy of character, to the faithfulness of God at every time.

Moreover, scripture seems to assume throughout that God has a history, that there is 'a story to be told about God'[58] that involves, as all stories must, seriality and the interplay of characters with one another. Nowhere is this clearer than in the passages that speak of biblical characters praying to God (whether it be Hezekiah praying for his life or Elijah summoning help on Carmel) for that which is yet to be. This is consonant with the more general summaries that emerged from our earlier study of God as personal, accessible, dialogical. Proponents of the 'timeless eternity' position are bound to claim that such passages that depict interaction are, in Calvin's words, merely an accommodation to our human limitations,[59] but they also open themselves to the charge that they portray God as deceitful, as only *seeming* to respond.

It might also be argued that temporality is a necessary property of persons, and that – because God is understood to be personal – this also suggests that God must be

---

[58] See Nicholas Wolterstorff, 'Unqualified Divine Temporality' in ibid., pp. 203ff.
[59] 'For because our weakness does not attain to his exalted state, the description of him that is given to us must be accommodated to our capacity so that we may understand it.' Calvin, *Institutes*, 1/17/13, p.22.

temporal. Sometimes characteristics such as remembering, anticipating, reflecting, deliberating, deciding, intending and acting intentionally are suggested.[60] While the predication of some such characteristics may not be entirely straightforward, the deliberative and conscious thought and interaction which goes with intentional agency does seem important. Following our discussion of the Trinity we may consider that temporality may seem to be an important part of what it is to be a person interacting with other persons. Such interaction involves responses and changes: change requires duration. The person, interacting with other persons (by responding to their prayers, for instance), would seem to be involved in the temporal sequence. The Trinity leads to the temporality of God.

These themes of biblical witness, the nature of person-hood and the Trinity, converge in the thinking of Barth. Barth began with revelation. The problem with beginning anywhere else is that there is a tendency to decide in advance who or what God is. Instead we have to allow God to speak. In revelation God speaks triply in the voices of Father, Son and Holy Spirit.[61]

According to Colin Gunton, for Barth revelation has a dynamic character – it is an *event*, a *happening*, in and amongst human lives and human history. It is 'God happening'.[62] 'For Barth, God is temporal, because revelation is God, taking place in time.'[63] Barth's exposition concerns itself with the threefold Lordship of God. But to be Lord means being able to make decisions about God's own being and relationships. To be Lord, for instance,

---

[60] e.g. William Lane Craig, 'Timelessness and Omnitemporality' in Ganssle (ed.), *God and Time*, p. 136ff., referring to R. C. Coburn's article 'Professor Malcolm on God', *Australian Journal of Philosophy* 41 (1963), pp. 152–73.

[61] See Richard Roberts, 'Karl Barth' in P. Toon and J. D. Spiceland (eds), *One God in Trinity* (London: Bagster, 1980), p. 83.

[62] Colin E. Gunton, *Becoming and Being* (Oxford: OUP, 1978), p. 129.

[63] Ibid., p. 140.

means not being bound by any metaphysical necessities beyond God's self, such as not being able to change, or not being able to become part of creation, and even that the 'eternal God' can elect to become part of the temporal creation – these are the exercising of divine Lordship.

> That God is capable of what the Bible ascribes to Him . . . that God can become unlike Himself in such a way that he is not tied to His secret eternity and His eternal secrecy but can and will and does in fact take temporal form as well; the fact that God can and will and actually does do this we now understand as a confirmation of our first statement that God reveals himself as the Lord.[64]

Not to believe this is to fall foul of a natural theology – to believe, in effect, that although the Bible *seems* to suggest that God meets us in time that in fact this is unworthy of God, or that it is impossible for God. Barth here punctures the claim that such moves 'protect God's dignity' – after all, how can it protect God's dignity to suggest that God is *incapable* of electing to be in time out of love for us? This is to bring an idea of God *to the Bible*, instead of discovering who God is by *listening to the Bible*.

Eternity is for Barth not an abstract concept that takes its definition apart from God who, as it were, 'inhabits' it. Just the other way, in fact – as we might expect! – *God defines eternity*. So just as time is the form in which God creates human existence, 'eternity is God himself';[65] it is the dimension of God's own life. God is not to be defined – or *con*fined – by any terms imported from outside. God gives these words their definition.

For Moltmann,[66] again like Barth, God's eternity is more than a negation of time – it is the fullness of divine creative life. This makes it possible to conceive of 'an opening for

---

[64] Barth, C.D. I/1, pp. 319f.

[65] Barth, *C.D.* III/2, p. 526.

[66] Jürgen Moltmann also uses 'event' language about God, and in a more explicitly Trinitarian way: *The Crucified God* (London: SCM, 1974), pp. 294–6.

time in eternity'.[67] God's eternity then need not be 'time-less'. To insist that it is may be to import an abstract definition from elsewhere once more. Like Barth, Moltmann speaks of 'before and after' in the eternity of God's free choice to create. In the beginning God acts inwardly on God's self, and then externally in creation.[68] If this is the moment when what we call time comes into being out of the (temporal?) eternity of God, there is a corresponding eschatological moment. God's purpose to be 'all in all' will mean that *temporal creation* will become *eternal creation*, and the 'end of temporal history' will be the 'beginning of eternal history'.[69]

God and time: the question of divine action
Scripture appears to depict God as 'planning, deliberating, acting and reacting within the temporal'.[70] But the sort of account of prayer which we saw given by Origen at the end of the previous chapter clearly does not envisage God being involved temporally in the world. In such a view God appears to pre-programme responses to our prayers, and indeed any other divine actions, into the whole completed canvas of time at the outset. In fairness it has to be said, however, that proponents of 'timeless eternity' do not think in quite such terms. After all, it is hardly proper to suggest that God pre-programmes temporal actions 'before time'. What would 'before' mean in the expression 'before time'? 'Before' only makes sense when there is time. If we try to think in terms of 'timeless eternity' we seem to have to conceive of God acting as it were 'once' upon every time, and simultaneously once. By eternal act God responds to every prayer, determining where and what to do simultaneously. Such a conception stretches to the limits our language and attempts at sense. 'What could it mean to say that Caesar crossing the Rubicon, Napoleon living in

[67] Jürgen Moltmann, *The Coming of God* (London: SCM, 1996), p. 281.
[68] Ibid., p. 282.
[69] Ibid., pp. xi, 294f.
[70] Pinnock, *Most Moved Mover*, p. 96.

Paris, and Churchill being the Prime Minister of Britain are simultaneous? How can God be a person and deal with us if outside time? His thoughts would be one thought that somehow lasts forever.'[71]

All thoughts and actions, all prayers and their answers, experienced at once and lasting forever? Suppose we think about God's responding to every prayer simultaneously. This seems to rely on conceiving of time by analogy with space:[72] all the events of time are present at once, rather as when someone looks down from the Eiffel Tower on the landscape around. They can look in one direction and see the Bois de Boulogne, or in another and see Notre Dame; or they can see traffic on the Champs-Elysées. All these 'landscape events' are present at once, and the 'timeless eternity' idea of God and time envisages something similar: all the landscape of time is present at once and simultaneously to God. It is such a view that Boethius imagines and which has shaped most Christian thinking on the matter: 'Eternity . . . is the complete, simultaneous and perfect possession of everlasting life.'[73]

There are a number of difficulties here beyond the difficulty of just thinking such thoughts. One relates to the question of the status of the future. If the future does not exist yet, if it is not yet actualised, then how can it 'be there' for anyone to see? This is, critics argue, the fundamental problem with envisaging time in this spatial way. For Notre Dame, the Bois de Boulogne and the Champs-Elysées are *there* in a way that 4 July 2024 (to pick a date at random) is not. If it *is not* yet, how can it be seen? Changing the perspective of the spatial analogy makes the point: if we imagine travelling along the Seine in a pleasure boat we

---

[71] Ibid., p. 98.
[72] e.g. Vincent Brummer, *What Are We Doing When We Pray?* (London: SCM, 1984), p. 41ff.; Alan D. Padgett, 'Eternity as Relative Timelessness' in Ganssle (ed.), *God and Time*, p. 99. See John Polkinghorne, *Science and Providence* (London: SPCK, 1989), p. 79.
[73] Boethius, *The Consolation of Philosophy*, V. E. Watts (tr.) (Harmondsworth: Penguin, 1969), 5.6.

may travel first past the heliport to the south-west of the Eiffel Tower. At this point we cannot see Notre Dame, it is not within our line of vision, but is further along and around a large bend. Of course, *it is there*, but we can't see it yet. The 'timeless eternity' notion suggests that our experience of time is like this pleasure craft trip. We travel into a future which is there but which we can't see because we have not yet arrived at it: only God, as it were, on the top of the tower, can see Notre Dame!

Any understanding of God as thoroughly temporal needs to redefine 'omniscience' somewhat in order to retain real openness to the future. This may be through such concepts as 'prediction', analogically applied; but it is also more likely to be through asking 'What is there *really* to be known about the future?' If the future really is not yet 'there', in the way that Notre Dame really is upstream, does it make sense to say that God can see it from the top of the Tower? Some who have difficulty with divine temporality object that what is being proposed is that God 'knows less' than in the traditional, timeless-eternity position. But to complain that God knows less because God does not know the as-yet-unactualised future is like complaining that 'God does not know that England won the 2002 World Cup.' God doesn't know this because England didn't win it. It isn't actual.[74]

Another difficulty here relates to the way in which divine action is configured, and in particular how it may be thought of as being responsive. Paul Helm, advocating the 'timeless eternity' view, uses an illustration:

> The correct way to think of God eternally willing something in time is to think of one eternal act of will with numerous temporally scattered effects. As an analogy, we may think of a person's action in setting the time on her central heating system. This is (we may

---

[74] David Hunt, for instance, calls the view I am suggesting 'diminished foreknowledge': 'The Simple Foreknowledge View' in J. K. Beilby and P. R. Eddy (eds), *Divine Foreknowledge: Four Views* (Downers Grove: IVP, 2001), p. 66ff.

suppose) one action, analogous to God's eternal willing. But this one action has numerous temporally scattered effects, analogous to the effects in time of God's one eternal act of willing; as a result of this one act, the system fires at 7:00 a.m., goes off at 12:00 noon, fires again at 2:00 p.m., goes off again at 10:30 p.m. day after day. The basic point is: there can be one decision to bring about different effects at different times. This decision may be in time, as in our example, or it may also be timeless.[75]

At first sight the illustration may seem a strong one: one act which has many subsequent effects. But if we think about domestic realities for a moment it appears less strong.[76] It illustrates perhaps how God may indeed act eternally 'once', but at the cost of divine responsiveness to experienced temporal realities. When our central heating fails to come on on a cold winter morning because the timer is at fault, my wife does not blame me (not when things have been explained properly, anyway), even though I programmed the timer. Similarly, my wife would not normally tell our neighbour that her husband turns the heating on every morning. We would say, 'it comes on', or perhaps that 'the timer turns it on'. For turning on the heating to be *my* action I would normally be thought to have to have a closer, more direct relationship with the turning on. Central heating timers can be wonderful boons, but they are devices with no personal qualities and no discretion. The timer may be overridden, for instance, by the thermostat. But similarly we know those occasions when the thermostat comes on or stays off but our *experience* of the room temperature is that it is not satisfactory. Our system may be programmed to go off at 10:30 p.m. but the weather is so cold that we want to it to stay on longer. We manually override the system, we respond to the moment. This is precisely what seems to be lacking in Helm's illustration. He may argue that these blips may be foreseen, and that

[75] Helm, 'Divine Timeless Eternity', p. 53.
[76] cf. Wolterstorff, 'Response to Paul Helm', pp. 76ff.

with an extraordinary timer (and God would have one, of course) the system can be programmed to stay on an extra hour on this night, or go off early on the night I have been at the gym and come home perspiring and hot. But the more one finesses the illustration, the more remote it all seems to become: remote from the now of our experience, and remote from what we normally mean by 'responsiveness' and 'personal interaction', and indeed 'intentional action'.

When we come to talk of any sort of action we must have in mind something that is only fully explicable by reference to intention.[77] Divine action, we may assume, is more supremely action than ours and so would be even more obviously and fully intentional. Intentions, in contrast to motives, are *future oriented*.[78] Even allowing for the special way in which we are invited to configure such a one-off eternal action, the 'timeless eternity' position would seem to find it difficult to account for this deliberate and specific future orientation of God. Granted that we speak of divine action only by analogy with human action, nevertheless it may be best to avoid using the language of action at all if the illustration of the central heating timer is any useful indicator.

God: temporal but transcending time?

Readers will by now understand that I want to advocate an understanding of God that sees God as involved with and in time. The question now arises as to whether we may wish or be able also to affirm that God in some respects transcends time.[79]

---

[77] On action as fundamentally intentional see, for example, Jennifer Hornbsy, *Actions* (London: Routledge & Kegan Paul, 1980), p. 36; Anthony Kenny, *Action, Emotion and Will* (London: Routledge & Kegan Paul, 19792), p. 87; Robert Ellis, 'God and Action', *Religious Studies* 24 (1989), pp. 463–82.

[78] Kenny, *Action, Emotion and Will*, p. 86; see also G. E. M. Anscombe, *Intention* (Oxford: Blackwell, 1957), pp. 86, 34f.

[79] I have not entered the discussion which attempts to define time itself, a discussion which often focuses on the so-called A-series or Process theory of time, and B-series or stasis theory of time. See the various references in Ganssle (ed.), *God and Time*, and in view of comments here, Padgett's essay, 'Eternity as Relative Timelessness', pp. 92ff. Like most contemporaries, I have implicitly opted for the A-series view.

One way in which God transcends our experience of time may be considered if we contemplate the theory of relativity, which suggests that there is no such thing as absolute creaturely simultaneity.[80] God is temporally related to all creatures – but God also transcends creaturely temporality. So, as Keith Ward suggests, 'God must exist in a number of different time-sequences, not relatable to each other by relations of absolute simultaneity.'[81] God will exist simultaneously to each event in each system as it occurs. Just as God may be said to be in every space, though is not confined to space or located to space in a bodily way, so God may be said to be present at every created time, though not confined to any. So God is not simply temporal, but is *multi-temporal*. This multi-temporality might be one way in which we need to think of God as transcending time, and even being the Lord of Time.

But we must go further. God must be temporal while transcending temporality.[82] When we reviewed Barth and Moltmann earlier we came across language that suggested two different sorts of time: to put it crudely, our time and God's time, or our time and 'eternal-time'. While those writers like many others seemed to want to say that God experienced our time in a real way – indeed Barth affirms that God elects to be just this kind of God, who knows and shares time with us – they also seemed to want to speak of a divine experience of another sort. As Alan Padgett says:

> there must be a sense in which God is temporal . . . [but] God remains Lord of time and the Creator of our (measured) time. This means, first, that God is the Creator of our time (space-time universe). Our time takes place within (and only because of the prior existence of) God's own time. Second, even God's own time, eternity, exists only because God exists (and not the other way around). Even eternity is dependent, ontologically, on God's very

---

[80] Keith Ward, *Rational Theology and the Creativity of God* (Oxford: Blackwell, 1992), p. 164.
[81] Ibid., p. 166.
[82] See Padgett, 'Eternity as Relative Timelessness', p. 93.

Life and Being. The Being of God is thus rightly at the heart of the whole of reality in history or eternity, in heaven and on earth. Third, God's own time is infinite and cannot be measured by our time. Eternity is infinite and immeasurable.[83]

In a way similar to our account of Barth and Moltmann, Padgett distinguishes between the creaturely experience of time and God's, while still insisting that 'there must be a sense that God is temporal'. Furthermore, the basic move, to define eternity from God and not subject God to a previous definition of eternity, seems to be a crucial move. It allows the reality of God (who must in some sense be temporal) to fill the meaning of that concept rather than restricting the divine nature within an alien idea.[84]

But what might this actually mean, and how might we avoid the charge of simply wanting to have our cake and eat it? We would need to begin by saying that it is essential that any proposed 'solution' takes seriously the genuine interaction, personal responsiveness and real involvement of God with creation in a temporal way. I would want to go further and suggest that it must also mean that the future, which is 'not yet there', remains open and *relatively unknown in detail* even to God (and I shall have more to say about this when we consider omniscience). However I also want to affirm that God transcends our time as its Creator and Lord, and affirm that God is never the victim of time, and always has the resources to meet every moment. (The Process notion of God's Primordial and Consequent Natures is one way in which theologians have attempted to explicate this dialectic of time transcending temporality, and there are others.)[85]

---

[83] Ibid., pp. 106f.

[84] John Macquarrie has something similar in mind when he formulates his dialectical concept of God: *In Search of Deity*, pp. 181ff.

[85] See Whitehead's *Process*, pp. 134f., 528f., and Charles Hartshorne, *The Divine Relativity* (New Haven: YUP, 1948). For another, different account of how we might describe the temporal God as transcending time, see Paul S. Fiddes, *The Promised End* (Oxford: Blackwell, 2000), pp. 202–7, 246–58.

Earlier I suggested that a proper understanding of God as Trinity, in which we took account of God's revelation and activity in history, required that we understand God as temporal, as in time. But we might make an argument the other way from the doctrine of the Trinity also. For if the Son and the Spirit are fully divine, the Fathers were surely right to argue that the generation of the Son and the procession of the Spirit cannot be 'events' which occur at some point in time, as it were, 'after' the Father has already existed! If this were the case then Arius may have been right all along: that 'there was a time when he [the Son] was not', and that therefore the Son was not as fully God as was the Father. To most readers the idea that the Son might be divine but not quite as divine as the Father will seem as absurd as the notion that someone might be a little bit pregnant. God the Son, the second person of the Trinity, and God the Spirit, the third person, are fully divine. The Fathers adopted the notion of eternal generation to account for this: the generation of the Son and the procession of the Spirit are not events in time but are 'eternal events'. This seems necessary to ensure the divinity of the second and third persons, and it puts us, together with the argument I put forward earlier, in a strange position: the doctrine of the Trinity requires both the temporality and the atemporality of God. God must in some sense be temporal yet also transcend our creaturely temporality. 'Whatever God's eternity is like, it includes the possibility of time and the capacity to relate to us in time.'[86] This time-transcending temporality seems to me to be required by what we generally believe and scripture suggests to us about intercession, and about the answering God.

Exploring Further the Nature of God's Omniscience

As I have indicated, the question of divine omniscience relates to many other questions. Discussion of God and

---

[86] Pinnock, *Most Moved Mover*, p. 99.

time led us into omniscience (most notably with our cruise up the Seine) and many of our concerns about God's eternity focus on the question of divine omniscience. If omniscience means knowing everything, including the future, from all eternity – because the future is already present to God – then omniscience may lead down a narrow track to determinism. Does God's knowledge of a decision I have not yet taken determine that decision in some way? Does God's knowledge of a future free event make that event inevitable?

We have already also considered a number of biblical texts that impinge on the discussion. One strategy now could be to gather them all together and attempt exegesis which would steer our discussion – texts like 1 Samuel 15, Genesis 9 and Isaiah 46, which in different ways are taken to support complete foreknowledge or not. Writers such as Gregory Boyd and Bruce Ware do just this, but while neither exegesis is, in my view, wholly satisfactory, Ware especially seems to homogenise biblical texts in a way that is unhelpful. Ware's sometimes convoluted exegesis[87] fails to own up to the fact that the position is more complex and less clear than we would like, and that all readers and exegetes are influenced by factors which are *extrinsic* to the text. This is, I suggest once more, what Barth meant when he warned us of the dangers of doing natural theology rather than biblical theology – of not allowing the Bible to speak, to tell us who God is.[88] There is an irony in those who insist on their evangelical credentials actually importing their view of God to scripture, from some philosophical source, though it would be wrong to suggest that only writers like Ware do this (to some extent, everyone does).

I would argue that the temporality of God which I have already sought to establish is *at least* as reliable an interpretation of biblical texts as other positions (given the

---

[87] e.g. on 1 Sam. 15:11,35 in Ware, *God's Lesser Glory*, pp. 32–4.
[88] Barth, *C.D.* I/1 pp. 319f.

dynamic and personal nature of God in the Old and New Testament, the incarnation, and the doctrine of the Trinity), but because dealing with the texts alone is unlikely to facilitate progress we need to examine some of these other assumptions. It is true, as Ware points out, that the church has not generally held to this position through many centuries: evangelicals ought to be especially aware, however, of taking scripture seriously, and be ready to call the church out of another Babylonian captivity.

The contemporary Thomist Brian Davies puts the logic of the argument for traditional omniscience *and* free will clearly, if somewhat algebraically![89]

> If God knows at time 1 that P will freely do X at time 2 then what God knows is that P will freely do X. In other words, if God knows at time 1 that P will freely do X at time 2 then God's knowledge at time 1 is dependent on P freely doing X at time 2 . . . For if P were not free at time 2, then God could not know at time 1 that P would be free at time 2.

This argument has a certain merit. My free acceptance of the invitation to be Tutor in Pastoral Theology at Regent's Park College in 2001 is known by God at time X as a free acceptance; God's knowledge of it is dependent upon my free action; my action is not dependent upon his knowledge.

There are two problems with this, though. (1) One comes when omniscience takes its place as part of the nexus of attributes, in particular alongside omnipotence. For as traditionally conceived God has the power to do all God decides to do. This alliance of omniscience and omnipotence gets us into the difficulty that God could alter/ determine the course of events before finally knowing it! God orders all events, and even if God permits it, it is done with God's permission, and the element of free choosing

---

[89] Brian Davies, *Introduction to the Philosophy of Religion* (Oxford: OUP, 1982), p. 86.

takes on a somewhat illusory aspect. (2) The second problem is that Davies seems now to be speaking of God as 'in' time. God knows things at time 1 and 2 in this illustration: the feasibility of this understanding depends upon the temporal nature of God which, espousing the 'traditional' relationship of God and time, he has already rejected! It is not at all clear that the illustration works as well with a God who knows timelessly from all eternity.

Even God cannot know (in the strongest sense) in advance what the choices of self-determining creatures will be. This might be said to enhance God's knowledge, for 'when they have chosen, God will know something that he could not have known before, the choices they freely make . . . It is not a defect that God knows temporally; on the contrary it involves the addition of certain sorts or property to God which he might otherwise have lacked.'[90]

Let us put two questions: has God always known that there are quarks (if there are)? And has God always known that I would be the Pastoral Theology Tutor at Regent's Park College? If there are quarks, there have presumably always been quarks. In speaking of God's omniscience it may be necessary to make a distinction between knowledge that is temporally dependent, and that which is not – like knowing whether there are quarks.

Knowing whether I would become Pastoral Theology Tutor would appear to be temporally dependent, however. The 'neo-classical' or 'open' view would be that God has not always known that I would be the Pastoral Theology Tutor, even if God had *planned* it from all eternity (a mind-boggling thought!). My appointment requires the operation of free creaturely wills, and God could not *know* whether I would be invited, and whether I would accept, until it had happened. This is the implication of the temporality of divine knowledge.

However, we may want to say, paralleling our discussion of God and time, that while God's knowledge of

[90] Ward, *Rational Theology*, p. 151.

temporally contingent events is temporal, that in some ways God's knowledge transcends such temporal contingency. What might this mean? God's knowledge of non-temporally contingent facts (whether there are quarks) is supreme and complete at every moment. We might include within this the divine knowledge of every possibility for creatures for every future moment, with knowledge of how 'real' such possibilities are for them. God is never mistaken; God never forgets or overlooks. God's knowledge is perfect. God's knowledge of temporally contingent events also transcends that of creatures. God again knows every actual fact at any moment: God's perspective is not partial or distorted but complete and whole. But we may want to go further than this, for God's knowledge of all creatures is also supreme: closer to me than my own breathing, God knows me better than I know myself, and God knows every other person and circumstance with which I interact with equal fullness and supremacy. We might want to suggest therefore that God can 'predict' the future with supreme confidence. 'Predict' may seem a rather weak word, but this is no ordinary human prediction. It is not knowledge of the future as actual, and it is not quite certain knowledge perhaps. It is, however, rather more than simply 'not knowing'.

So, dialectically, we might want to say this: that God's intimate knowledge of creation and creatures is such that God's power to predict, even perhaps infallibly predict, that I would be Pastoral Theology Tutor (even if God had not planned it from all eternity!), is something we cannot fathom. It would be possible, it seems to me, to make a case for God's knowledge of the future based upon such divine predictive power that would retain something of the more traditional position even in a thoroughly temporal understanding of God and divine knowledge. Take a football illustration. If Manchester United plays Arsenal next week, is it possible for me to say that I know the result? Of course it is not. An ardent fan of one team may claim to 'know' that their team will win, but they would be foolish to place their life savings on the result. However, if Manchester United sends their best team to play our local school under-11 team next Saturday, do I know what the result will be? I would be unable to predict the actual score with any certainty, but I feel confident that I do indeed know the result because I know enough about the participants: this time an ardent fan of either side might not be foolish to place their life savings on a Manchester United win! This is again reminiscent of Cullman's decisive battle: the moves may be uncertain, but the victory looks guaranteed.[91]

God's Power

The question of divine power has become a hotly debated one in contemporary theology, and its relevance to a discussion of intercession will be readily apparent. If God is conceived of in a deterministic way, as one who has already determined what is to be, then the most that might be said for intercession is that – as we saw suggested by Augustine – it readies us to receive what God has already decided to give. A negative evaluation of this position suggests that prayer is a waste of time because God has already decided what God will do and what will happen. If God's power is conceived of as in some way responsive but nevertheless as coercive or overwhelming, then we might also assume that if God determines to do something – whether or not it is in response to our prayer – it will be done: God is irresistible.

That could make prayer either infallibly efficacious or useless. In the former, my prayer for you, if 'heard', could change your circumstances even against your will: God would just do it. In the latter, we might argue that the all-controlling God will just do to you and your circumstances

---

[91] cf. Phillip Yancey, 'Chess Master' in *Christianity Today* (22 May 2000), on line at http://www.christianitytoday.com/ct/2000/006/35.112.html.

what God wants to do, whether I pray or not. Or if God's power is conceived in terms of persuasion so that, to pursue the example, your circumstances are not changed wholly against your will, does that in effect, as critics of this newer perspective have argued, make prayer an ineffectual waste of time?

Issues of power connect with some of the other matters we have discussed. If God in some way becomes part of time, and if indeed time in some way becomes part of God, the question arises of whether God can change. And if God can change, can God *be changed*? The ancients wanted to affirm neither, because of their particular views about perfection and being. Yet it has seemed to many more recently that if God is to be truly personal, truly involved in creation, truly responsive to it, then God must be able to change. More than that, if God is to be responsive – if, for instance, God is to answer prayer – it must be possible for God to *be changed by* creatures. What is the answering of prayer, if not the willingness to be changed in some way by those who pray? For God to be, as Barth boldly says, determined by our prayers?

What sort of view of divine power emerges for those who take the centrality of the history of the Father, Son and Spirit seriously? In particular, what sort of idea of divine power do we gain if we put the suffering of the cross at the centre of our considerations?

God's omnipotence has traditionally been qualified in a number of ways. A first type of qualification is that of logical possibility – not even God can make a square triangle, for instance. Similarly, God cannot create creatures with free will while at the same time withholding free will from them. Such a claim would be non-sense.

Another type of qualification suggests that God cannot do anything that is inconsistent with God's own nature – for instance, tell lies.[92] Do such assertions have the same status as those about square triangles (are they mere logic),

---

[92] But see Exodus 1:15–20 for God approving lies!

or are they more to do with the divine will and/or character? Some opt for the former because they suggest that otherwise God seems too arbitrary, too *wilful*, as it were. Some prefer the latter because they are reluctant to suggest that God is bound too much by a logic or necessity apparently outside of God's self.[93]

A further qualification, affirmed at least from medieval times, opines that if God chooses to do a particular thing, that inevitably means God cannot also choose to do something else which contradicts it in some way. So, for instance, before the Exodus God could choose to liberate the Hebrew slaves in this way or not. Once God has acted, however, the 'not to liberate' option is no longer available. Within the created world, chosen courses close off other possible choices – just as they do for human agents. Paradoxically, to suggest otherwise may be to say God is unable to choose and commit to a particular course of action at all.

But even after such accepted qualifications have been made, it has nevertheless been assumed that God is able to do anything God wants with God's creatures apart from these defined technicalities. 'Omnipotence' has usually been taken to mean that, within the historic-creative process, God either directly wills or permits everything that happens. Anything God wills to happen will happen; and because God could in theory deviate the chain of cause and effect at any point, even those events not directly willed, God must be said to permit. What is more, this position entails an implicit understanding that God's power is to a greater or less extent coercive: that God compels creatures including human persons to behave in certain ways or to actualise certain outcomes, even when this is expressed in terms of secondary causes which have a freedom which is compatible with divine coercion. Such a position has come under increasing pressure from a number of angles.[94]

---

[93] See the discussion in Alister McGrath, *Christian Theology: An Introduction* (Oxford: Blackwell, 1994), pp. 222–5.

[94] This pressure is not an entirely recent phenomenon, as John Macquarrie shows in his *In Search of Deity*.

Before we consider the question of divine power in general, a word about 'willing and permitting' is in order. An appeal to divine 'permission' is usually made for two reasons. On the one hand, it seems to preserve the freedom of creatures, who are not determined in their every action. On the other hand, it seems to absolve God from moral responsibility for human misdeeds, which turn out to be freely chosen by sinful creatures and allowed rather than compelled by God. But Calvin saw that this distinction was ultimately fraudulent. 'But why shall we say "permission" unless it is because God wills . . . I shall not hesitate to confess with Augustine that "the will of God is the necessity of all things."'[95] For if God has the power to intervene and directly cause an(other) action and does not do so (that is, if God *permits* it) then 'permission' must in some sense represent God's will – the distinction does not satisfactorily absolve God of responsibility for the way the world goes. Permission is only intelligible as a concept in conjunction with the power to prevent. If God has the power to prevent and fails to do so God must at least share responsibility for what occurs; if God has no power to prevent (perhaps, to 'intervene') then the distinction is meaningless when used in its usual way. But the concept is almost as unsatisfactory in defending human freedom. For this freedom turns out to be exercised in a realm where God might at any moment suspend it. The fact that human beings do not know in advance, or indeed in retrospect, when such suspensions take place hardly mitigates the undermining effect.

Many who defend traditional divine foreknowledge as not undermining human freedom argue too atomistically: that is, they treat single events rather than sequences, and they treat omniscience apart from an omnipotence that includes divine permission. For it is one thing to say that God foreknows I will accept the invitation to the be Tutor in Pastoral Theology as a one-off event; but when we factor

---

[95] Calvin, *Institutes*, 3/23/8, p. 956.

in all other (also foreknown) events around it, and add that God could intervene to compel any particular outcome should God wish, it is difficult to avoid the conclusion that everything happens because God chooses that it should. The world is now merely an expression of the divine omnipotence. We have pantheism by the back door!

To return, then, to consider the nature of divine omnipotence, as we have said, the traditional concept of absolute power is now somewhat less secure. It can be critiqued from a number of directions.

A biblical perspective on the God of the cross

A strong case can be made out that coercive elements in divine nature have been overplayed. God is personal, accessible, dialogical, allows time for persons to respond; and in the New Testament, and in Jesus' ministry in particular, a picture of God seems to be given which is, at the least, more ambivalent: this is the Christlike God. The cross is a sign of weakness and vulnerability, of a God who in Bonhoeffer's memorable phrase allows God's self to be edged out of the world on to a cross.[96] The God revealed by Jesus does not 'frog-march' people into the Kingdom, but works by consent.[97] Similarly, Paul walked along a *via crucis*, boasting of his weakness, witnessing that God's power is made perfect through suffering. But these insights about power have often been lost in a tradition that has tended to see only a more absolutist power – and indeed has exercised such power in ecclesiastical and political life! Alfred North Whitehead shrewdly observed of the development of Christian doctrine in the early centuries that 'the brief Galilean vision flickered throughout the ages, uncertainly . . . But the deeper idolatry of the fashioning of God in the image of the Egyptian, Persian, and Roman imperial rulers, was retained. The church gave

---

[96] Dietrich Bonhoeffer, *Letters and Papers from Prison* (London: SCM, 19673), p. 360.

[97] Timothy Bradshaw, *Praying as Believing* (Oxford: Regent's Park College, 1998), p. 124.

unto God the attributes which belonged exclusively to Caesar.'[98] The charge is that Christianity took over the 'tyrant God' from the ancient political world. While it is true that certain texts seem to be open to a more absolutist reading, the tradition has not balanced helpfully these other insights. Scripture recounts a relationship of covenant, of personal fellowship. Such personal relationships are not at their highest quality when marked by compulsion or domination by one side. We might even say that there is, in the evangelical insight that God desires – but will not force us into – fellowship, a clear suggestion that at root divine power is not coercive but persuasive.

The theological discussion about the self-limitation of God
The theme of divine self-limitation received important consideration during the development of so-called 'Kenosis Christology' in the nineteenth century,[99] but it soon became a commonplace of treatment of the doctrine of creation too. Thinkers spoke of the way in which, in the act of creation, God limits his own power in order to make it possible for creation to exist and for it to exercise any freewill. Just as God 'makes room' spatially for creation, it is sometimes suggested, so also God 'makes room' in terms of power. There are two differentiated variations of this position, however. Sometimes this is expressed to convey a deliberate *choice* to be limited – as a matter of will or volition; sometimes it is expressed more as a matter of *logical necessity*.

The 'Open Theists' make this difference the crucial one that distances their position from the Process one: that God chooses to limit the divine power rather than being constrained by necessity external to God's self.[100] It is an important differentiation, but one of the threads running

---

[98] Whitehead, *Process*, p. 529.
[99] See John Macquarrie, *Jesus Christ in Modern Thought* (London: SCM, 1990), pp. 245–50.
[100] e.g. Clark Pinnock, 'Systematic Theology' in Pinnock et al, *The Openness of God*, p. 110.

through the argument of this book may suggest that the
difference between them is not as great as it may at first
appear. I have suggested that in a determinist understanding of divine power the world becomes in effect an
expression of the divine will; it reflects the divine purpose.
If the distinction between willing and permitting is
untenable, as again I have suggested, this 'pantheistic
implication' becomes even clearer: if the world is a
reflection of the divine without any freedom to be anything
else, we are in virtual pantheism. This clearly is not what
the champions of predestination have had in mind, but it
is, I believe, where we end up. The Open Theists, who want
to retain some capacity of God to act coercively,[101] are as
likely to fall into this trap as their more conventional
protagonists: if God retains the capacity to override
freedom (whether exercised or not) what actually happens
is what – actively or passively – God has chosen will
happen. To this point, I believe that the critique of
traditional theism is cogent. However, the Process position
of 'persuasion alone' seems rooted at least in part, in their
disavowal of creation *ex nihilo*, God's creation of the
universe *from nothing*. It is difficult to conceive of God
persuading something from nothing: an act of creative
coercion seems to be necessary. But if, as I would want to
argue, *ex nihilo* with its implication that the universe
depends on God for its reality is non-negotiable (though
the argument would require another book!), there may not
be such a difference between the two positions. The Open
Theists argue, with traditional theists, that God chooses to
limit divine power; the Process Theists argue, with other
more radical thinkers, that God is bound by a metaphysical
necessity such that God's power cannot coerce creaturely
power. But suppose we conceive of God freely choosing to
create a universe that is genuinely independent of God's
self? In creating a world that is genuinely independent God

---

[101] See, e.g., William Hasker, 'A Philosophical Perspective' in ibid.,
p. 140.

is seeking to create those who are in God's image, free persons in community (and free creatures in the community of creation) capable of love and fellowship with others – and indeed with God. In choosing to do this God freely chooses to create a world in which he does not possess all the power there is, and in which he cannot override creatures. It may be more as the Process Theists suggest but not because of some external metaphysical necessity, but instead because of the free and gracious choice of God to create this sort of world – to create us. In the very act of creating free creatures, God – as it were, by definition – limits God's self. This possibility dovetails with the previous biblical perspective: the Christlike God who is willing to be edged out of the world on to the cross is the God who voluntarily excludes possibilities of domination and other less than fully personal modes of relationship. This is a 'metaphysical necessity' that exists because God chooses that it should.

I am not yet suggesting this as a last word on this tension between divine coercion and persuasion, but it is a perspective to be taken seriously in considering the divine self-limitation.

The argument relating to a community of powers, or agents
This is an argument we have already encountered and it is related to some perspectives on the Trinity as a community of persons. A number of thinkers have examined the nature of power and agency to come to similar results. Process thinkers have analysed the concept of power and concluded that omnipotence as 'all the power there is' does not make sense. 'A being that was supposed to have a complete monopoly of power would really have no power for there would be nothing over which to exercise it. It could also be a being that could have nothing to relate to and so could not be a creator.'[102] Rather, *power has to be used*

---

[102] David A. Pailin, *Groundwork of the Philosophy of Religion* (London: Epworth, 1986), pp. 153f.

in a community of powers – even if the other powers are lesser (though still real) ones. Omnipotence does not then mean 'all the power' or 'absolute power' (as in tyrant) but 'supreme' or 'greatest power', or 'greatest possible power given the existence of other powers'.

The sort of 'personalist' arguments that have also been of use to us in understanding the nature of Trinitarian persons are significant here. For just as a person, to be a person, requires other persons; so also a power, to be a power, requires other powers. All sorts of lines of argument and investigation about the 'personhood' of the Triune God converge with other arguments that put a question mark against 'omnipotence' as traditionally understood. Most significantly there is a similar argument from the nature of agency: if God is to 'act' in response to our prayers, does it make sense for God to act as one with 'all the power there is'? 'The possibility of action', says John MacMurray, 'depends on the Other being also agent, and so upon a plurality of agents in the field of action. The resistance to the Self through which the Self can exist as agent must be resistance of another self.'[103] If MacMurray is correct then any idea of God being an agent in the world requires that there be other agents exercising power, a power of potentially effective resistance.

Persuasion and coercion

These three critical perspectives on divine power lead us into an important debate about the nature of divine power, about coercion and persuasion. The trajectory established by these critical perspectives suggests that an understanding of divine power as persuasion is likely to be the more satisfactory: the centrality of the cross, a sign of power made perfect in weakness; the divine choice to create a truly independent world of other powers, thus restricting God's power; the person-among-persons, and the agent-among-agents, who requires other persons and

---

[103] John MacMurray, *The Self as Agent* (London: Faber, 1957), p. 145.

agents in order to make their own agency real. The Process theologians are at the forefront of those who argue that God's power is only exercised by persuasion; more traditional theists have argued that God's power is properly conceived as potentially coercive. The Open Theists attempt to occupy the middle ground again here. They prefer to speak of God's power as generally persuasive, as if this were preferable. So Pinnock argues that God has no monopoly on power but creates genuinely self-determining creatures. God is still 'omnipotent' but this should not mean that everything happens according to the divine will, but rather that God has the resources to respond to every eventuality. God's power woos us rather than compels us, and yet persuasion is not the only power available to God, says Pinnock.[104] Pinnock wants to leave open the possibility that God may coerce when circumstances require it, though in doing so he opens his position up to the critique of willing and permitting: if God could ever coerce and chooses not to, on each specific occasion when God chooses not to then it may be said that everything that happens does so because God chooses – actively or passively – that it should happen.

It is in the area of necessity that the Process position is again distinguished from Open Theism. Process theologians argue that God cannot coerce because God does not have the facility to do so: it is the nature of reality that creatures are self-determining, not the *ad hoc* decision of the Creator. Just as the Open Theists pay a price – that God may be held responsible for all that happens – the Process thinkers also pay a price. In their case it may be thought to have two aspects: first, that God appears to relinquish overall control over the process, and thus any chance of guaranteeing its final outcome; second, that God cannot unilaterally bring about any particular outcome within the process. Process Theists seem content to pay up, but others are less comfortable at the purchase. In the

---

[104] Pinnock, 'Systematic Theology', pp. 113–17.

position I explored above transposed into this issue, God would have relinquished the facility to coerce in the decision to create genuinely independent creatures. God evades the charge of not choosing to coerce (even when he could), but it is true that the problem has been shifted back another level. It could be argued that any given state exists in the universe because God has chosen to allow creatures genuine independence. However, it could not be argued than any *particular* state of affairs was the responsibility of God, because God cannot coerce on an *ad hoc* basis, choosing where and when to persuade or otherwise compel.

David Basinger is critical of the Process Theists, arguing that their *moral* argument for persuasion is suspect – they argue that persuasion is superior to coercion.[105] He suggests that it is not clear that coercion is always morally inferior to persuasion, as when a parent prevents a child from harming him or herself, or the state forcibly restrains a violent offender. I will argue in the next section of this chapter that it may be possible to construe the Process system such that, while other beings have relatively more or less power over one another, it may in fact be possible to construe divine power in process thought as more compelling, while still remaining ultimately persuasive.

We find a nuanced Trinitarian argument for persuasion in David Cunningham's *These Three Are One*. Cunningham works from what he calls the Trinitarian Virtue of Polyphony, which accepts and celebrates an enriching difference rather than pursuing a bland uniformity. The biblical witness points both to God's power and to God's willingness to forfeit that power for the sake of humanity.[106]

Cunningham examines the 'dialectic of power and gift' in several biblical passages, arguing that 'a polyphonic reading of these narratives would recognise that supreme

---

[105] David Basinger, *Divine Power in Process Theism* (New York: SUNY, 1988), pp. 27–54.
[106] Cunningham, *These Three*, pp. 143f., italics his.

power can still be compatible with submission to the will of the other'.[107] Instead of contradicting one another these different elements coexist like the notes of a chord – 'they can be sounded simultaneously, without compromising the unity of the whole'.[108] Mary sings of the God who scatters the proud, but has to give her consent to God's action in the incarnation; Jesus teaches and heals with authority, but chooses to accept the cross. Mary is thus the consenting peasant girl *and* the glorified Queen of the Universe, and Jesus is the perfectly dutiful servant *and* Lord of all. Jesus Christ shows us something of the polyphonic nature of God and belies the worldly insistence that 'obedience must denote a corresponding loss of power'[109] – instead the two are held together dialectically.

Just as we found ourselves wanting to affirm that God is temporal and yet in some way transcends time, so also we seem to have to hold together some apparent opposites when speaking of divine power: we have dialectically to affirm that 'God's purpose is assured' and that 'God acts by persuasion'. Just as in the case of time, where we had to affirm the temporality first and then imagined ways of transcending this reality, so here we have first to state that the God and Father of our Lord Jesus Christ, the God of the cross, acts by persuasion and patient love – is edged out of the world on to the cross. But the God and Father of the Lord Jesus Christ is also the God of resurrection, of triumphant new beginnings, of radical new starts which burst into our causal sequences with the power of the future Kingdom. This God chooses to create a genuinely independent world, which he cannot simply compel to any particular outcome within the process. But the creator *ex nihilo* (the coercive act by which God graciously compelled our world into being) is the One on whom that process depends for its existence at every moment. God could, as it

---

[107] Ibid., p. 149.
[108] Ibid., p. 150.
[109] Ibid., p. 151.

were, call off the whole project of creation, rolling our time into God's time once and for all, beginning again (or not); and in the resurrection of Jesus we see a glimpse of God's final purpose to 'begin again' with a New Creation. Indeed, the resurrection of Jesus is a foretaste and pledge of this future act of love when all things will be made new and brought to their fulfilment. Until this final and fulfilling compulsion God has made us as we are, independent and self-determining. But as I have already hinted, even this persuasion of God may be sometimes something quite compelling. If it is objected that a God who works by persuasion cannot guarantee the final outcome we will have to respond (in a way not so dissimilar to more traditional accounts) that this is an Easter hope: that we who live in between Good Friday and Easter Day also live in the hope that the God who raised Jesus from the dead will indeed prevail, meanwhile with all creation we groan in eager longing for God's end (Rom. 8).

In the meantime, when we speak of divine omnipotence in relation to our world in the here and now we are making at least two very positive assertions: (1) that *God's power is supreme in its scope* – God exerts power over all things; (2) that *God never fails to perform God's own actions in the most perfect way*. But because God is truly personal and has made creation truly something apart from God's self, God may have to wait for my response and is unable completely to compel that response; but God issues the call to me with unswerving accuracy and attraction. I also have to wait on the response of others, but unlike God I'm not always able perfectly to express my own wishes to them, or realise my own private purposes. God, omnipotently, is.

In creating a genuinely free creation, creatures have wills of their own over which God has less 'control' than theologians have sometimes wanted to say. This means that the world is not a mere pantheistic cipher for God's own being, but interacts genuinely and freely with God. No wonder then, that there is a cross at the intersection of this interaction, and at the very heart of God.

Imagining Divine Action

Before we proceed to our final chapter one more task must detain us: that of trying constructively to imagine God's action in the world in a way congruent with the Trinitarian and dialectical considerations we have outlined. In order to do this I will work through two phases: first, revisiting the philosophy of action to examine a pair of key concepts; second, sketching the Process conceptuality of divine action and discussing some adjustments to it.

Agency and Action: Clues from the Philosophy of Action

One of the things we notice when we try to describe the actions of human agents is a kind of 'Russian doll effect'. Certain actions seem to contain within them other actions, and this works in at least two different ways.

(1) On entering a room I raise my arm, flick a switch and turn on the light. What have I done? Three things or one? Raising my arm does seem to be a separate action in a sense: it is sequentially more 'basic' than flicking the switch – I had to raise my arm before I could flick the switch – but flicking the switch and turning on the light are just two different descriptions of the same action. It is sometimes suggested that flicking the switch is more 'basic' in a causal sense than turning on the light. Philosophers of action speak of some actions as 'basic' in these ways in their analysis of action.[110] Like a Russian doll that contains smaller dolls inside larger ones, actions sometimes contain within them 'smaller' actions, as turning on the light contains flicking the switch or raising an arm. Those who argue for divine timelessness are arguing for something like the causal basicness indicated here. God's action somehow precedes our creaturely actions not temporally

---

[110] cf. e.g. Arthur C. Danto, 'Basic Action' in A. R. White (ed.), *Philosophy of Action* (Oxford: OUP, 1968), p. 45; Hornsby, *Actions*, pp. 66f.; Anscombe, Intention, pp. 37–41.

but in an underlying enabling sense. However, I want to argue that it is the sequential sense of an action being 'basic' which is also important for our thinking here, and I want to move from the language of basic actions to simple and complex actions.

(2) Some actions I perform are simple, others more complex. Turning on a light is pretty simple: I enter a room, I raise my arm to flick the switch: there is light. There are no other human agencies, only I am involved. If the electricity supply is good and the switch not faulty, it would take a bizarre hitch to thwart me. Despite the number of component parts which analysis may expose, this action is relatively simple. But take other examples: George W. Bush has invaded Iraq, Tony Blair has reformed the NHS, Arsene Wenger has created a formidable Arsenal team. The language we use about these actions seems exactly like the language we used to describe me turning on a light, but these latter examples are considerably more complex. When Bush invaded Iraq, the decision to invade may have been solely his, but he relied utterly on the assistance of others to complete his action. The same may be said of Blair's NHS reforms, though another factor may creep into analysis: Bush has invaded Iraq, of that there is no doubt; but opposition parties may dispute the extent to which Blair has reformed the NHS. Wenger is an impressive coach, but while journalists may say that he has created a formidable Arsenal team, once again we know that this act of creation has relied upon the cooperation of coaches and players (and their initial availability) as well as the financial and structural environment at the club. Wenger is credited with the creation of a formidable Arsenal team, but he has not acted alone, nor has he been in control of every important factor.

It's possible to think of more prosaic examples. We may say of a pastor that she has reinvigorated a congregation, of a headteacher that he has 'turned around' his school, of a manager that he has balanced the books, of a single mother that she has done a wonderful job in bringing up her children alone, or of a daughter that she has put on a successful surprise party for her parents. All these actions, though simply described, are in their ways extremely 'complex' – that is, made up of many component parts and involving the agency of other people working with and for the principal agent. In each case we would admit that the agent has not been in total control of every aspect of his or her situation, though sometimes we know that his or her success is rooted in an ability to exert more influence over every component part than is customary or expected.

What such analysis shows us is that in the way we usually speak of actions that have significance (for generally, the simpler the action, the less broad significance it has) often masks the fact that they are actually complex series and combinations of actions involving more than one agent and being somewhat risky by nature. The more complex, we might suspect, the more risky: landing a boat on the beach is usually simple enough; pulling off the D-Day invasion much more complex and dangerous. Simpler actions seem 'safer'; complex actions are fraught. Indeed, we might suggest that there is something inherently vulnerable about all action, but especially about complex actions – actions of greater significance.[111]

But something else may be observed in the analysis just given. We say 'President Bush invaded Iraq,' but we all know that he stayed in Washington. While we are willing to ascribe the action to him we are aware that others have acted at his behest and on his behalf. In ordinary speech the word 'agent' is commonly reserved for one who acts on behalf of another.[112] This illumines many of the examples given above. Large-scale complex actions are not only fraught with elements of risk, they are also inevitably multi-agent actions. It would not surprise us if, in terms of active participation, the person credited with the larger-

---

[111] cf. Robert Ellis, 'The Vulnerability of Action', *Religious Studies* 25 (1990), pp. 225–33.

[112] J. R. Lucas, 'Freedom and Grace' in J. R. Lucas, *Freedom and Grace* (London: SPCK, 1976), pp. 6f.

scale complex action is relatively little involved. Compared to the work of those who prepare troops and equipment and fight battles, President Bush is in some ways relatively inactive. Blair briefs his aides and ministers but does little directly to change the management or staffing of the NHS. Both leaders may be said to originate their actions and provide important ongoing energy, but even though the invasion and the reform are 'their' actions their direct participation is relatively small.

The usefulness of such analysis is clear when we come to consider God's action. It may be straightforward to describe God's more basic actions (the leading of an individual, the forgiveness of my sin, the calling of someone to a particular ministry, even perhaps the healing of a person's body), and such simpler actions might be thought to be not only less complicated but also (given what we have said about divine power as persuasive) more easily assured. But more complex actions become increasingly less assured. As other free agents are needed to cooperate with God, and if a genuinely independent creation is not wholly under God's control, divine action for the end of apartheid or the freeing of Hebrew slaves from Egyptian bondage, for just peace in Iraq and Palestine and Northern Ireland, is more fraught with risk and difficulty. God has the resources with which to respond to every changing situation, a new plan to put in place for every old one that must be discarded, a resurrection to work from every cross. But God does not act alone even when we ascribe acts to God's agency: Moses, the slaves, the sea and the Egyptians all play their part cooperating with God. Praying for such complex acts is more fraught than praying for simpler ones.

Process Theology and Divine Action

It is beyond our scope here to give an account of the system of Process Theology based on the philosophies of Whitehead and Hartshorne, let alone the critique of the system that would be required. My purpose is only to outline the Process notion of divine action – one of the system's most appealing features – and to probe its possibilities for an understanding of intercession. In the next chapter we will look at a typical Process understanding of intercession.

Whitehead believed that the basic building blocks of the universe are 'actual entities' and that all actual entities (i.e. everything that is actual) can be described by using the same generic language. Most things we observe (human persons, dogs, walls, footballs) are large-scale societies of entities – but the actual entities themselves are the energy events to which all reality is ultimately analysable. The universe is in a constant state of becoming, or process, and all actual entities participate in this process in their own becoming and perishing. Each entity 'prehends' those entities which come before it in the sequence of reality, and then 'decides' what to do in its own moment of existence. Its own aim for its existence is formulated by reference to the possibilities available to it, and also by reference to the divine purpose. It then 'becomes' and is part of the data made available to the next actual entity in the process of reality.

Whitehead was unwilling to 'use' God to fill the gaps of understanding. Nevertheless, he found it necessary to speak of God in his system in order to make sense of reality, and in particular to account for novelty – for the reason why anything changes at all, to explain why the primeval soup did not remain just that.

God is spoken of by Whitehead as an actual entity like all others: the same generic language can be used of God as about any other entity, though in certain respects God is significantly different from other entities and transcends them. In the process by which every actual entity comes to be and then passes into the history of the universe God is present in a number of significant ways. In particular, for our purposes, it is God who mediates to every actual entity the possibilities which are open to it as it becomes, and it is

God who imparts to each entity its 'initial aim' – God's preference for that entity, God's will and purpose. God lures each entity to actualise God's preference, its initial aim, through an act of persuasion. The actual entity is free, however, to determine itself, not necessarily following God's aim or responding to divine persuasion. It may choose another possibility, or it may simply repeat the past. When the actual entity does actualise the divine aim it may be said to have followed God's will and, in the terms of our discussion above, to have been an agent of the divine purpose.

This account of divine agency is often thought appealing because of its universal application and coherence. It applies to me as I sit thinking these thoughts, the molecules comprising the word processor I write on and the paper on which this chapter is printed; it applies to each and every component part of every example of action we considered in the previous section, from invading Iraq to flicking a switch; it applies to the parting of the Red Sea and the Gospels' healings; to the growth of the tree outside my window, the flight of the bird which alights in it, and the behaviour of the soil in which it is planted. It also works satisfactorily within the various dialectics we have explored. God is thoroughly involved in the temporal process but transcends it, and really responds to the particularities of each given moment. God is the actual entity who prehends and is prehended by all other entities and thus knows all there is to be known about the actual world as well as all that is possible. God's power provides stability and novelty, and is persuasively at work always to enable creatures to actualise the best for themselves and the greatest harmony of the whole at any moment, but all genuinely independent creatures can resist it. Such an account is a helpful model as it seeks to help us imagine what Austin Farrer called the 'causal joint' and H. H. Farmer the 'rapport' between God and the world.

Process theologians make virtue of the necessity that God may only persuade in this system, arguing that persuasion is morally superior to coercion. But as Basinger suggests, we are not clear that this is always actually so. Sometimes it seems that coercion can be the kindest thing: either for the one coerced (the child prevented from running into the street) or for others (the murderer incarcerated). It is possible, however, that within the Process system the account of God's action may be strengthened, so that while it remains formally persuasive it may sometimes be said to be close to compelling. This would blur somewhat the disputed distinction between coercion and persuasion as well as reflecting the biblical dialectics of power and gift noted by Cunningham. If it can legitimately be done from 'within' the system it may allow this useful model to be more helpfully used by others not convinced by the totality of the system. How would such an adjustment be made? There may be a number of ways in which we could understand God's power to be rather more than 'softly persuasive' within the Process system, and the first two certainly are already present if not prominent in Whitehead's own thought. As forms of coercion they are all weak; but as forms of persuasion they may all be thought to be rather strong!

(1) 'Each temporal entity . . . derives from God its basic conceptual aim, relevant to its actual world, yet with indeterminations awaiting its own decisions.'[113] God provides the initial aim for each actual entity and God does this without, as it were, consultation. While the entity is not compelled to follow the divine aim it is compelled to receive it. This aim should be within the range of genuine possibility for the entity but God chooses and gives it. Given that the meaning of 'coercion' is sometimes understood to be 'the power unilaterally to bring about a state of affairs',[114] here is a universal instance of God doing just that.

---

[113] Whitehead, *Process*, p. 343.
[114] Basinger, *Divine Power*, pp. 28ff.

(2) In offering to each actual entity the range of possibility God includes all possibilities (such as simple repetition) inherent in the past as well as novel possibilities for the future. But Whitehead suggests at places that God might restrict this choice of available possibility for each entity in some way,[115] thereby unilaterally closing off possibilities for an entity. He is quick to add that complete determinism is avoided because of the entity's freedom of choice, but this divine limiting of available choice would represent a unilateral limiting of possibility.

(3) God presents possibilities to all actual entities in their becoming. We may consider developing Whitehead's thought to suggest that at particular moments God might offer a radically new possibility to an entity such that it did not arise naturally from its past. In a stronger form this might be rather like C. S. Lewis's account of a miracle that he explains as an event that fits into the causal sequence forwards but not backwards.[116] A radically new possibility is offered which is introduced only by the divine will. It remains true, however, unless God were to restrict all possibilities except one, that the creature is free to choose this new possibility or not to choose it. This freedom of the actual entity is so deep-set in the system it is difficult to believe that it could be adjusted without calamitous effects. Moreover, if we are to maintain that God in gracious freedom chose to create a genuinely independent world it would appear that a corollary of this is that God cannot over-limit possibilities.

(4) In Basinger's critique of the Process position he not only claims that coercion may at times be justified and kind, he also suggests that sometimes persuasion can be *all but* compelling, as in cases of blackmail or psychological manipulation.[117] Others have noted this possibility that

---

[115] Alfred North Whitehead, *Religion in the Making* (New York: Meridian, 1974), pp. 91f.

[116] C. S. Lewis, *Miracles* (London: Collins Fontana, 1960), p. 64.

[117] Basinger, *Divine Power*, p. 32.

'lures might be made so attractive that they are effectively irresistible'.[118] Just as parents sometimes might physically constrain a child from running into danger, so at other times they might persuade the child with something close to manipulation. This word has pejorative connotations and we might usually use a more wholesome-sounding term, but it amounts to the same thing: X exercising very strong influence on Y, sometimes making them do what that X wants though Y's motives are different. This may account for the Old Testament affirmation that God uses Cyrus to perform God's will: it is not coercion, but persuasion seems too weak a word. In this vein Farrer speaks of 'the openness of men's thoughts to pressures of which they are unaware'.[119] It might be possible, while still insisting on the genuine independence and therefore ultimate freedom of the creature, to suggest that God acts in such strongly persuasive ways just as a parent might strongly persuade her child for his own good.

These four developments of Whitehead's conception of divine action provide a cumulative case for suggesting that while divine action remains persuasive and creatures remain independent and free, that divine persuasion may at times be almost *compellingly persuasive*. Perhaps this is something like Farrer meant in speaking of 'over-riding persuasion'.[120]

---

[118] David A. Pailin, *God and the Processes of Reality* (London: Routledge, 1989), p. 94.
[119] Farrer, *Faith and Speculation*, p. 61.
[120] Ibid., p. 62.

4

Towards a Theology of Intercession

Praying In, With and To the God who Answers

We began this study by reading and reflecting on inter-cession as scripture seems to portray it. We then examined a number of key historical thinkers before more explicitly seeking answer to the question 'Who is God?'. In this chapter I will move towards some conclusions by attempting to gather up the insights we have garnered along the way and proposing a way forward towards a theology of intercession. This theology will have something of the character of our previous thinking: we will find ourselves having to push towards the edges of mystery, sometimes dialectically holding together insights which pull in different directions. First I will examine some of the more important accounts of intercession (the 'usual suspects'); then I will propose an integrated account that draws to some extent on all of them. Then we shall reflect on why and when our prayers seem not to be answered; before moving on to consider again praying for the Kingdom and 'praying in Gethsemane'.

Interrogating the 'Usual Suspects'

For the purposes of discussion I will divide accounts of intercession into two categories: subjective and objective. In the subjective accounts the stress is placed on what intercession 'does' to the pray-er: in effect it configures

intercession as 'us answering God' in some way. In the more
objective accounts intercession is understood as affecting
God in some sense, intercession leads to 'God answering
us'. This may be a convenient methodological tool, but we
must also be aware that it is a relative distinction. Some
accounts of prayer fall into both sides of this distinction – as
indeed does the account I will want to offer.

'Subjective' Accounts of Intercession: We Answer God

Under this heading we will consider two related accounts:
Augustine's view (and Schleiermacher's) of 'praying as
preparation'; and Kant's view of prayer as a form of
'therapeutic meditation',[1] with its modern version in the
thought of D. Z. Phillips.

Praying as preparation: Augustine and others
We do not need to say much more about Augustine's view,
replicated in other writers, that our intercession is basically
a means by which we prepare ourselves to receive what
God has already decided to give – we have already
commented upon it in chapter 2. It is an account widely
held in the Christian tradition. Augustine said that:

> . . . the Lord our God requires us to ask not that thereby our wish
> may be intimated to Him, for to Him it cannot be unknown, but in
> order that by prayer there may be exercised in us by supplication
> that desire by which we may receive what he prepares to bestow.[2]

I noted in the earlier discussion that Augustine had
believed it appropriate to pray for a broad range of things –
wisdom, but also friends, and even, within limits,
prosperity. But he is suggesting that such prayers will be to
no avail unless God has already decided to give these

---

[1] This expression is borrowed from Brummer, *What Are We Doing?*, pp.
16ff.
[2] Augustine, 'To Proba', VIII/19, p. 155.

things to us and unless the praying comes in fact to make us ready to receive that for which we pray. We will consider later the additional complications caused by Augustine's timeless view of God, and the problems this may raise in particular for human freedom. Suffice for the moment to note again that God has 'already' determined what we will receive, and knows when we will pray for it and when we will be ready to receive it. God's will cannot be changed: not by us, and not by God.

While I believe that this is an unsatisfactory account of intercession, we also need to observe that there are facets of Augustine's account that need to be part of any account of prayer. I have challenged the assumptions made about God's relationship with time, and the static metaphysical unchangingness predicated of God. But two features in particular strike me as vital.

The first is Augustine's insistence that something about praying affects the pray-er. We saw when reviewing Jacob and the prophets in chapter 1 how in different ways prayer is costly. To pray and to mean it changes us. To pray for justice without becoming ourselves more just would be a sham. As we long for our prayers to be heard by God, so God's Spirit works in us through our praying, and those prayers also affect us. By praying we begin, strangely, to answer God, in some ways to allow God to use us to answer our own prayers. Denise Carmody remarks that 'one cannot pray well and not love the light. Dishonest prayer is a contradiction in terms.'[3] Prayer changes things, and it begins, in true prayer, with the pray-er. If we don't 'love the light' when we begin, by praying for it we should come to love it, long for it, seek it out. When we pray for justice God's Spirit makes us more just and enlists us in the struggle for justice. All this is true prayer.

The second is the affirmation (though I would want it reframed) that God has a preveniently gracious will for us,

[3] Denise L. Carmody, *Christian Feminist Theology* (Oxford: Blackwell, 1995), p. 237.

a purpose for us and our lives and our world that pre-exists any prayer we may offer. We might go further, without I think contradicting the dialectical statement I will want to make in due course (along the lines of our being able to 'argue with God and win'), and say that this preveniently gracious will is in absolute terms the best that might be purposed for us. In Process Theology terms, this is the initial aim given by God from amid every conceivable possibility. Before we pray, God knows us, loves us and has plans for us.

Praying as 'therapeutic meditation': Kant and Phillips

Kant considered any attempt to influence the deity as 'mere superstition': such are Enlightenment sensibilities. In some respects the idea that God cannot be affected by human desires has a rationalistic rather than biblical pedigree. Kant's 'moral reading' of intercession is to make private prayer a means of meditating upon the good and so become good, while public prayer becomes what he calls a 'moral ceremony'. There are two reasons for this move: the first is the inability to conceive of God acting in or upon our world – with such a rationalistic, Newtonian view of the world, our universe is closed off to God. In fact, like many of our contemporaries, Enlightenment thinkers had an implicitly deistic view of the world, and of prayer. The deists believed that God had created the world as a watchmaker might make a clock, then, having wound it up, had just let it run. It has run ever since without 'interference' – whether in answer to prayer or of other sorts. The second reason is an inability to conceive (or desire to conceive) of our being able to affect the divine will. Such an account at first looks very like the Augustinian one already considered in that the praying affects the pray-er rather than God. But there are two differences that soon become obvious. One is the rather restrictive understanding of the end of prayer, confining it to petition for moral traits; the other is the relegation of God from the process altogether! We *change ourselves* by praying according to Kant, rather than God's Spirit working upon and within us to effect change. I suppose there may be minimal truth in this, but we would surely be better here – if not in an Augustinian account – to abandon the language of intercession altogether and call it meditation. There seems something dishonest about 'pretending' that I am using words like 'Lord, we pray for John' when we are in fact intending something which directly relates to ourselves, and only very indirectly to John.

D. Z. Phillips shows signs of Kant's influence in his important philosophical treatment of prayer first published in the 1960s. In fact, Phillips' thought is deeply affected by Wittgenstein's thinking and this is one of the reasons why he insists that philosophy as philosophy cannot deal with the religious question of the reality of prayer or whether God answers prayer: philosophy deals with meaning rather than truth.[4] It does not stop him venturing some Kantian thoughts on petitionary prayer, however. When prayer resembles incantation, it is simply superstition, he observes. This is surely true: anything that appears to reduce intercession to formulae, and therefore to depersonalise it, turns prayer into superstition, magic. This is a danger perceived in set forms of prayer by many an ardent reformer like my Baptist forbears, though they were wrong in overreaction to assume that all set forms, and however used, had to teeter over into such abuse. It may also be a danger in forms of prayer that assume that a particular form of meeting, or vigil, or chain, is somehow more likely to produce a 'result'. In so far as there is an implicit understanding that 'it's just a matter of getting the form right' prayer is descending again into incantation and superstition. As Phillips remarks, the idea that if prayer is offered hard enough, often enough, or correctly enough it will work is on the way to superstition.[5]

---

[4] D. Z. Phillips, *The Concept of Prayer* (Oxford: Blackwell, 1981), p. 27.
[5] Ibid., pp. 118f.

But he goes on to work at the example of prayer for a sick child. 'If the prayer is not to be regarded as superstition, it cannot be thought of as an attempt to influence God.'[6] Here surely he has moved from examining meaning to adjudicating truth? If he does not believe it appropriate to think of influencing God, what is the purpose of our praying? – for there is, Phillips assumes, a purpose in praying. In praying for the child, the believers:

> recognise their own helplessness, that the way things go is beyond their control, and seek something to sustain them which does not depend on the way things go, namely, the love of God . . . the prayer of petition is best understood, not as an attempt at influencing the way things go, but as an expression of, and a request for, devotion to God through the way things go.[7]

There is something positive to be said about this account, and it is this: at bottom, praying to God, asking God for healing for a child or yearning for the Kingdom, is just this – an awareness of our utter dependence on God, of God's 'Godness'. It is certainly in some sense an implicit desire to be sustained by God through 'the way things go'. We noted in the Old Testament the importance of the recognition of God's divinity, and the Lord's Prayer proceeds in similar mood. Schleiermacher's sense of 'absolute dependence' is indeed close to the heart of prayer. But this cannot be all it is. If it were, once more, the way we use language would be seen to be inappropriate, even dishonest. When we use words like 'Lord, please heal this child' Christians generally understand themselves to be asking God to heal a child, not keep them, the ones praying, safe through a difficult outcome.

That Phillips should miss this is perhaps the more remarkable given his stated starting point: philosophy, he says, leaves things as they are (in Wittgenstein's phrase),

---

[6] Ibid., p. 119.
[7] Ibid., pp. 120f.

not trying to provide a basis for prayer, but just to give an account of it.[8] But his account has reframed it radically. His treatment alerts us then to a fundamental criterion about intercession: that any account should adequately explain the way people who pray use words. Any account of prayer should give substance to the words used. This highlights a problem with those more traditional accounts that suggest that 'really' such language is not about asking God to heal a child but something more subtle. Such accounts risk dishonouring prayer, and even calling the God who commands us to pray a liar! The very language of intercession suggests an image of God that is dialogical, personal and responsive.

Prayer as accepting God's will: back to Gethsemane
Calvin, it will be recalled, spoke vividly of God 'bridling our prayers': there is a process at work in our prayers whereby – even though God may respond to our petitions ('even if God grants our prayer')[9] – our will is brought into conformity with God's. Augustine had spoken in a similar way, also suggesting that we use words in our prayers partly because this externalising and articulating allows us to observe the sort of progress we are making.[10] Jesus taught his disciples to pray 'your will be done on earth as in heaven', and it is impossible to avoid the conclusion that this is an important part of intercession. There is something counter-intuitive about this in that it once more suggests that in part language which seems to be about praying for others in fact refers back to ourselves: words about praying for John turn out to be about me accepting God's will (for John, perhaps). Sometimes our prayers proceed with such formulae as 'if it be your will' in order to make clear this sense of bringing our purpose into line with God's.

The prayer of Jesus in Gethsemane is the epitome of such praying. We saw in our first chapter that the prayer in

---

[8] Ibid., p. 3.
[9] Calvin, *Institutes*, 3/20/52, p. 919.
[10] Augustine, 'To Proba', IX/18, p. 155; XI/121, p. 157.

Gethsemane, interpreted as one of meek submission, is seen sometimes as the model of all petitionary prayer. But I also suggested that we can move too quickly to such a position: that in fact, as Cullmann suggests, the prayer of Jesus, 'My Father, if it is possible, let this cup pass from me' (Mt. 26:39), implies that it *may* be possible – that events are not necessarily fixed in stone. However, Jesus does conclude 'yet not what I want but what you want'. Primacy is given to the Father's will over Jesus' present wishes.

In the account that follows I will want to suggest that it is possible that intercession sometimes may 'persuade God'. However, it is necessary to allow this prayer to take its central place in our account. Our petitions never overpower God, they never talk God round to do something against God's better judgement (as sometimes I might be talked round!). *If* God responds to our prayers by deciding to do something other than he might first have intended, God does this because he wants to. It might be true that we can sometimes 'argue with God and win', but God is always in control of the divine response, never at our mercy. If in God's grace he chooses to respond to our requests, that is God's prerogative. In our discussion of Exodus 32 we also observed that God does not simply buckle to human requests!

Nevertheless, we need to hear clearly that part of what it is to pray is also to 'argue with God and *lose*': to become convinced and possessed by God's gracious will, to learn more faithfully to discern it and to do it. An examination of the process by which such discernment is practised and appropriated is the task of another book.

While acknowledging that we also concede that sometimes to pray meekly 'your will be done' may be to turn aside from the command of God to pray persistently and vigorously, to entreat God like a friend in the night or the widow who persists with the judge (Lk. 11:5, 18:3). We are *commanded* to ask, seek, knock (Mt. 7:7), to bring our intercessions for everyone (1 Tim. 2:1), to pray without ceasing (1 Thes. 5:17). 'We owe it to the command of God to pray . . . we should and must pray if we are to be Christians.'[11] So while the prayer of submission to God's will is at the heart of all our praying, it must not generate a sort of spiritual false modesty by which we avoid the genuine dialogue into which the living God calls and commands us. Indeed, we might note that the Gethsemane prayer suggests to us that it is false to ask whether God or the pray-er is changed by prayer: there will be a sense in which, at different moments, both may be.

'Objective' Accounts of Intercession: God Answers Us

Under this heading we will consider two main accounts, giving us the opportunity to examine a Process Theology view and a much more traditional, 'Origenist' account.

Prayer as 'opening doors for God': Process Theology and others
Some 'objective' accounts of intercession suggest that in some sense our petitions allow God to do what otherwise God would not have been able to do. But the way in which this is imagined and explained varies. Sometimes this is spoken of in terms of 'opening doors for God', or some similar image of enablement. It can be a characteristic of such positions that language remains rather vague as to how doors are opened, and what that means, so I intend to consider this sort of imagery mainly by examining Process approaches to intercession, where we will find such ideas given a degree of precision.

In Marjorie Hewitt Suchocki's account of intercession there are four main strands.[12] Intercession is spoken of as a means by which we open ourselves to God's will and seek to come into conformity with it.[13] Process thought has particular language to articulate this in terms of the divine initial aim and our prehension of it, but the idea is similar

---

[11] Barth, *C.D.* IV/4, p. 44; cf. III/4, p. 97.
[12] Marjorie Hewitt Suchocki, *In God's Presence: Theological Reflections on Prayer* (St Louis: Chalice, 1996), pp. 43–56.
[13] See Tiessen, *Providence*, p. 64.

to the common one we have just reviewed. Suchocki also suggests that intercession is a means of allowing God to work in and through us: we become in a sense the answers to our own prayers.[14] Again this is a familiar idea, though given a particular 'Process spin'. For Process thinkers, our praying for X makes us more open to receive an initial aim from God which, when actualised, makes X more likely.

But the other two (related) strands in her account are more Process specific. In the first, intercession is spoken of as a kind of 'meeting place' – our prayers connect us, through God, with those for whom we pray. God prehends all actual entities at every moment so that 'all things and all persons eventually meet in God through God's feelings of them and for them'.[15] Process Theology postulates the ultimate connectedness of every entity: reality is fundamentally social in nature. But in prayer we begin to feel with those for whom we pray with special intensity through our connectedness in God.[16] This 'connectedness' does not remain simply an experience of mystical fellowship. Rather, the desires we express to God in prayer in fact allow God to offer different possibilities for actualisation in the world, including for those for whom we pray. Our prayers change the given world with which God works in sifting and presenting possibilities. 'Our prayers change what is possible.'[17] In *Praying for Jennifer*, John Cobb puts this in non-technical language:

> When we align ourselves with the Spirit within us and are led by that Spirit to direct our prayers to the healing of another person, that general effect on all the cells in the world becomes focused on that other person . . .
>
> The result is not to persuade God to do what otherwise God is not willing to do. The result is to work with God in the healing of the other person. God is already at work but the conditions are hostile.

---

[14] Suchocki, *In God's Presence*, pp. 51ff.
[15] Ibid., p. 45.
[16] Ibid., p. 47.
[17] Ibid., pp. 49f.

Perhaps the other person is choosing death. Our choice can make a difference . . .

The doctors remove obstacles and open up channels for God's more effective working . . . intercessory prayer works in a similar way.[18]

Important to this suggestion is the notion that God can offer only 'relevant' or 'real' possibilities to actual entities at any given moment (an idea I attempted to undermine gently in the previous chapter). The pray-er affects what counts as real possibility by changing the context of the prayed-for. This seems to be a helpful if somewhat minimal insight, and we might well ask whether what we have called the 'Godness' of God is reflected in it. Does such an account circumscribe too closely what God is able to do (in offering possibilities) and when God is able to do this (when we pray)? It does reflect something of what we will later underline as important: that our prayer be a necessary if not a sufficient condition for any event X to be brought about by God. But despite this, and considering it is such a strongly relational account, the Process account does seem somewhat impersonal. God may be caricatured as a kind of divine telephone exchange or world wide web, providing the connectiveness required with little by way of personal involvement. The impression is given that prayers are processed rather than personally responded to.

Paul Fiddes suggests a slightly different Process-type idea that we might note. Working from an understanding of God's action as persuasive, Fiddes suggests that when we pray, in effect, we 'can add the persuasive power of our love to God's'.[19] As we pray for others God takes our desires and wishes for them into the divine desire and wishes. Our prayers 'are assumed into God's own persuasion, augmenting and amplifying the urging of God's Spirit, so that

---

[18] John B. Cobb Jr, *Praying for Jennifer* (Eugene: Wipf & Stock, 1985), pp. 72f.
[19] Fiddes, *Participating in God*, p. 136.

together God and the interceders begin to work transformation'.[20] Fiddes wants to maintain the divine initiative in this process – our prayers are not required to 'get God started',[21] and God's persuasive love is always at work – but something seems to be added to it when we pray.

As it stands this seems a suggestive but problematic account. Fiddes' protecting the divine initiative seems to suggest more 'Godness' than Suchocki, but given the vast range of God's own love, the supremacy of his persuasive power and omniscience, what can I realistically 'add' to that by my prayers? Is very much added to the divine persuasive power when we add our prayers to it? At first sight Fiddes seems to suggest that our prayers make God more powerful, but in terms of 'quantity of power' this surely cannot be the case. God's perfect persuasive power does not need our prayers to become more powerful: given its persuasive nature, it is already maximally powerful.

But in fact Fiddes means to suggest that our creaturely persuasion adds something to the *character* of God's persuasion that otherwise it would not have. Our empathetic praying 'gives a particular character to the initial aims that God offers'. This is in two ways: similar to Suchocki, Fiddes suggests that our prayers change the world and thus make new possibilities real for God to offer to others – again perhaps making the actualisation of novelty a more real possibility; additionally, our human perspectives give divine persuasion a character fitted to human life.[22] So God's power is augmented with different rather than supplementary powers. Fiddes suggests that our prayers may join us with those for whom we pray through the fellowship of the Trinity, thus making *our* persuasion directly present to them.

There is surely a sense in which our prayers do create openings for God's persuasive love: a sense in which our

---

[20] Ibid.
[21] Ibid., p. 138.
[22] Ibid., p. 137.

prayers may make God's power more effective. To begin with, our prayers make a difference in us, as we have already seen. But it may also be that in some strange way our prayers, as it were, open doors for the power of God in our world. Charles Elliott offers an evocative illustration of this based on an aerial view of Punjabi agricultural irrigation: prayer opens the sluices that release the creative, transformational water.[23] Walter Wink has more dramatic imagery:

> Prayer is rattling God's cage and waking God up and setting God free and giving this famished God water and this starved God food and cutting the ropes off God's hands and the manacles off God's feet and washing the caked sweat from God's eyes and then watching God swell with life and vitality and energy and following God wherever God goes.[24]

Suchocki stresses that our prayers add to the options that are real for God in any situation; Fiddes suggests that our prayers somehow augment God's persuasive power. What neither suggest is that our prayers might actually influence God to do something different. Suchocki's account has God able to offer new aims because our prayers have changed the world; but our prayers do not change God such that God decides to offer different aims from those which previously might have been, as it were, in God's mind. In other words, these Process accounts do not appear to know of intercession as sometimes being like 'arguing with God, and winning'. This is the more remarkable, perhaps, when one considers the Process stress on God's being affected by the world at every moment, but it may also underline the suspicion God is not responding here in a personal way, but in some other more remote way.

The Process view has its problems, then, but in its proposal that our prayers alter the world and open doors

---

[23] Elliott, *Praying the Kingdom*, p. 20.
[24] Walter E. Wink, *Engaging the Powers* (Minneapolis: Fortress, 1992), p. 303.

for God it does offer a rich and suggestive, if minimal, insight – that there is a sense in which God 'needs' our intercessions to further God's own purposes. There is something problematic and yet also attractive in the suggestion that our prayers somehow 'strengthen God's hand' as God works out his purpose.

Prayer as part of God's prearranged plan: from Origen to Tiessen
We concluded the second chapter of this book by examining Origen's ancient account of intercession, an approach that underlay all the accounts we considered there to a greater or lesser extent. The idea that intercession is part of the way in which a divine plan that is pre-arranged and/or pre-determined is actualised has been persistent and appealing. In part, this is because of certain understandings of God's relationship to time, and divine knowledge and power that I have questioned. There are a number of variations of this basic idea, and one is set out in Tiessen's 'Middle Knowledge Calvinist Model of Prayer'. In some variations God exerts more predetermination than in others, and a key question is the extent to which divine foreknowledge necessarily implies divine determination; or to put it another way, the extent to which divine foreknowledge necessarily curtails creaturely freedom.

According to such a view – in its strong form – God has *foreordained* each event, but has also planned how each particular event will come to pass: God has predetermined that some events will be brought about in response to prayer. Says Tiessen, commenting on Calvin, 'God has thus given petitionary prayer an effective role in the outworking of his purposes. There are many things that God does providentially, whether or not anyone asks him to do them. But there are also things that God has purposed to do precisely as answers to prayer.'[25] Why do things this way? Because it enables God to involve us in establishing the Kingdom, because it inculcates a spirit of dependence on

---

[25] Tiessen, *Providence*, p. 233.

God, and because when prayers are answered in this way it also fosters thankfulness in us. A somewhat weaker form of this theory may suggest that God knows, rather than simply determines, our free choices and fits in the answers to prayer alongside other divine actions in order to achieve the desired end result.

In this account as I have summarised it, there is no particular theory of how God actually acts in the world to achieve divine ends, predetermined or otherwise. Various theories have been suggested,[26] the more satisfactory generally being variations on Aquinas' two-cause theory, where a 'natural' cause has alongside it (or within, or above, it) a divine cause. It is the relationship between these causes, the 'causal joint', that is difficult to explain. Inevitably, where the divine purposes are seen as *inevitably* actualised, there must be a degree of coercion posited: the divine cause must have compelling power over natural causes. What unites all the variations on this basic and 'classic' account of intercession is the divine knowledge of what will be done and prayed, and the assurance that the divine purpose *will* be actualised.

In terms of the account of intercession specifically then, this account portrays God as having determined in advance that certain things will be actualised in response to prayer, in the context of God having decided what will happen in general. But what value can then be given to the idea that God decides to achieve certain things in response to prayer?

I am still praying for John. God may have decided to heal John, and he may have decided to do so as a response to my prayer. But surely here we are playing games, or rather, God is? For the crucial decision is whether or not John will be healed. After that has been made God can choose to actualise that in any way he chooses. God could decide to heal John in response to prayer. In the stronger version of

---

[26] There is an excellent discussion of the main theories in Fiddes, *Participating in God*, pp. 116ff.

such a theory, God could make sure I pray by predetermining that I do: formally the claim might be made (in a compatibilist account) that God's determining will has determined this along with my free choice to pray, but it matters little. God has determined it: I follow along, unwittingly cooperating in actualising the divine purpose. In the weaker version of the theory, where God only foreknows my prayer rather than determining it, God knows that I will pray and therefore builds in the answer to my prayer. But by the same token, if God knows that I will not pray and still has determined that John is to be healed, God will find another way of doing it – perhaps without any prayers at all. My prayer is convenient, but hardly essential. If God is all determining, willing or permitting all occurrences, with a controlling omnipotence over (or potentially over) every event, prayer and answers to prayer take on a somewhat illusory quality. Particular outcomes are guaranteed. (If the view is 'weakened' further so that God wills to heal John, but determines to do it only if I pray, but foreknows that I will not pray and so does not heal John – what kind of God is this, who acquiesces in John's fate because of my negligence?)

Tiessen debates whether such a position as his own 'Middle Calvinist' one adequately addresses the linkage between petition and outcome. Referring to James 4:2 ('you do not have, because you do not ask') and the 'explicit connection between our asking and our receiving'[27] he argues that what this means is that sometimes prayer is a necessary factor among a whole cluster of factors which will bring about a given outcome. He goes on to illustrate this by reference to his running case study involving prayer for 'Richard Henderson', who has been abducted:

> God could have predetermined that he would act to deliver Richard Henderson and his colleagues from harm and that he would do so even though no one had prayed about it or even knew that Richard

---

[27] Tiessen, *Providence*, p. 344.

had been captured. On the other hand, God could have determined that this particular act would be one that would rightly be discerned by his people as a response to their prayers and that would elicit appropriate praise of God for his greatness and kindness.[28]

Here we see the problem quite clearly. Prayer becomes an illusion planted in the system in order to make human pray-ers thankful. If God had determined *in any case* to free the captors, there is no explicit connection between our asking and receiving; and if God had determined not to free them, the prayer would have availed nothing anyway. In this account, prayer becomes a game God plays with us, sometimes. Our thanks are a manipulated and redundant quasi-response.

A satisfactory account of intercession must include what Geach and Brummer call 'two-way contingency'. The event must neither have been inevitable without the prayer, nor after it. A meaningful account of intercession requires that God orders events not simply 'as we wish' but (sometimes and not necessarily) 'because we wish'.[29] This should not be understood to mean that our prayers compel God to act: that would lead us off into magic rather than the personal relationship that is prayer. But here we see the importance of distinguishing between Tiessen's variables: whether 'prayer affects the outcome' and whether 'prayer changes God's mind'. Tiessen is able to argue, even if unsatis-factorily as I maintain, that his position demonstrates the former but not the latter. For a satisfactory account, there has to be possibility that prayer 'changes God's mind', that one might 'argue with God and win'! Otherwise we end up in the circular loop by which prayer is credited with something that would in any case and by other means have happened anyway. Geach presents the example of the father who resolves to give his son a pony; when the boy

---

28 Ibid., p. 345.
29 P. Geach, *God and the Soul* (London: Routledge & Kegan Paul, 1969), p. 87.

asks for a pony, we cannot also say that the boy got the pony because he asked.[30] It is no answer to argue, as Ganssle suggests is possible, that if the father knows the request before it is made, then the gift of the pony may still be understood to have been made 'because the son asked': it may *appear* to be in response to the request, but the father had in any case decided to make the gift.[31]

God does hold the initiative. God may heal John with or without my prayer. Usually we might assume, God is working to heal John anyway, and in such situations the insights of Fiddes and Suchocki suggest how our prayers 'open doors for God'. But not everything for which we pray has such a clear, exclusive, good (from our limited perspective) goal. Sometimes we might pray for an outcome X when Y or Z appear equally wholesome. God may have opted for Z, and yet may graciously decide for X in response to prayer. With Barth we might suggest that God 'shares' his initiative!

What distinguishes the positions I have called the weaker and stronger variations is the question of whether God's knowing the future means God also determines the future. Suppose that God knows that I will pray for John on Sunday morning: does that mean I am free *not* to pray for John on Sunday morning? Advocates of the weaker position argue that it does, saying that God only knows that I will pray for John on Sunday because in fact I will – it is not that I will pray for John on Sunday *because* God knows it. My action is not dependent on God's knowledge of it, but the other way around – God's knowledge of my action is dependent on my doing it.

Some argue that by conceiving of God timelessly these problems are eased. A temporal God who foreknows that I will pray for John on Sunday, who allows or directs every event leading up to my prayer and following from it, and whose purpose will be actualised anyway, seems either to

---

[30] Ibid., p. 88.
[31] Ganssle's 'Introduction' in Ganssle (ed.), *God and Time*, pp. 21f.

limit or at least to trivialise my freedom to pray. But a timeless God, who knows my praying for John simultaneously with John's recovery or relapse, and who again decides eternally what will be at any given moment and precisely how divine purposes will be fulfilled, seems once more to undermine the meaning of my praying. I have argued that, for reasons associated with God's Triune being and with God's identity as an agent active in the world, God has to be conceived of as experiencing time in some way. In particular I argued that for God to be understood as personal and responsive, a view that pictures God as knowing and experiencing all things at once (and therefore not 'acting' at all in any sense we might recognise) is deeply problematic.

As Geach shows in discussing C. S. Lewis, once such a timeless view is accepted, praying for things that have already happened seems to be possible.[32] But such prayers make no sense: if I prayed *now* that John *not* be victim to the accident *last summer* that threatens his health *now*, and God 'answered' this prayer affirmatively, then *now* I would not be praying this prayer because the accident would not have happened! This makes as much sense, says Geach, as a schoolboy praying that *pi* will have the value 3.1416 in his maths test. This leads Geach to observe that in such a view time itself seems ultimately unreal. Time is just a matter of 'our perspective', it is *timelessness* which is real, or more real: and we are back entrapped in a particular philosophical world which has little essential relationship to the God who is revealed in scripture, the God and Father of our Lord Jesus Christ.[33]

But even beyond all these objections, supposing them all to be dealt with, it is still unconvincing to think that the God who eternally knows and experiences all things simultaneously – my writing this now and my praying for John next Sunday – does not somehow curtail my freedom for next Sunday to do otherwise. Prayer becomes a futile

---

[32] Geach, *God and the Soul*, p. 90.
[33] See also Brummer, *What Are We Doing?*, p. 42.

illusion. Presumably even my realisation that that is the case, and so my disillusioned abandonment of prayer to let God just get on with it, is foreknown (maybe foreordained) and worked around from all eternity.

What may be said positively about this account of intercession? It does point us towards something very significant, even if it does so by overstating its case in trumps. What this view reminds us is that God has a purpose that in detail applies to every situation and person and moment. This purpose is part of the great plan of salvation history that God determined to actualise when the project of our universe was begun. The confidence in the success of that plan, which radiates from this account (in a way which actually damages God by making creation an extension of God's own being, a mere cipher for the divine will), is one we would do well to contemplate: it will have to be reframed, but it echoes the eschatological confidence of scripture. And in its stress on the final purposes of God this account also draws us back to the eschatological theme we saw running through scripture: that all prayer is in some sense a praying for God's will to be done, God's Kingdom to come, on earth as in heaven.

Prayer as a Response to the Gracious Command of God to Participate in the Action of the Trinity in the World

I come now to begin to draw together the threads of a coherent account of the nature and purpose of intercessory prayer, of moving towards a theology of intercession. Something of all the positions reviewed so far will be reflected in it, and readers may also discern similarities with accounts of prayer given by some writers in the Open Theism movement: indeed their position and the one I will now outline are close enough not to warrant a separate review of the Open Theism position here. As with other positions outlined, however, Open Theists do not all agree, and there is no one agreed 'Open Theist account of intercession', so that the account I offer will jostle among the various accounts already on offer. Where I think my account may be somewhat distinctive is in a particular combination of emphases – including the Trinity; in asking whether certain Open Theists go far enough in their descriptions of divine power and human interaction on the one hand, but also whether they go far enough in affirming what might be said of divine knowledge – what I have called the dialectics of omniscience and omnipotence; the possibility of resistance to the divine purpose as both a mark of creation's independence but also its complexity and its thrall to what scripture calls the 'principalities and powers'. Other strands will doubtless emerge – but enough of the trailers, it is time to begin.

Intercession as participation in the open Trinity
I want to begin with the doctrine of the Trinity: with the Christian answer to the question 'Who is God?' We may recall how it was the experience of prayer and worship that was a significant factor in the development of the doctrine of the Trinity. The Christian experience was such that it had to be articulated in Trinitarian terms. Looked at from the other side, so to speak, with Barth, the voice with which God speaks in revelation is the triple voice of Father, Son and Spirit. The Christian experience of praying to the One God is that of stepping into a dynamic relationship whereby the Spirit catches us up into a movement with the Son to the Father. This same Spirit helps us in our prayers, and intercedes for us when we do not know how or what to pray with sighs too deep for words (Rom. 8:26); or as Hebrews 7:25 and Romans 8:34 put it, Jesus at the Father's right hand intercedes for us. Jesus gives us the words to pray with the Lord's Prayer and continues to speak for us and with us; the Spirit helps us when words seem to run out.

Fiddes' dynamic and relational account of the Trinity speaks of God as One whose 'life consists in relationships' which are 'love in movement'[34] These relationships can best

---

[34] Fiddes, *Participating in God*, pp. 115f.

be characterised in terms of *perichoresis*, and the image which is most helpful for us is that of the dance – a divine dance into which we are invited, caught up in the life of the Trinitarian persons who are 'love in movement'.

Such language immediately and vividly illumines the act of praying. Because God *is* Father, Son and Holy Spirit, and because the Spirit helps us in our prayers to the Father through the Son, any account of intercession must have a Trinitarian perspective, though few accounts accord such considerations a prominent place. This is, in part, because of the temptation to treat the subject of petitionary prayer in a more abstract way, as a problem of philosophy of religion in general, a problem for any theistic thinker. But the Christian has to reframe the issue dramatically: the Trinitarian dimensions we have been considering cast this 'problem' in a new light.

The Trinity is important in at least two ways, firstly because it suggests that prayer is not so much something offered *to God* as something that takes place *within God*. The Trinity is an open Trinity; God draws us into the dance, into the life of the Trinity. Secondly, not only do we begin to see more clearly how our wills (and our prayers) might begin to be moulded by the will of God through such an interactive indwelling, we also see more clearly how it is that our desires might be taken seriously by the Triune God. Cunningham argues that the doctrine of the Trinity suggests that God is not simply uniform, 'mono': rather, as his accounts of polyphony and difference show, God's being is complex, is community, is one where difference (while still arising from and returning to an underlying unity) is welcomed and celebrated.[35] Polyphony is a 'Trinitarian virtue' that we are called to model; Fiddes would go further, suggesting that it is a divine movement in which we are called to participate. This stronger language is helpful when thinking about prayer. The Father, Son and Spirit are not uniform but various,

---

[35] Cunningham, *These Three*, pp. 127ff., etc.

different. And into this open Trinity we are called, with our differentness.

When we considered the doctrine of the Trinity earlier we heard Kasper affirm that the Trinity was the only viable form of monotheism because of this unity that includes differentiation.[36] We indicated that the very existence of God as Agent requires other active and (relatively) powerful agents, and as we saw how the definition of God as Person requires other persons with whom to be in fellowship, so as the Triune God goes about the divine purpose in the world our different wills and desires are invited into the Triune Fellowship. The potential 'affectedness' of God may be argued for from a number of different angles. Cunningham is concerned with a form of community which makes space for different 'melodies or voices'. The Trinity is such a community, and human community becomes part of it and is modelled by it. But it is not difficult to see how, with Moltmann's critique of 'monarchical' notions of God in our minds, this analysis of difference might suggest that it is in the very nature of God the Trinity not to require us always to conform to God's will but to allow space for our own wills to become part of God's life and purpose. Cunningham does not make the connection, but it seems to me that the doctrine of the Trinity leads to an affirmation that our different desires are somehow welcomed and made part of the rich fellowship and purposes of God.

At the forefront of such discussions is often the theme of freedom: the freedom of persons to respond or not, the freedom to pray or to resist. But what is also at stake here is the freedom of God, as Barth suggested – divine freedom to respond to God's creatures. Traditional doctrines may jeopardise this freedom, but we are required to keep these various freedoms (divine and creaturely) in balance. As Barth says, God has the freedom to 'give to the requests of this creature a place in His will . . . he lets the

---

[36] Kasper, *The God of Jesus Christ*, p. 295.

creature . . . participate in His omnipotence and work'[37] precisely because God does not have the 'immovability of an idol'. This is who God is; this is who God has chosen to be, God has chosen to make room for us in the divine governance of the world.

Moltmann speaks of prayer in terms of expressing friendship with God with a tone echoing Barth's language about God's freedom and shared sovereignty:

> The prayer offered in the assurance that prayer will be heard therefore becomes the expression of life lived in friendship of God. God can be talked to. He listens to his friend. Thanks to his friendship there is room in the almighty liberty of God for the created liberty of man. In this friendship there is the opportunity for man to have an effect upon and with God's sole effectiveness.[38]

The act of prayer is a way of claiming God's friendship for those who sigh and groan, it is even, we might suggest, a way of drawing others more really into the Trinitarian fellowship, or into greater participation in the 'dance'. This may be a Trinitarian reworking of some of the ideas we encountered in Suchocki's Process account: our prayer changing the context of the prayed-for by drawing them into the life of God, and thus making what was previously impossible possible.

Intercession and relationship
Speaking of our desires and petitions being 'welcome' within the Trinitarian fellowship is one thing, but how might we understand the way in which the God whose knowledge is perfect and whose wisdom supreme 'hears' such prayers? How might it be true that, as Barth says, God 'does not act in the same way whether we pray or not'?[39] Theologians who object to relational-responsive accounts

---

[37] Barth, C.D. III/4, p. 109.
[38] Moltmann, *The Church in the Power of the Spirit*, p. 118.
[39] Karl Barth, *Prayer and Preaching* (London: SCM, 1964), p. 16.

of prayer often find some difficulty here, so it is necessary to explore more fully what it means to be in relationship.

God relates to human persons (pray-ers) in a reciprocal way: not behaving coercively, like a dictator (benevolent or otherwise).[40] As Brummer says, God *could* always notice our needs and meet them without reference to us. But this would be to depersonalise us: it would be treating us more like plants on a windowsill to be watered than people. While God meets most of our needs without our asking, God cannot do this all the time or in everything without degrading the personal nature of our relationship with him. Petition then creates the conditions necessary for God to be able to give us what we need or desire. But this much might be said by an advocate of an Augustinian position: that God has decided to give us X, but waits for us show our readiness for X by praying for it. God gives what God always wills to give, but has to wait for us to ask. But an understanding of intercession as fundamentally relational has the potential of further development.

Brummer himself opens up this possibility by building a case for three necessary pre-requisites of a satisfactory account of petitionary prayer:[41] (1) the existence of a personal agent God with ability to make real responses to the events or creation and the requests offered to him – this, we have already tried to argue, makes sense in a thoroughly Trinitarian account; (2) two-way contingency in the world – in terms of my praying for John next Sunday, this requires that his recovery be neither impossible nor inevitable for my prayer to matter; (3) the petition must be a necessary but not sufficient condition for the event prayed for to take place, that is, for John's recovery to be explained with reference to my prayer, we would have to be able to say that it happened *because* I prayed – though not *just because* I prayed – the prayer was necessary, but not on its own enough.

---

[40] Brummer, *What Are We Doing?*, pp. 45ff.
[41] Ibid., pp. 29ff.

Our prayers, therefore, matter. God does not deal with us like plants to be watered, or indeed as anything less than fully personal. The three-personal God who created human persons in the divine image insists on treating us as active agents, called to participate in the life of God and the life of God's world. Persons relate to one another with flexibility. Friends and lovers *adapt* and *modify* their wishes in relationship. Might we not be able to suggest that God is able to respond, to adapt and modify the particulars for which we pray, and that this involves God changing his short-term but not his long-term purposes for us? In other words, God remains mutable/flexible in the particular, while God's final purpose for us remains immutably great? Two illustrations may help.

A father decides to do some work in the garden, altering the layout a little. His young children are desperate to help. Because he enjoys their company, and because he thinks it would be good for them to help, he allows them to do so. However, the original plans for the garden work might now not be feasible. Perhaps it is because some of the tools or manoeuvres are too dangerous to use with the children involved, or maybe they are just too difficult for children to do. So the father amends his plans: he allows them to have a patch the way they like it, and generally adjusts things all round. The end result is still a re-jigged garden as intended, but not in all details. These have been tweaked to allow others to participate with their particular resources, and maybe even some of these revised plans have not been perfectly actualised. But the father decides that the value of doing it this way is greater than barring the children's contribution and simply doing it all himself. Is intercession illumined by this story? It seems to me that it is. It is often stated in giving accounts of God's providential activity that God works to redeem human failures and weave them back into the divine plan. Prayer is an instance of this: through prayer we express our desires and wishes to God, and while we may assume God would never collude with a really 'bad' idea (instead working to move us away from it, or mitigate its worst effects), God will allow human persons the freedom to do things their way if in fact that is likely to produce (directly or indirectly) the kind of creation and the sort of persons which is God's ultimate aim. Such accounts of providence and prayer see God's penultimate aims as flexible and continuously renegotiated with creation, changing like a kaleidoscope with every moment from one divinely beautiful pattern to another slightly different divinely beautiful pattern. But God's ultimate goals remain firm and fixed.

The second illustration might make this clearer. The films of movie director Mike Leigh are well known (including *Secrets and Lies*, *Topsy-Turvy* and *Life is Sweet*), and his style is idiosyncratic. Leigh is usually listed as the 'writer and director', but the actual process is more complex. Each scene is planned on the storyboard of the film, and is given basic content, and an outline of its relationship to the whole. However, the actors are not given scripts in the normal sense. They are encouraged to play the scene over and over, to experiment with lines and gestures and movements. Finally, usually in a series of first-takes, Leigh shoots the scene as the actors have created it, perhaps ending up quite different in important ways from the material they started with. I doubt the plot ever changes very significantly – Leigh still remains in charge to this extent – but the project becomes more collaborative. Is prayer illumined by this? I believe it may be. The analogy of God as director of a play is familiar in the literature of providence,[42] but the added dimension which considering Leigh's practice brings is this: the scenes are genuinely the result of creative improvisation and interaction between actors and director, while at the same time the overall shape of the scene, and indeed its relation to the whole plot, remain more or less fixed. These improvisations take place within certain limits. *Topsy-Turvy* being based on the real lives of Gilbert and Sullivan, for

---

[42] See Bradshaw, *Praying*, pp. 98f.

instance, the actors are not free to create wholly new lives for these men.

It may be objected that it is inconceivable that the supremely wise God should seek or pay attention to our desires and wishes.[43] God needs no counsellor, Isaiah 40:13f. tells us. This text suggests that God's wisdom is never lacking, that God's knowledge never needs supplementing – but I am not suggesting that we are in any position to advise or enlighten God, simply that God may choose graciously to allow our wishes to influence the divine will. It truly is remarkable that the supremely wise God might attend to the petitions of human persons. But this is not to 'diminish God': rather it is the glory of God to decide to be and to do just this, God for us, God with us, the three-personal God in fellowship with the persons God creates. Why should it, after all, be considered more consistent with divine honour for God's will to be unchanging and unaffected by prayer? Rather, as H. H. Farmer puts it:

> Without abating in the least its essential consistency or the assurance of its ultimate victory, [God's will] can take up into itself responses to the personal needs and petitions of men. Nay, just because the end it is seeking is personal, such personal relationship must be included ... The essence of a personal relationship is ... that one will act differently from what it would otherwise act because it meets another will. The objection is in fact a projection onto God of our own egotistic and mechanical conception of will-power as power to ignore or override other wills; under cover of zeal for God's honour, it depersonalises him.[44]

Intercession and the dialectics of time, knowledge and power
In the previous chapter we explored what I called the dialectics of God's relationship with time, and God's knowledge and power. I want to add some brief comments

---

[43] Ware, *God's Lesser Glory*, pp. 170ff.
[44] Farmer, *The World and God*, pp. 138f.

now to relate these topics to our current discussion. It will be useful, I hope, in particular as a way of clarifying the position I am suggesting alongside or apart from typical 'Open Theist' positions.

I suggested that God had to be understood to have temporal experience, but that also in some ways God transcends our experience of time, and time itself. The Process resource of the primordial and consequent nature may be one way of conceptualising this, and Wolfhart Pannenberg suggests another in terms of the 'economic' and 'immanent' Trinity,[45] which may be similar to my suggestion that the Trinity requires time-transcending temporality. It may be truer to say that God is multi-temporal rather than simply temporal, and God's time (which sometimes we call eternity) embraces experience of time and its surpassing. All of this is important when discussing prayer because, as again we discovered in this chapter when considering the idea that God has prearranged events including our prayers and God's answers, we pray for events in time. If God is to be truly personal and truly responsive, then it seems likely that God answers *in time*.

This leads naturally to a discussion of God's relationship to the future. In theories 'of timeless eternity' God knows the future as already present, as the Paris landscape is present at one moment to someone on the top of the Eiffel Tower. But if the future is not yet there to be known, if the future is contingent upon our free decisions, God's relationship with the future seems to be somewhat risky. It must be true that it is relatively more risky to think in these terms (though it would be quite wrong, of course, *not* to think it simply because it is safer or more comforting not to do so). God knows the future, then, at any given moment, as *possible* rather than *actual*. We might say that God knows that I might, or that I intend to, pray for John on Sunday.

---

[45] Wolfhart Pannenberg, *Systematic Theology*, vol. 1, G. Bromiley (tr.) (Edinburgh: T & T Clark, 1991), p. 407.

Until I do, that is 'all' God can know. But we also wanted to say that God knows all the possible futures together with an assessment of how realistically possible they are at any given moment. Generally, Open Theist positions want to go this far and a little bit further: they want to suggest that the future is 'partly settled'[46] and partly not, though they rarely tease this out in detail. I am not sure, for instance, what that does to God's knowledge of my praying for John on Sunday, or of John's final earthly outcome, or of John's eternal state – not sure at all, short of being sure that Open Theists mean to say the 'big thing', that God's eternal purpose is safe.

I am not too concerned about what may or may not be a typical Open Theist agnosticism here, instead I want to suggest on the basis of the dialectics of God's omniscience that we discussed previously, that while God certainly does not know the unactualised future as actual he knows every possibility together with an assessment of its likely actualisation. God also knows, because God 'knows' every person and creature and situation better than they know themselves, what are all the likely reactions and responses in each and every moment. This may be a weaker sense of 'know' than we are used to employing, but it strikes me as a very strong weak sense! God knows our reactions as well as I know that Manchester United will beat that school football team, perhaps. This knowledge may be technically closer to 'prediction' than the kind of knowledge we think we have about '2+2=4', but it is real knowledge. We may be close here to what Craig calls a 'conceptualist' account of foreknowledge rather than a 'perceptualist' one: where, instead of foreknowledge being a looking at the future, it is instead more self-contained within the mind of God.[47]

Creatures have freedom in their future acts, and this freedom may in theory be exercised in a way that God had

---

[46] e.g. Pinnock, *Most Moved Mover*, p. 108.
[47] William Lane Craig, 'The Middle Knowledge View' in Beilby and Eddy (eds), *Divine Foreknowledge*, p. 133.

not foreseen as the most likely. But because God knows every possibility and knows us too, such choices never surprise God, though they may disappoint (or gladden) God. God 'knows' that it is extremely likely that I will pray for John – or perhaps that I won't, being the sort of forgetful, self-centred person I am. Whichever it is, God knows the truth about me and my praying.

At this point we might consider another objection. God may not know the future according to such an argument, but God does know the present and the past, everyone and everything – how could we conceive that our prayers somehow impart to God our desires and wishes, is God not bound to know these already?[48] In one sense of course God is bound to know. Scripture addresses the question of why we pray if our Father in heaven knows what we need already (Mt. 6:8). The common spiritual insight that our whole lives should become a prayer suggests among other things that our desires should be integrally related to the way we live our lives, and God knows *all* about our lives. But we are back here to being treated like plants to be watered rather than persons. God *could* meet all our needs and answer all our desires (or the appropriate ones, anyway) without them being articulated – however, the same scriptures that remind us that God already knows what we want also command us to pray, and to bring our petitions and requests to God. That is because prayer is relational, and we might add dialogical: it may well be that in praying *our desires change* as we listen as well as speak. As Augustine said, sometimes we need to articulate our prayers so that we can see them in a more detached and proper way. This objection then seems to me to miscon-strue the fundamentally personal nature of intercession.

A sometimes related problem arises when someone objects that, if too much weight is given to our petitions, God appears to be unduly inhibited when we do not pray. Will God not heal John unless I pray for him? Surely a good

---

[48] See Ware, *God's Lesser Glory*, pp. 167ff.

and gracious God will not allow John's wellbeing to depend upon my fickleness? I have been careful to try to avoid any such suggestion. With Fiddes, and with more conventional accounts, I agree that God retains the initiative at all times. God is always at work in God's world – the Process conceptuality of divine action, whatever its weaknesses may be, stresses this too, and the Process account of intercession also suggested (with its 'opening doors' imagery) a way of understanding how divine prevenience marries with petitions. John's recovery does not depend on my prayer, if by that we mean that God will not act on John's behalf without my prayer. However, God's purposes for John may be open to influence by my prayer, and we may even say with Suchocki, Fiddes and Wink that our prayer adds something to what God is already seeking to do.

Open Theists often seem to speak of God using coercive force as a sort of emergency measure.[49] This seems to me to surrender the real theological advantages of insisting on a model of divine action based upon persuasion. If God still can, in theory, coerce at any time and only withholds by choice, then we are back again in a situation where everything that happens does so because God chooses it should happen – either actively, by coercively overriding; or passively, by not doing so. The world becomes again a cipher for the divine being. I suggested a model of divine action drawing upon the conceptuality of Process Thought which used persuasion as the model for all action, but which also sought to assert dialectically that such persuasion could at times be quite compelling; further, using the Process conceptuality, it seemed possible to speak of God 'setting the limits' of action in a way more appropriately considered compelling. The usefulness of the conceptuality is that it appears to allow such thinking in a

---

[49] For instance, Pinnock, 'Systematic Theology', p. 116 and David Basinger, 'Practical Implications' in Pinnock et al, *The Openness of God*, p. 159.

coherent way, while protecting the true independence of the world, God's creation.

The God who uses Cyrus (Is. 41:25, 45:1–3) sometimes persuades people to do things by relying on them following their own instinct to best interest, or maybe even (as in the Pharaoh of the Exodus) giving them up to their own obstinate hardness of heart. Usually it will be subtler. I do not think that we need to be too squeamish about this: we often persuade people to do things by appealing to different priorities and motives from those we ourselves have. This need not be called 'manipulation', though the moment we label it thus it alerts us to some of the dangers, some of the less than fully personal ways in which human persons experience human relationships, which can be experienced as exploitative and abusive, as well as fulfilling. In the recently filmed Graham Greene novel *The End of the Affair*[50] a major plot point is a prayer-bargain, where a character prays for a miracle and makes an 'offer' to God in return. Is this personal, relational behaviour? Maybe so, but not *good* personal, relational behaviour – not the way we would like others to deal with us, and not the way one might expect a relationship founded on grace to function. It cautions us against assuming that talking about 'personal' language and the relationship of prayer is entirely straightforward.

Divine power is not always and everywhere coercive. This means that sometimes, perhaps often, the initial aim offered by God to creatures is not actualised: God's will is not always done, just as the director's wishes are not always followed by the actors, or the children working in the garden do not always follow their father's instructions. In events that we might think of as more complex divine actions, as opposed to very 'simple' ones (in philosophy of action terms), it becomes more difficult that God's will be actualised in every respect and detail – more free creaturely wills are involved. Sometimes God's will is not done, and

---

[50] Colombia Pictures, 2000; directed by Neil Jordan.

that means that sometimes God may seek to answer our prayers but is frustrated from doing so. We must now turn to ask about those situations where our prayers seem to receive the answer 'no'.

The answering God seems to say 'yes' but also 'no'
We have argued for an account of intercession in which the three-personal God is free, by gracious resolve, to respond to our petitions and take account of our desires. We have argued, in short, that the answering God seems sometimes able and willing to say 'yes' when we pray. But, as we heard in the Old Testament, while it may be wondrously possible to 'argue with God and win', this is by no means assured every time we turn to God in prayer. It may even be an exception. However, without dawdling over the 'success rate' of petitions let us also freely acknowledge that in every situation and in hearing every prayer it is very much the case that God always knows what is best, which prayer may and may not be responded to. Sometimes, often, usually, who are we to say which, the answering God may yet say 'no'. However, because of what we have just said about the power of God and the independence of the world we have to think more carefully about those situations where our prayers seem not to be answered.

When I pray to God for wisdom God may give me the wisdom I may be capable of using wisely. However one debates the possible outcomes here, the action, if God decides to perform it, is 'simple' – only God and I are involved. When I pray next Sunday for John's recovery things are more complex: John's body and mind are involved, as are his carers, his family, and things as obscure as the hospital generator which has to keep life-saving equipment working. Nevertheless, it remains a relatively simple action with all individual wills working for a similar outcome, compared, say, to bringing peace to the Middle East, or ending world poverty. Such events are much more complex, from our perspective infinitely more complex. If events are more vulnerable to frustration the more complex they get, and if we are serious that God-given free will remains free will in more than name, might not one of the reasons that the answer seems to be 'no' when we pray for an event is that there are too many free wills involved which are working in conflict with one another and God?

This is something like Oscar Cullmann hints at when he talks about the setbacks of contingency and sin.[51] It is also something that Walter Wink has in mind when he talks – rather more full-bloodedly – about the 'principalities and powers' that thwart the penultimate purposes of God. But just as he conceives of this temporary limitation on God's power, so he also gives a very positive and strong place to intercession. 'Those who do not believe in [prayer's] efficacy simply illustrate the effectiveness of the Powers in diminishing our humanity.'[52] Rationally there are few real objections to the 'efficacy of prayer' – instead it is rooted in one's world view, and that is seldom constructed entirely from rational sources. He suggests that Revelation 8:1–5 offers a vision where prayers 'intervene in the heavenly liturgy' and the 'uninterrupted flow of consequences is dammed for a moment'. Because people have prayed, 'new alternatives become feasible'.[53]

However, Wink goes on, most of us were taught that unanswered prayer is a result of either our failure or God's refusal. Either we lacked faith (or were too sinful and impure or asked for the wrong thing), or God said 'no' out of some inscrutable higher purpose.[54] 'What we have left out of the equation is the Principalities and Powers. Prayer is not just a two-way transaction. It also involves the great socio-spiritual forces that preside over so much of reality.'[55]

---

[51] Oscar Cullmann, *Prayer in the New Testament*, p. 35 and *Salvation in History* (London: SCM, 1967), pp. 122ff.
[52] Wink, *Engaging the Powers*, p. 297.
[53] Ibid., p. 299.
[54] Ibid., p. 309.
[55] Ibid.

For instance, Wink argues, in the Book of Daniel the angel of Persia is able to block God's messenger from answering Daniel, and God's angel wrestles with the angel of Persia. This is an accurate, though mythological, description of our praying experience.[56] The Bible does not seek to justify such delays – it is simply a fact of experience. The Principalities and Powers are able to resist the divine will *'and, for a time, prevail'*.[57] What is remarkable, once we understand the effects of the principalities and powers, is that prayers are *ever* answered – not that sometimes they are not. The divine purpose is not just constrained by human freedom but by more sinister forces.[58] According to Wink, God hears our prayers for justice and liberation immediately, but prayer involves God *and* people *and* the Powers, so 'God's ability to intervene against the freedom of these rebellious creatures is sometimes tragically restricted in ways we cannot pretend to understand. It takes considerable spiritual maturity to live in the tension between these two facts: God has heard our prayer, and the Powers are blocking God's response.'[59] Despite this, because of this, and without any assurance that prayer will always produce the result we seek when we seek it, prayer is the means God uses to establish this 'ultimate act of partnership with God', a partnership in which 'God allows no grovelling'.[60]

There is, of course, another explanation for why there sometimes seems to be the answer 'no'. This is the idea that God refines our prayers, makes them what they should have been, before answering them. Here, the answer seems to be 'no' because we have underestimated how much our prayers needed to be refined! Of intercessors, Barth writes that:

---

[56] Ibid., pp. 309f.
[57] Ibid., p. 310.
[58] cf. Gregory A. Boyd, *God at War: The Bible and Spiritual Conflict* (Downers Grove: IVP, 1997) and *Satan and the Problem of Evil* (Downers Grove: IVP, 2001), also www.gregboyd.org.
[59] Wink, *Engaging the Powers*, p. 311.
[60] Ibid., p. 312.

They ask for this and that. Inevitably they do so according to their own estimate and opinion of what they and others need . . . of what, according to their own thinking and program, God ought to be doing to be a Supporter, Helper, and Saviour . . . No request by any child of God is not fulfilled by God his Father. Fulfilled! According to the meaning and intention with which it is brought before him, the petition might be largely and even mostly an empty, short-sighted, arbitrary, unreasonable and even perverted and even dangerous one. Already as request it needs fulfilment, that is, correction, amendment, and transformation by the one to whom it is directed and before whom it is brought . . .[61]

Barth tells us that God answers our prayers in their 'perfected' form, that is, after his grace has made them into the prayers we would have prayed had we known, had we seen things from his perspective, had his grace really worked on us through and through. This applies to all prayers, for great and small. In its benign aspect this recalls the conclusion of one of Garrison Keillor's *Lake Wobegon* stories where he remarks, not about prayer, but with words that may have an application for us: 'Good luck lies in not getting what you thought you wanted but getting what you have, which once you have it you may be smart enough to see is what you would have wanted had you known.'[62]

But it does not always seem so benign. C. S. Lewis tells the story of the boy who is told by his father that he may ask for anything, and his father will give it to him. The boy duly asks for a bicycle, but the father gives him an arithmetic book with the explanation that he knows the boy's needs better than the boy himself, and that the arithmetic book will be better for him in the long run. The problem seems to be not so much in accepting and living with the Father's superior judgement, but in the apparently cruel extravagance of the original offer.[63] While

---

[61] Barth, C.D. IV/4, p. 107, italics mine.

[62] Garrison Keillor, *Lake Wobegon Days* (London: Faber, 1987), p. 337.

[63] C. S. Lewis, 'Petitionary Prayer: A Problem without an Answer' in C. S. Lewis, *Christian Reflections* (London: Fount, 1981), pp. 188f.

a satisfactory account of prayer must establish the responsiveness of God, it cannot but also concede the 'God knows best' argument, nor should it want to do anything else. Any satisfactory account of intercession must also include within it the sense that our prayers should bring us more closely into line with God's will. However, if God is to be a truly responsive God, then God must be responsive to prayers that are genuinely and recognisably *our* prayers.

We recall that Calvin had already wrestled with these problems too. Assuring us that God answers our prayers, he deals with apparently unanswered prayer. 'Besides, even if God grants our prayer, he does not always respond to the exact form of our request.'[64] He suggests that sometimes God answers by giving us something else (the arithmetic book!) – 'what was expedient'[65] – and sometimes God delays responding to the request until the right time – 'seeming to hold us in suspense'.[66] It is difficult to think of any reason to disagree on either count. If God sometimes answers 'yes', sometimes the answer might also be 'no, instead this', or 'yes, but not yet'. When we face moments when prayer seems *not* to be answered we are reminded of the difficulty of knowing whether any particular prayer has been answered, or not.

Praying for the Kingdom, and praying for a parking space

If God is sometimes able and willing to say yes to our prayers, though is in no way bound or constrained by them, for what sorts of things should we pray? A Christian bookshop I used to know was run by an earnest couple from one of the local churches. From time to time their friend came in to help in the shop and I remember him telling me one day how he and his church were hard at prayer for a new car for him. His old Cortina was pretty

---

[64] Calvin, *Institutes*, 3/20/52, p. 919, italics mine.
[65] Calvin, *Commentaries*, on 2 Cor. 12:8; cf. *Commentaries*, on Heb. 5:7 and Ps. 78:26.
[66] cf. Calvin, *Commentaries*, on Ps. 10:17, 25:6, 6:9–11, and the sermon on Lk. 1:26–38 (Wallace, *Calvin's Doctrine*, p. 292).

beaten up, and while it still went, it didn't glorify the Lord very much. Something a bit smarter would be more suitable, and he felt the Lord had put this on his heart. I hope my memory does not caricature this conversation too much, but it has stuck in my mind. I remember Dennis Bennett's prayer for a parking place in *Nine O'Clock in the Morning*,[67] but I don't remember him praying for the vehicle to put in it. The following month when I went into the shop the friend's new Sierra gleamed outside, and he waxed lyrical about the 'answer to prayer': someone in the church had a spare, apparently. The Lord moves in mysterious ways.

Should we pray for a new car, or for fine weather for the church fête, as many a church leader has done, I am sure, while I have been writing this book? Should we pray for our son's job interview, for revival in church, for John's recovery? Augustine encouraged Proba to pray for mundane needs, and even for material prosperity (a new Ford?), especially if it could be used for the good of others. But there are clear dangers of self-centredness involved in any of these examples – the sun (and rain) will shine (or fall) on everyone, and my motives in wanting employment for my son or even John's recovery may be quite muddy. Such requests also imply questions about our conception of God's relationship to the world – in 'arranging weather', or healing someone, or helping an interview go well. In our prayers we often seem to run the risk of asking God to remake the universe around us, and some of our prayers (even when extremely commendable) request immensely complex actions in response. Questions of proportion also arise: should I pray for fine weather for the fête rather than relief from floods in Bangladesh or from drought in Africa?

Is the weather at the church fête then too mundane for prayer? Here the answer surely must be 'no'. We believe in the God who is the Father of the Lord Jesus Christ. He

---

[67] D. Bennett, *Nine O' Clock in the Morning* (London: Coverdale House, 1974).

assured his followers that the hairs on their heads were numbered (Mt. 10:30), and spoke of his providence over the lilies of the field and birds of the air (Mt. 6:28). Nothing is too small for God's notice and concern, though that does not mean we should ask God to remake the universe around us in answer to our prayers. We observed in Augustine a readiness to pray for 'the competency of things necessary', and Christians have generally thought that they should pray for everyday things. Our faith is an incarnational one: God became part of everyday life, and the everyday things around us are made holy by his presence in and with them. Barth suggested that it is always better to pray for something and risk it being inappropriate rather than not to pray at all.[68] God will forgive us (even when we pray for the weather), though God hopes we will learn and grow. But not to pray at all is to be too thoroughly secularised, too lacking in expectation and hope. It is, Wink might say, to have capitulated to the principalities and powers.

So with Augustine we should pray for 'a happy life'. This should include all the things that surround us and engage us – everything that is important to us, which we enjoy, which we are concerned about. It is only through praying for ordinary things that our prayers, and our spiritual lives, take on any reality.[69] Love of God takes flesh in our lives through love of our neighbours; satisfaction of the spirit goes hand in hand with satisfaction of the body.

However, that is not to say that we have free rein on what to pray for, and expect to receive. The collection of *Children's Letters to God* includes the 'prayer', 'Dear God, O.K. I kept my half of the deal. Where's the bike?'[70] But there can be no such deals, and God writes no such blank cheques. We recall Calvin's vivid image from a day when

---

[68] Barth, *C.D.* III/4, pp. 99ff.
[69] Farmer, *The World and God*, p. 137.
[70] Eric Marshall and Stuart Hample, *Children's Letters to God* (Glasgow: Fontana, 1975), p. 28.

the horse was the most common form of transport, of the Spirit 'bridling' our prayers, bringing them under God's control. Which insight brings us back to Barth and Garrison Keillor, to God answering the prayers we would have prayed, had we known.

'Not my will, but yours be done'?
In the mysterious dialectic of prayer we may pray in the confident hope that God will hear and respond to our petitions, while also accepting that God's purposes for our lives represent our deepest good. That said, a less monarchical view of God might also lead us to note that we may have been too ready to think of God's will in rather exclusive terms, as if God has only *one* thing for us at any moment when actually God might offer to us a number of equally 'good' possibilities and be as concerned for the 'how' of our decisions and actions as the 'what', wanting us to grow as parents hope children will grow, through taking responsibility and becoming adult. A looser sense of God's will is, of course, also consonant with the idea that God may allow us through prayer and other decision-making to 'do things our way' rather than insist on one way as the sole and absolute one.

There are other perspectives here too. When a human father has just one aim that his child *must* accomplish, we often speak of that person as being rather weak and insecure, or as controlling. God is surely not this sort of neurotic? Again this suggests that while God may seek to persuade us to the best for any given moment, even this may need some qualification in terms of there being more than one possible good outcome, or of God being willing to give us freedom and work with our choices as much as always insist on the divine choice. After all, love does not always insist on its way (1 Cor. 13:5). Obversely, while we may be confident that God is concerned about all the details of our lives, we may also assume that part of our growing into maturity (Eph. 4:13) is being able to make some decisions for ourselves: we do not usually need to take questions of interior decoration or dinner party menus to God in prayer.

All *this* said, the prayer in Gethsemane proves truly central (Mt. 26:39). 'If it is possible' – *sometimes it may yet be possible* that God will respond to our desires and pursue the ultimate divine purposes by another way. But finally it is indeed that divine purpose which is our good and our healing, and for which in our prayers – even when we do not know it – we yearn and long. As the Spirit of God prays within us the prayers we cannot know or articulate, but which stretch after God's will in our world and our lives, we are sometimes caught up in the answers to our own dimly perceived requests; and our working, being and praying brought more nearly into harmony and union with the Son's. The Triune God is indeed an answering God; and yet just as strangely, though still by God's grace – through the answers 'yes', 'no', or 'not yet' – we turn out to be answering God in our praying and our living.

As God perfects our prayers, enables and inspires them, so God also gives us a model for prayer. In the Lord's Prayer we pray 'your kingdom come, your will be done' (Mt. 6:10) and whatever penultimate shape our prayers take, ultimately all prayer is directed to this end: to the coming Kingdom of God. In prayer, we may be praying in our self-centred way for a parking place right *now*, and maybe even for the car to park in it; or with relatively more other-centredness for John's recovery after his accident, for our son's job interview, for our church's revival, or for peace in Jerusalem – but all prayer is ultimately being caught up by the Spirit in creation's eager longing for deliverance and the perfect fellowship of the Triune God.

Bibliography

Anscombe, G. E. M., *Intention* (Oxford: Blackwell, 1957).

Aquinas, Thomas, *Summa Theologiae* (London: Burns & Oates, 1922); on line at http://www.newadvent.org/summa/.

Augustine, *On the Trinity*, http://www.ccel.org/fathers2/NPNF1-03/npnf1-03-06.htm#P163_49810

——, *To Proba* in Dods, Marcus (ed.), *The Works of Aurelius Augustine*, vol. 13, Cunningham, J. G. (tr.) (Edinburgh: T & T Clark, 1875).

Balentine, Samuel E., *Prayer in the Hebrew Bible: The Drama of Divine–Human Dialogue* (Minneapolis: Fortress, 1993).

Barbour, Ian G., *Myths, Models and Paradigms* (London: SCM, 1974).

Barr, James, 'Abba isn't Daddy', *Journal of Theological Studies* 39 (1988), pp. 28–47.

Barrett, C. K., *The Epistle to the Romans* (London: A & C Black, 1957).

Barth, Karl, *Church Dogmatics*, Bromiley, G. W., Torrance, T. F and Thomson, G. T. (eds and trs), vols I/1, I/2, II/1, III/2, III/3, III/4, IV/1, IV/4 (Edinburgh: T & T Clark, 1936–1977).

Barth, Karl, *Karl Barth: Theologian of Freedom*, Green, Clifford (ed.) (London: Collins, 1989).

——, *Prayer and Preaching* (London: SCM, 1964)

——, *The Epistle to the Romans* (Oxford: OUP, 1933).

Basil the Great, *Letter 38/2*, http://www.ccel.org/fathers2/NPNF2-08/Npnf2-08-56.htm#P3098_1005192.

Basinger, David, *Divine Power in Process Theism* (New York: SUNY, 1988).

——, 'Practical Implications' in Pinnock, Clark, Rice, Richard, Sanders, John, Hasker, William and Basinger, David, *The Openness of God* (Carlisle: Paternoster, 1995).

Beare, F. W., *The Gospel According to Matthew* (Oxford: Blackwell, 1981).

Beilby, J. K. and Eddy, P. R. (eds), *Divine Foreknowledge: Four Views* (Downers Grove, Illinois: IVP, 2001).

Bennett, D., *Nine O' Clock in the Morning* (London: Coverdale House, 1974).

Boethius, *The Consolation of Philosophy*, Watts, V. E. (tr.) (Harmondsworth: Penguin, 1969).

Bonhoeffer, Dietrich, *Letters and Papers from Prison* (London: SCM, 19673).

Boyd, Gregory A., *God at War: The Bible and Spiritual Conflict* (Downers Grove, Illinois: IVP, 1997).

——, *God of the Possible: A Biblical Introduction to the Open View of God* (Grand Rapids: Baker, 2000).

——, *Satan and the Problem of Evil* (Downers Grove, Illinois: IVP, 2001).

Bradshaw, Timothy, *Praying as Believing* (Oxford: Regent's Park College, 1998).

Brown, R.E., *The Epistles of John* (New York: Anchor/Chapman, 1983).

——, *The Gospel According to John*, 2 vols (New York: Anchor/Chapman, 1971).

Brummer, Vincent, *What Are We Doing When We Pray?* (London: SCM, 1984).

Calvin, J., 'Catechism of the Church of Geneva' in *Calvin: Theological Treatises*, vol. XXII, Reid, J. K. S. (tr.) (London: SCM, 1954).

——, *Commentaries*, Pringle, W., Anderson, J. et al (trs) (Edinburgh, Calvin Translation Society, 1845-1853); on line at http://www.ccel.org/c/calvin/comment3/comm_index.htm.

——, *Institutes of the Christian Religion*, McNeill, J. T. (ed.), Battles, F. L. (tr.) (London: SCM, 1961).

——, *Opera Selecta*, vol. 1, Barth, Peter and Niesel, Wilhelm (eds) (Monachii: Kaiser, 1926)

Carmody, Denise L., *Christian Feminist Theology* (Oxford: Blackwell, 1995).

Clements, R. E., *The Prayers of the Bible* (London: SCM, 1986).

Cobb Jr, John B., *Praying for Jennifer* (Eugene: Wipf & Stock, 1985).

Cocksworth, Christopher, *Holy, Holy, Holy – Worshipping the Trinitarian God* (London: DLT, 1997).

Craig, William Lane, 'The Middle Knowledge View' in Beilby, J. K. and Eddy, P. R. (eds), *Divine Foreknowledge: Four Views* (Downers Grove, Illinois: IVP, 2001).

——, 'Timelessness and Omnitemporality' in Ganssle, G. E. (ed.), *God and Time: Four Views* (Downers Grove, Illinois: IVP, 2001).

Cullmann, Oscar, *Christ and Time* (London: SCM, 1951).

——, *Prayer in the New Testament* (London: SCM, 1995).

——, *Salvation in History* (London: SCM, 1967).

Cunningham, David, *These Three are One* (Oxford: Blackwell, 1998).

Danto, A. C., 'Basic Action' in White, A. R. (ed.), *Philosophy of Action* (Oxford: OUP, 1968).

Davies, Brian, *Introduction to the Philosophy of Religion* (Oxford: OUP, 1982).

Davis, Dale Ralph, *2 Samuel* (Fearn: Christian Focus, 1999).

Davis, Stephen, Kendall, Daniel and O'Collins, Gerald (eds), *The Trinity* (Oxford: OUP, 1999).

Dibelius, Martin, *A Commentary on the Epistle of James* (Minneapolis: Fortress/Hermaneia, 1976).

Dulles, Avery, *Models of Revelation* (Dublin: Gill & MacMillan, 1992).

Dunn, James D. G., *Jesus and the Spirit* (London: SCM, 1975).

——, *Romans 1–8* (Waco: Word, 1988).

——, *The Evidence for Jesus* (London: SCM, 1985).

Eichrodt, Walther, *Theology of the Old Testament*, vol. II (London: SCM, 1967).

Elliott, Charles, *Praying the Kingdom* (London: DLT, 1985).

Ellis, Robert, 'God and Action', *Religious Studies* 24 (1989), pp. 463–82.

——, 'The Vulnerability of Action', *Religious Studies* 25 (1990), pp. 225–33.

Farmer, H. H., *The World and God* (London: Nisbet, 1936²).

Farrer, Austin, *Faith and Speculation* (London: A & C Black, 1967).

——, *The Freedom of the Will* (London: A & C Black, 1958).

Fiddes, Paul S., *Participating in God* (London: DLT, 2000).

——, *The Promised End* (Oxford: Blackwell, 2000).

Finkel, Asher, 'Prayer in Jewish Life' in Longenecker, Richard N. (ed.), *Into God's Presence* (Grand Rapids: Eerdmans, 2001).

Fretheim, Terence E., *The Suffering of God: An Old Testament Perspective* (Philadelphia: Fortress, 1984)

Gaiser, Frederick J., 'Individual and Corporate Prayer in Old Testament Perspective' in Sponheim, Paul R. (ed.), *A Primer on Prayer* (Philadelphia: Fortress, 1998).

Ganssle, G. E. (ed.), *God and Time: Four Views* (Downers Grove, Illinois: IVP, 2001).

Geach, P., *God and the Soul* (London: Routledge & Kegan Paul, 1969).

Geisler, N., *Creating God in the Image of Man?: The New Open View of God – Neotheism's Dangerous Drift* (Minneapolis: Bethany House, 1997).

Green, Joel B., *The Gospel of Luke* (Grand Rapids: Eerdmans, 1997).

Gunton, Colin E., *Becoming and Being* (Oxford: OUP, 1978).

——, *The Promise of Trinitarian Theology* (Edinburgh: T & T Clark, 1997²).

Harnack, Adolf von, *History of Dogma*, vol. 1 (London: Williams & Norgate, 1894).

Harrington, Daniel J., *The Gospel of Matthew* (Collegeville: Liturgical Press, 1991)

Harris, W. S., Gowda, M. and Kolb, J. W. et al, 'A Randomized, Controlled Trial of the Effects of Remote, Intercessory Prayer on Outcomes in Patients Admitted to the Coronary Care Unit', *Archive of Internal Medicine* 159 (1999), pp. 2273–8, on line at http://archinte.ama-assn.org/cgi/content/abstract/159/19/2273.

Hartin, Patrick J., *James* (Collegeville: Liturgical Press, 2003).

Hartshorne, Charles, *The Divine Relativity* (New Haven: YUP, 1948).

Hasker, William, 'A Philosophical Perspective' in Pinnock, Clark, Rice, Richard, Sanders, John, Hasker, William and Basinger, David, *The Openness of God* (Carlisle: Paternoster, 1995).

Heiler, F., *Prayer: A Study in the History and Psychology of Religion* (Oxford: OUP, 1932).

Helm, Paul, 'Divine Timeless Eternity' in Ganssle, G. E. (ed.), *God and Time: Four Views* (Downers Grove, Illinois: IVP, 2001).

Herrmann, J., 'Prayer in the OT' in Kittel, G. (ed.), *Theological Dictionary of the New Testament*, vol. II, Bromiley, G. W. (tr.) (Grand Rapids: Eerdmans, 1964).

Hill, David, *The Gospel of Matthew* (London: Marshall, Morgan & Scott, 1972).

Hornbsy, Jennifer, *Actions* (London: Routledge & Kegan Paul, 1980).

Hughes, Gerard, *God of Surprises* (London: DLT, 1987).

Hunt, David, 'The Simple Foreknowledge View' in Beilby, J. K. and Eddy, P. R. (eds), *Divine Foreknowledge: Four Views* (Downers Grove, Illinois: IVP, 2001).

Jay, Eric G. (ed. and tr.), 'Introduction' in Origen, *Treatise on Prayer* (London: SPCK, 1954).

Jeremias, Joachim, *The Prayers of Jesus* (London: SCM, 1967).

Johnson, Luke T., *The Gospel of Luke* (Collegeville: Liturgical Press, 1991).

——, *The Writings of the New Testament: An Interpretation* (London: SCM, 1992).

Kant, Immanuel, *Religion Within the Limits of Reason Alone* (New York: Harper Torchbooks, 1960).

Kasper, Walter, *The God of Jesus Christ* (London: SCM, 1984).

Keillor, Garrison, *Lake Wobegon Days* (London: Faber, 1987).

Kelly, J. N. D., *Early Christian Doctrines* (London: A & C Black, 1968[4]).

Kenny, Anthony, *Action, Emotion and Will* (London: Routledge & Kegan Paul, 1979[2]).

Klein, Ralph W., *1 Samuel* (Waco: Word, 1983).

Lewis, C. S., *Mere Christianity* (Glasgow: Fount, 1977).

——, *Miracles* (London: Collins Fontana, 1960).

——, 'Petitionary Prayer: A Problem without an Answer' in Lewis, C. S. *Christian Reflections* (London: Fount, 1981).

Lincoln, Andrew T., 'God's Name, Jesus's Name, and Prayer in the Fourth Gospel' in Longenecker, Richard N. (ed.), *Into God's Presence* (Grand Rapids: Eerdmans, 2001).

Longenecker, Richard N. (ed.), *Into God's Presence* (Grand Rapids: Eerdmans, 2001).

Longenecker, Richard N., 'Prayer in the Pauline Letters' in Longenecker, Richard N. (ed.), *Into God's Presence* (Grand Rapids: Eerdmans, 2001).

Lucas, J. R., 'Freedom and Grace' in Lucas, J. R., *Freedom and Grace* (London: SPCK, 1976).

MacMurray, John, *The Self as Agent* (London: Faber, 1957).

Macquarrie, John, *In Search of Deity: An Essay in Dialectical Theism* (London: SCM, 1984).

——, *Jesus Christ in Modern Thought* (London: SCM, 1990).

Manson, T. W., *The Sayings of Jesus* (London: SCM, 1950).

Marshall, Eric and Hample, Stuart, *Children's Letters to God* (Glasgow: Fontana, 1975).

Marshall, I. H., 'Jesus – Example and Teacher of Prayer in the Synoptic Gospels' in Longenecker, Richard N. (ed.), *Into God's Presence* (Grand Rapids: Eerdmans, 2001).

——, *The Gospel of Luke* (Exeter: Paternoster, 1978)

Mays, James L., *Psalms* (Louisville: Westminster John Knox Press, 1994).

McGrath, Alister E., *Christian Theology: An Introduction* (Oxford: Blackwell, 1994).

McKane, W., *1 & 2 Samuel* (London: SCM, 1963).

Moltmann, Jürgen, *History and the Triune God* (London: SCM, 1991).

——, *The Church in the Power of the Spirit* (London: SCM, 1977).

——, *The Coming of God* (London: SCM, 1996).

——, *The Crucified God* (London: SCM, 1974).

——, *The Source: The Holy Spirit and the Theology of Life* (London: SCM, 1997).

——, *The Trinity and the Kingdom of God* (London: SCM, 1981).

Montefiore, Hugh, *The Epistle to the Hebrews* (London: A. & C. Black, 1964).

Morris, Leon, *The Epistle to the Romans* (Grand Rapids: Eerdmans, 1988).

Moule, C. F. D., *The Origin of Christology* (Cambridge: CUP, 1978).

O'Donnell, John, *Trinity and Temporality* (Oxford: OUP, 1983).

Origen, *On Prayer*, Curtis, William A. (tr.), http://www.ccel.org/o/origen/prayer/prayer.htm, X. Also available in Origen, *An Exhortation to Martyrdom, Prayer, and Selected Works*, Greer, Rowan A. (tr.), (Mahwah: Paulist Press, 1979).

Padgett, Alan D., 'Eternity as Relative Timelessness' in Ganssle, G. E. (ed.), *God and Time: Four Views* (Downers Grove, Illinois: IVP, 2001).

Pailin, David A., *God and the Processes of Reality* (London: Routledge, 1989).

——, *Groundwork of the Philosophy of Religion* (London: Epworth, 1986).

Pannenberg, Wolfhart, *Systematic Theology*, vol. 1, Bromiley, G. (tr.) (Edinburgh: T & T Clark, 1991).

Parker, T. H. L., *John Calvin* (London: Dent, 1975).

Phillips, D. Z., *The Concept of Prayer* (Oxford: Blackwell, 1981).

Pinnock, Clark, 'Systematic Theology' in Pinnock, Clark, Rice, Richard, Sanders, John, Hasker, William and Basinger, David, *The Openness of God* (Carlisle: Paternoster, 1995).

Pinnock, Clark, Rice, Richard, Sanders, John, Hasker, William and Basinger, David, *The Openness of God* (Carlisle: Paternoster, 1995).

Pinnock, Clark, *Most Moved Mover: A Theology of God's Openness* (Carlisle: Paternoster, 2001)

Plato, *The Republic*, Jowett, Benjamin (tr.), on line at http://classics.mit.edu/Plato/republic.html.

Polkinghorne, John, *Science and Providence* (London: SPCK, 1989).

Rahner, Karl, *The Trinity* (New York: Herder & Herder, 1970).

Rensberger, David, *1 John, 2 John, 3 John* (Nashville: Abingdon Press, 1997).

Rice, Richard, 'Biblical Support', in Pinnock, Clark, Rice, Richard, Sanders, John, Hasker, William and Basinger, David, *The Openness of God* (Carlisle: Paternoster, 1995).

Roberts, Richard, 'Karl Barth' in Toon, P. and Spiceland, J. D. (eds), *One God in Trinity* (London: Bagster, 1980).

Sanders, John, *God Who Risks: A Theology of Providence* (Downers Grove, Illinois: IVP, 1998).

Schaefer, K., *Psalms* (Collegeville: Liturgical Press, 2001).

Schleiermacher, Friedrich and Clements, Keith W. (ed.), *Friedrich Schleiermacher: Pioneer of Modern Theology* (London: Collins, 1987).

Schleiermacher, Friedrich, *Selected Sermons of Schleiermacher*, Furilion, Mary (tr.) (London: Hodder & Stoughton, 1890), reprinted in Schleiermacher, Friedrich and Clements, Keith W. (ed.), *Friedrich Schleiermacher: Pioneer of Modern Theology* (London: Collins, 1987).

——, *The Christian Faith*, Mackintosh, H. R. (tr.), from the second German edition of 1830 (Edinburgh: T & T Clark, 1928)

Schnackenburg, R., *The Gospel According to St John*, 3 vols (New York: Crossroads, 1968, 1982).

Schweizer, Eduard, *The Good News According to Matthew* (London: SPCK, 1976).

Seitz, Christopher R., 'Prayer in the Old Testament or Hebrew Bible' in Longenecker, Richard N. (ed.), *Into God's Presence* (Grand Rapids: Eerdmans, 2001).

Smith, C. W. F., 'Prayer' in Buttrick, G. A. (ed) et al, *Interpreter's Dictionary of the Bible*, vol. 3 (Nashville: Abingdon, 1976).

Soares-Prabhu, G. M., 'Speaking to "Abba": Prayer as Petition and Thanksgiving in the Teaching of Jesus' in Duquoc, Christian and Florestan, Casiano (eds), *Asking & Thanking* (London: SCM, 1990).

Sponheim, Paul R. (ed.), *A Primer on Prayer* (Philadelphia: Fortress, 1998).

Suchocki, Marjorie Hewitt, *In God's Presence: Theological Reflections on Prayer* (St Louis: Chalice, 1996).

Swete, H. B., *The Ascended Christ* (London: Macmillan, 1910).

Tastard, Terry, *The Spark in the Soul* (London: DLT, 1989).

Taylor, John V., *The Christlike God* (London: SCM, 1992).

Tertullian, *Against Praxeas* in Roberts, A., and Donaldson, J. and Coxe, A. C. (eds), *The Ante-Nicene Fathers*, vol. 3 (Grand Rapids: Eerdmans, 1985); on line at http://www.ccel.org/fathers2/ANF-03/anf0343.htm#P10374_2906966.

Tiessen, Terrance, *Providence and Prayer* (Downers Grove, Illinois: IVP, 2000).

Toon, P. and Spiceland, J. D. (eds), *One God in Trinity* (London: Bagster, 1980).

Torrance, James B., *Worship, Community, and the Triune God of Grace* (Carlisle: Paternoster, 1996).

Verney, Stephen, *The Dance of Love* (London: HarperCollins, 1989).

Wallace, Ronald S., *Calvin's Doctrine of the Christian Life* (Edinburgh: Oliver & Boyd, 1959).

Ward, Keith, *Rational Theology and the Creativity of God* (Oxford: Blackwell, 1992).

Ware, Bruce A., *God's Lesser Glory: A Critique of Open Theism* (Leicester: Apollos, 2001).

Wendel, François, *Calvin* (London: Collins, 1953).

White, A. R. (ed.), *Philosophy of Action* (Oxford: OUP, 1968).

Whitehead, Alfred North, *Process and Reality* (New York: Macmillan, 1929).

——, *Religion in the Making* (New York: Meridian, 1974).

Wiles, Maurice, *The Making of Christian Doctrine* (Cambridge: CUP, 1967).

Wink, Walter E., *Engaging the Powers* (Fortress: Minneapolis, 1992).

Wolterstorff, Nicholas, 'Response to Paul Helm' in Ganssle, G. E. (ed.), *God and Time: Four Views* (Downers Grove, Illinois: IVP, 2001).

——, 'Response to William Lane Craig' in Ganssle, G. E. (ed.), *God and Time: Four Views* (Downers Grove, Illinois: IVP, 2001).

——, 'Unqualified Divine Temporality' in Ganssle, G. E. (ed.), *God and Time: Four Views* (Downers Grove, Illinois: IVP, 2001).

Wright, N. T., 'The Lord's Prayer as a Paradigm of Christian Prayer' in Longenecker, Richard N. (ed.), *Into God's Presence* (Grand Rapids: Eerdmans, 2001).

Yancey, Phillip, 'Chess Master' in *Christianity Today* (22 May 2000), on line at http://www.christianitytoday.com/ct/2000/006/35.112.html

Ziesler, J., *Paul's Letter to the Romans* (London: SCM, 1989).

Other cited web sites

http://sol.sci.uop.edu/~jfalward/ThreeTieredUniverse.htm.

http://www.tiscali.co.uk/reference/encyclopaedia/hutchinson/m0002193.html.

http://www.gregboyd.org

Index of Scripture Passages

Index of Names and Subjects

If worship is God-centred and God is the Trinity then worship should be Trinity-centred. This book explores the meaning and implications of that simple claim.

Written for church leaders, worship leaders and songwriters as well as those interested in theology, Robin Parry looks at why the Trinity matters and addresses pressing questions such as:

- What is the relationship between theology and worship?
- Why is the Trinity central to Christian living and believing?
- Can understanding the Trinity help us understand what we do when we worship?
- How should we worship the Father, the Son and the Spirit?
- How can we write and select songs that foster an awareness of the Trinity?
- How can we learn to pray more trinitarianly?
- How can we make the Trinity central through Holy Communion, spiritual gifts, preaching, and the use of the arts?

Practical and realistic, *Worshipping Trinity* shows how we can maintain the centrality of the Trinity in a fast-changing worship culture.

ISBN: 1-84227-347-7
Price: £7.99